BUILDING DIGNIFIED WORLDS

Diverse Economies and Livable Worlds

Series Editors: J. K. Gibson-Graham, Maliha Safri, Kevin St. Martin, Stephen Healy

1 *Building Dignified Worlds: Geographies of Collective Action*
GERDA ROELVINK

BUILDING
DIGNIFIED WORLDS

GEOGRAPHIES OF COLLECTIVE ACTION

GERDA ROELVINK

Diverse Economies and Livable Worlds 1

UNIVERSITY OF MINNESOTA PRESS

MINNEAPOLIS • LONDON

Portions of chapter 2 were previously published in "Broadening the Horizons of Economy," *Journal of Cultural Economy* 2, no. 3 (2009): 325–44. Portions of chapter 3 were published in "Collective Action and the Politics of Affect," *Emotion, Space, and Society* 3, no. 2 (2010): 111–18. Portions of chapter 5 were published in "Rethinking Marx's Species Being in the Anthropocene," *Rethinking Marxism* 25, no. 1 (2013): 52–69.

Published by the University of Minnesota Press
111 Third Avenue South, Suite 290
Minneapolis, MN 55401-2520
http://www.upress.umn.edu

Library of Congress Cataloging-in-Publication Data
Names: Roelvink, Gerda.
Title: Building dignified worlds : geographies of collective action / Gerda Roelvink.
Description: Minneapolis : University of Minnesota Press, 2016. | Series: Diverse economies and livable worlds ; 1 | Includes bibliographical references and index.
Identifiers: LCCN 2015026040| ISBN 978-0-8166-7617-0 (hc) | ISBN 978-0-8166-8317-8 (pb)
Subjects: LCSH: Social movements. | Social change. | Organizational change. | Economic development—Social aspects. | Marketing—Social aspects. | Globalization—Social aspects. | Social sciences—Research.
Classification: LCC HM881 .R64 2016 | DDC 303.48/4—dc23
LC record available at http://lccn.loc.gov/2015026040

For JULIE GRAHAM

Contents

Introduction

Geographies of Collective Action

I sometimes think of social science as being a bit like coming up with constellations in the night sky. You step out under this vast sky and there are thousands of stars. The human brain picks out eight of them, and turns them into a stick figure, and calls it Orion. The issue is not only that some people get out there and say, "Hey, that is not a mighty hunter, it's a saucepan!" It is also that once someone has taught you the constellations, each time you step under the night sky, you look for that constellation. There are millions and millions of stars. But our minds will gravitate to trying to find those eight stars and will focus on them, filtering everything else out.

—LINDY EDWARDS at the Sydney Writer's Festival, 2007

Pondering Contemporary Alignments

While there is a long history of social movement struggle, contemporary forms of collective action centered on political economic concerns and joining diverse groups together can be linked back to what was and still is popularly known as the antiglobalization movement or, in more technical language, a movement against neoliberal capitalist globalization. The antiglobalization movement has been a struggle against a powerful alignment of economy and society, an association so strong that it has been dubbed TINA, "There Is No Alternative." Just as the eye is drawn to the same constellations of stars once they are given a name and description, the alignment called neoliberalism can be seen in most areas of life. Jamie Peck and Adam Tickell (2002, 381) take this as evidence that neoliberalism has become a "commonsense of the times":

1

Although Margaret Thatcher was never right to claim that "there is no alternative" to the neoliberal vision of a free economy and a minimalist state, two decades later the global hegemony of this mode of political rationality means that the burden of proof has shifted: neoliberalism is no longer a dream of Chicago economists or a nightmare in the imaginations of leftist conspiracy theorists; it has become a commonsense of the times.

Never ones to take a commonsense view of the times at face value, scholars of political economy (such as regulation theorists like Peck and Tickell) have linked the neoliberal political project to a particular form of post-Fordist capitalism that is closely aligned with institutions of local governance that take names like community, social capital, partnership, entrepreneurialism, and local innovation (Moulaert et al. 2005; Peck and Tickell 2002). These diverse local and socially orientated institutions are viewed as subordinated to global processes of marketization and commodification (Peck and Tickell 2002). Put simply, in this representation of the alignment forming neoliberalism, the social is subordinated and subservient to the economic (Roelvink and Craig 2005).

Taking the global stage with the antiglobalization movement, contemporary social movements have worked to oppose this alignment and reconfigure political economy in new ways. The most noticeable early forms of collective opposition have been the diversely populated antiglobalization protests taking to the streets around the world in response to forums and meetings held by the G8, the World Trade Organization, the International Monetary Fund, the World Bank, the Asia Pacific Economic Corporation, and other representatives of powerful states and multinational corporations. These protests aim to politicize global processes of marketization and commodification by revealing among other things devastating social and environmental impacts, from increasing poverty and vulnerability of the poor to the destruction and enclosure of the commons. The antiglobalization protest movements were initially centered on a politics of resistance; they were against the "market," privatization, and the commodification of life. They have been prepared to burn crops; reclaim land, water, and electricity; and disrupt meetings of economic and political representatives.

Despite their media prominence and disruptive nature, the antiglobalization movements have been largely judged as insignificant and powerless in comparison with the global forces of neoliberal capitalism that they oppose

(Chandhoke 2002). This evaluation relates to the all-or-nothing approach to social transformation that Michal Osterweil (2005, 25) describes as the "universalizing" position. Scholars who take this position judge social movements according to their ability to match the scale and scope of that which they are against. In addition, antiglobalization movements have been criticized for their "anti-" political strategy and, in particular, for the way that this anti-ness reinforces the perceived power and hold on the imagination of that which they are against (Hynes, Sharpe, and Fagan 2007). This line of criticism argues that antiglobalization movements risk affirming the discursive power of neoliberalism and thus also contribute to public feelings of hopelessness. Like Eve Kosofsky Sedgwick's (1993, 5) description of "Christmas effects" in which language, institutions, practices, and other dimensions of social life all line up, this politics of resistance risks aligning multiple institutions of the state; sites of economy and community; and processes of imperialism, capitalism, and development with neoliberalism. This gives little hope or room for alternatives. Thus the anti- stance tends to align and conflate a whole range of institutions and processes under the banner of neoliberalism, especially aligning the "state" and the "market" with capitalism. Analysts of neoliberalism have also been criticized on these grounds, and in particular for their role in maintaining neoliberalism as a common reference point in the analysis of contemporary power (see Larner 2003 and, more recently, Weller and O'Neill 2014).

Because of the brighter alignments that constitute neoliberalism, the antiglobalization movement struggles to reconfigure sociocultural economic relationships in particular places initially less noticeable. Yet, for some time now, collective political economic struggle has been changing shape, shifting away from conjunctions centered on the capitalist economy, the nation-state, and working-class collectives to new forms of sociocultural economic associations. These associations are remarkably different from struggles of the traditional left and the social movements of the 1960s. In contrast to the massing together of working-class males and groups joined by a common singular identity (or indeed forced collectivization under a centralized state, as the *Dictionary of Human Geography* defines collectives; Johnston et al. 2000, 90–91), today collective associations gather diverse peoples, animals, the natural environment, technologies, and others around public matters or concerns, such as climate change, corporations, bush care, or the privatization of the commons (Latour 2005a). They have thus been described as hybrid collectives (Callon and Rabeharisoa 2008). For Latour, these hybrid collectives represent a new agent of social transformation; they operate as an assemblage that realigns diverse peoples and things around contemporary issues. It is this form of collective action that is the focus of this book. In other words, *Building Dignified Worlds* takes seriously these contemporary clusters around matters of economic concern (Latour 2004a). It does so by exploring the *making* of these new hybrid collectives—the making of a new body politic. I thus join other scholars in asking how contemporary matters, peoples, and things are currently being put together differently to change the world.

Although when I began working on this project, the political economic experiments undertaken alongside the politics of resistance characterizing the antiglobalization movement were largely unseen, the more recent collective experiments gathered under or linked to the Occupy movement have had a much stronger presence on the global stage. In fact, in light of Occupy and the many other experiments undertaken around the world, contemporary political economic collective action has exceeded the imagination of some of the key scholars rethinking capitalism to enable social movement experimentation to take flight. As J. K. Gibson-Graham (2006b, xxi) notes in her introduction to *A Postcapitalist Politics,*

> from our locations in academia at two ends of the world, we have a sense that events have overtaken us. Ten years ago, when we were writing *The End of Capitalism (As We Knew It): A Feminist Critique of Political Economy,* we imagined it as an invitation and perhaps a prelude to a new economic politics. . . . Today we see ourselves as part of a movement that is actively retheorizing capitalism and reclaiming the economy here and now in myriad projects of alternative economic activism. Our project has been gathered up in the whirlwind of inventions and interventions, resonating with some, amplifying or amplified by others, and above all sharing sentiments and stances with respect to the tasks of transformation.

Occupy is an excellent example of such an intervention. Beginning with Occupy Wall Street, the Occupy movement combined protests against income distribution with the practice of a different kind of economy; as Maliha Safri (2012, 1) puts it, "Occupy Wall Street (OWS) assumed both sides of the meaning of the word [occupy]: to take up the space, and to do work." OWS, for example, involved working committees that organized meals, education, media, bedding and showers, training in organization, and more (Safri 2012). Academics (including Safri and Suresh Naidu) were ready and armed with a range of rethinking economy tools to teach in the free classes provided during OWS (see Naidu 2012; Safri 2012). Yet the forging of alternative economic experiments within or alongside struggles of resistance has not always been so clear. A lot of work both inside and outside the academy has been undertaken to enable such possibilities. *Building Dignified Worlds* examines and is part of this collective work.

Part of my motivation for this project to theorize new kinds of collective association is a frustration with the way that the public feelings of hopelessness of which Latour (2005a, 14) writes led to the frequent dismissal of dimmer alignments:

> Some conjunctions of planets are so ominous, astrologers used to say, that it seems safer to stay at home in bed and wait until Heaven sends a more auspicious message. It's probably the same with political conjunctions. They are presently so hopeless that it seems prudent to stay as far away as possible from anything political and to wait for the passing away of all the present leaders, terrorists, commentators and buffoons who strut about the public stage.
>
> Astrology, however, is as precarious an art as political science; behind the nefarious conjunctions of hapless stars, other much dimmer alignments might be worth pondering. With the political period triggering such desperation, the time seems right to shift our attention to other ways of considering public matters. And "matters" are precisely what might be put center stage. Yes, public matters, but how?

Though these alignments are much brighter today, in this book I continue to call for those who wish for a better world to take collective experimentation seriously. I argue that scholars need to pay attention to the ways in which collective action is realigning institutions, processes, and sites linked to the contemporary "capitalist" economy with diverse social, cultural, and environmental struggles for justice.

Specifically, *Building Dignified Worlds* takes up Latour's question that, once we acknowledge that collectives matter, we need to ask how. I ask how contemporary collectives made up of people, things, and concerns have brought into being the huge number of alternative economies we can see today. In doing so, this book explores the geography of collectivization, that is, the way realignment and new compositions of political economy shape the world and what is possible within it. I argue that the relational and geographical nature of collectivization is central to understanding the way in which new alignments are creating alternative economies. This geographical lens on collective struggle also provides a view to the diverse forces through which social movements create change. Given this focus, I utilize and examine much research from within the discipline of human geography. Some of the key thinkers to *Building Dignified Worlds,* however (such as Eve Kosofsky Sedgwick, Judith Butter, Michel Callon, Bruno Latour, Paulo Freire, Adam Smith, and Karl Marx), come from fields outside the geographical tradition, and the movements I theorize, from the World Social Forum to farming innovation in Australia, will be of interest to scholars of social activism within and outside the academy. My argument about the relational geographical nature of collective action, then, is as much for geographers as for researchers in the social sciences more generally and activists interested in economic experimentation.

Without wanting to diminish the many achievements of a long history of left politics, from workers' rights to women's rights, from antislavery to decolonization, this book focuses on the kind of politics practiced by hybrid collectives. In contrast to the resistance-centered antiglobalization movements, hybrid collectives are focused on a politics of affirmation and the creation of alternatives (Hynes, Sharpe, and Fagan 2007). Social movements of this kind are less concerned with neoliberalism than they are with the creation of and experimentation with new ways of living and possibilities for "flourishing" (Berlant 2007). Collectively, these social movements could be described as social innovation (Gibson-Graham and Roelvink 2009). Premised on feelings of hope, which prompt action, social innovation aims to improve life through creating new, innovative projects like Live Aid, the Grameen Bank's microcredit schemes, the development of cooperatives, and neighborhood renewal projects (Moulaert et al. 2005; Westley, Zimmerman, and Patton 2006). Like the antimovements, social innovation stems from a realization of the unsustainability of the present (Westley, Zimmerman, and Patton 2006). Yet alongside this understanding, and in contrast to the antimovements, Westley, Zimmerman, and Patton (2006) argue that whenever the circumstances enable it, social innovation involves a decision to take change-orientated action. By taking action, social innovation realigns the entities that facilitated action and thus the kinds of projects that are possible (Westley, Zimmerman, and Patton 2006). Social innovation is able to initiate change through a number of different processes. One of particular interest to me is to make visible and broaden the field of action to include other people, things, spaces, and relationships. I describe this as part of a geography of collective action.

Although independently, such innovative social movements have been making real changes to improve the quality of life around the globe, aligned together, their collective vision was initially largely unarticulated. One way in which affirmative social movement struggles have experimented with articulating both their presence and vision has been through the World Social Forum (WSF) movement. This movement annually gathers together diverse social movement groups from around the globe to create "new worlds." From its inception in 2001, the WSF movement has shifted from an antipolitical stance to the affirmative form of politics that corresponds with the way of social innovation (Keraghel and Sen 2004). In line with this shift in focus from resistance and the struggle for an alternative, the WSF embraces multiple alternatives and new worlds. The WSF is an ideal site to explore the beginnings of an affirmative vision of contemporary collective action and techniques for realigning economies. It was, for example, at the 2005 WSF in Porto Alegre, Brazil, that I first heard about the diverse networks of trash collectors that are initiating or shaping recycling markets around the globe (discussed in chapter 4). Such alternative markets operating and/or represented at the WSF present a stark contrast to the "market" against which social movements rally. The 2005 WSF also gave me a glimpse of the processes whereby feelings and diverse experiences are combined to create new visions that are so vital to social innovation and change-making action (examined in chapter 3). Dignity was one area of concern that I discovered by attending the World Dignity Forum held during the 2005 WSF meeting. Here the use of the term *dignity* reflected a shift in focus from a politics of class opposition to exploitation to one centered on a more general concern that economic life be evaluated in terms of human dignity. By examining collective action responding to climate change, in chapter 5 of this book I ask how the concept of dignity might be broadened further to include not only human dignity but also a dignified world.

Many different kinds of researchers attended the 2005 WSF. Participation in the WSF movement motivated my thinking about the role of research in social movement struggles. Research and thinking are vital elements of social innovation; social innovators need to see where and how to act and how to respond to an evolving situation (Westley, Zimmerman, and Patton 2006). Yet analysis of the way that thinking and research work as a technique of social innovation requires an understanding of research as an active part of social movement activism. It is such an understanding that I aim to contribute to with this book. I examine the role of research in constituting social reality and argue that although the performativity of research is increasingly acknowledged, research remains an underutilized force with which to shape the world. As this is especially the case for research undertaken in academic institutions, I represent research as a way for activist academics to be part of social movement struggles. More specifically, inspired by Latour, I argue that research is a way to gather and represent contemporary matters of concern and diverse publics. This perspective has implications for intellectual work, adding weight to the increasing responsibility of researchers in relation to their impact on the research field.

Research That Changes the World

The value of research is often judged by one's response to a "so what" question such as "So what difference is your research going to make to the way people live their lives?" This evaluation is especially true in the discipline of geography, a discipline ethically committed to making a positive impact on the field site in which one gathers information about the world (Massey 2005). Traditionally, the field site is demarcated as external to the intellectual thinking and research undertaken inside the academy (Dewsbury et al. 2002; Sharpe 2002). This division of intellectual exercises from the field site is associated with other dichotomies, such as thinking and practice, theory and empirical evidence, or discourse and materiality. In each case, one's contribution to how people live their lives is primarily judged in terms of how the other has changed.

Recent developments, such as that known as the cultural turn, have opened up these dichotomies for debate (Sharpe 2002). In scholarship on epistemology and ways of knowing the world, the debate over one's analytical lens and social change initially took the form of a struggle for determination. This is exemplified by debates within Marxism over how best to theorize the relationship of class with other areas of social life, such as culture (Resnick and Wolff 1987). Put simply, this is a debate about the extent to which economic life determines all other parts of social life (Resnick and Wolff 1987). This debate also relates to the extent to which research can capture the rich nature of the world (Law 2004b). Resnick and Wolff (1987) argue that the Althusserian concept of overdetermination offers a resolution to the determination debate. Overdetermination has made a big impact on Marxist research, especially on how the relationships between economy and culture, theory and practice, and materiality and discourse are understood. From the perspective of overdetermination, there is no single determining aspect of social reality. Rather, as Resnick and Wolff put it, what is important is "the complex 'fitting together' of all social aspects, their relational structure, the contradictions overdetermined in each by all" (50). At any given moment, an entity is thus constituted by and in relation to all other entities (Gibson-Graham 2006a, 28). The concept of overdetermination also reformulates the relationship between theory and the knowledge research produces (Resnick and Wolff 1987). More specifically, one's entry point to thinking about the world, such as through the lens of class, can be distinguished from the knowledge produced so that, in this case, class is not viewed as *the* determining aspect of reality. Overdetermination equally applies to one's theoretical perspective in that it, too, will be overdetermined by other concepts as well as by nontheoretical elements (Resnick and Wolff 1987, 52). Overdetermination and other antiessentialist concepts have had a large influence on thinking about the relationship between theory and practice, giving theory and practice an interrelated and equally active role in shaping the world.

The dichotomy between theory–research and practice–intervention in the field site has also been challenged in debates about research methodology. Concerns about the ethical and political impacts of research on the field site and/or researched subjects have motivated scholars to rethink their research techniques. This rethinking has taken place in the context of growing attention to diverse identities and relationships of power, including those articulated through research projects (Kitchin and Hubbard 1999). In feminist research, for instance, concern about power has generated questions about the way particular groups are represented, about the validity of experience, and about who can speak for others (Butler 1990). Such debate has also raised questions about the aims and goals of research more generally and whether the outcome of research should serve academic interests or the interests of researched communities (Kitchin and Hubbard 1999). In sum, this debate has challenged long-standing assumptions about the separation between practices of thinking and doing research while also raising questions about the role of research in political struggles against oppression.

The problematic separation of research from action, theory from practice, has led to new practices of research, prompting, for example, researchers to adopt approaches such as participatory action research (PAR). PAR is an approach to research that aims to unsettle divisions between researchers and the researched by including research subjects as participants in the research project (Cameron and Gibson 2005; Kitchin and Hubbard 1999; Pain and Francis 2003). PAR generally takes the epistemological position that knowledge is the first step to liberation (Freire 1996). Participatory action researchers aim to draw out, extend, and in some cases transform participants' existing knowledge about the constitution of their worlds. To do so in a range of non-Western cultural contexts and diverse linguistic settings, they utilize a variety of linguistic and nonlinguistic techniques (Pain and Francis 2003).

Responding to the criticism of "abandoning politics and embracing the deconstruction of texts and images with little relevance to the 'real world,'" poststructural researchers who take an overdetermined approach to intellectual inquiry have further extended PAR as a means to create change in the field site (Cameron and Gibson 2005, 317). Jenny Cameron and Katherine Gibson (2005), for instance, develop three areas of PAR for poststructural research projects. First, moving away from the presumption of a predefined subject of history, they argue for an approach to research that recognizes multiple determined and ongoing processes of subjectification. Second, while Cameron and Gibson praise PAR's emphasis on diverse local knowledges, they also highlight the need to interrogate the effects of that knowledge on what action is possible. They suggest that research has a role in making visible new possibilities for action. Finally, though Cameron and Gibson affirm the role of knowledge and emotion in changing the world, they draw attention away from the knowledge of structural forces, such as those attributed to capitalism, and the affects and emotions of related collective struggle, such as the anger of a mobilized working class, to a micropolitics of subjects enabled by feelings of love, compassion, empathy, and joy.

The challenges of PAR continue to be debated, especially the problems of participation by mobile populations (Pain and Francis 2003) and the long-term effects of PAR projects on researched communities in contexts where there is little institutional support (Cameron and Gibson 2005). In addition, though researchers and the researched come together through the research project, the impact of research is often located in the field site. Thus, on completion of the research project, the effect of the project is judged in terms of long-term change in the field site. Although PAR challenges the division of researchers and the researched during the project, the division between the academy and the field site on which research acts tends to remain once the fieldwork component of the research is completed. Change is located in the field site and in the researched subjects. The researcher and her context, the academy, are not expected to change. This location of change affirms other divisions by which the impact of research has often been judged, including divisions between the academy and the field, between theory and practice, and between the position of the academic and the activist (see Kitchin and Hubbard 1999).

But what if one applies these insights to the disciplinary field of inquiry? How are the impacts of research on the field site and the disciplinary field of inquiry related, and how might these impacts be judged? Inspired by the insights of PAR on the way research can contribute to political struggle, in this book, I ask how research in and of itself might contribute to the realignments under way in contemporary social movement struggles. I aim to develop techniques of thinking, inquiry, and research practice with which to bring about change in the disciplinary field of inquiry. As I outline at the end of this introduction, these include techniques with which to spatialize the field of economy and techniques with which to translate knowledge held in the body into discursive consciousness and vision. In doing so, I take inspiration from scholarship that has begun to ask questions about the relationship between knowledge and struggles for alternative realities.

Research That Performs Diverse Economies

J. K. Gibson-Graham's (2006a) now classic (Leyshon 2010) book *The End of Capitalism (As We Knew It)*, first published in 1996, was motivated by concern about the relationship between theory and politics. As the author explains in the preface, while thinking about the book, she was stirred by a debate on industrial restructuring that represented people in diverse situations (and thus potentially disruptive to political economic alignments) as coping, adapting, and thus aligned with a changing global economy. Gibson-Graham writes:

It was clear to me that the refusal to explore disharmony—the things that did not line up and fit in with industrial change—had led to an unwitting economism or productionism in the social representation that was being constructed. As the process to which everything else was adapting and adjusting, industrial restructuring was the central and determining dynamic in the local social setting, though this kind of deterministic analysis was the very thing the researchers had wanted to avoid. I tried carefully to suggest that in attempting to uncover "what was happening" in their local case study, their research project had become part of the process of restructuring itself; it had produced a language and an image of noncontradiction between capitalist workplace changes, changes in household practices and the constitution of gendered identities, and in this way it contributed to consolidating the affinities it represented. (xxxvii–xxxviii)

Gibson-Graham goes on to ask what might happen if the contradictions and tensions, the things that do not "add up," are foregrounded in research and how this might change the way we see and live in the world. In doing so, she employs the concept of overdetermination to rethink economy without a singular defining structure, in other words, as essentially empty. In this and other work, Gibson-Graham (2008) offers a radically different relationship between research and the field of inquiry, shifting from "the goal of 'understanding the world in order to change it'" (2) to "change our understanding *is* to change the world" (3). She later refers to the "co-implicated processes of changing ourselves/changing our thinking/changing the world" (6). This is a stance in which research is understood as performative, that is, as playing an important role in constituting the world in which we live and the types of struggles that are possible. Gibson-Graham's work can therefore be situated in a broader poststructural tradition that places language and discourse more generally at the heart of explaining our social realities, from gender to the economy. *The End of Capitalism (As We Knew It)* begins with the realization that critical inquiry is complicit in the discursive constitution and power of its subject. Moreover, this realization suggests that intellectual inquiry is a way for researchers to initiate change. In *The End of Capitalism (As We Knew It)*, Gibson-Graham disrupts the discursive hegemony of capitalism by showing that the economy is full of diverse capitalist and noncapitalist enterprises, transactions, and labors.

Similarly, Wendy Larner and William Walters (2002, 1) criticize scholars of globalization for their epistemological realism and, in particular, for their presentation of globalization as a "set of changes . . . in the very structure of the world." Instead, quoting James Tully, Larner and Walters call for a move from the analysis of underlying structures and essences to the "surface aspects that give them meaning" (2). To counter the tendency of globalization research toward totalization and grand theory, Larner and Walters draw on the Foucauldian tradition to reframe globalization as govermentality. Globalization as governmentality focuses attention on systems of thought and the ways these systems problematize, and then seek to govern, different spheres of life, such as the economy (2). In taking this approach, Larner and Walters aim to

> draw attention to the field of relations and forces, of power/knowledge in terms of which the real is actualized in this, and not other forms. *But we are aware that in joining the globalization debate we are, in however small a way, adding to and extending the hold which this idea has upon the present. We become, in other words, complicit in this fascination. The problem is that engaging with globalization—however critically—we risk marginalizing other realities, other ways of describing the world, and the foreclosure of other political possibilities.* We need to map globalization if we are to understand how political power understands its present, its objects, and its problems. *However, mapping and critiquing globalization is not enough. We also need to ask how the world could be imagined otherwise, and what political consequences this might have.* (3, emphasis added)

Like Gibson-Graham, Larner and Walters emphasize the tensions and contradictions in the rationalities and practices of globalization to make room for other ways of seeing and being in the world. They also call for alternative narratives that highlight the impurity and constantly changing form of globalization, the way in which the globalization narrative has displaced other stories, and the globalizers' many failures to implement their vision of globalization in the world (20). Yet, as the quotation suggests, Larner and Walters still find themselves complicit in the story of globalization. Indeed, when it comes to actually creating alternative narratives from fields of diversity and possibility, many other kinds of work have had to be done.

Today, many scholars employ research as a way to contribute to social movement struggles against oppression and for new worlds (see Appadurai 2000; 2002; Callon and Caliskan 2005; Callon and Rabeharisoa 2003). And recent scholarship on the relationship between knowledge and political action has moved beyond just challenging essentialist thought (although it continues to do this) to using the idea of the performative to actively construct alternative realities from fields of diversity. This is the project of Gibson-Graham's (2006b) book *A Postcapitalist Politics,* as explained in the new introduction to the second edition of *The End of Capitalism*:

> Successful theory "performs" a world; categories, concepts, theorems, and other technologies of theory are inscribed in worlds they presuppose and help to bring into being. . . . Thus the ability of theory to describe and predict is not an outcome of accurate observations/calculations, but a measure of the success of its "performance." With this understanding of the performativity of theory, we have engaged in theorizing and researching diverse and community economies, hoping to help bring these into being by providing technologies for their conceptualization and enactment. (Gibson-Graham 2006a, xx–xxi)

Building on the book *The End of Capitalism, A Postcapitalist Politics* retheorizes the economy to bring into being a new economic politics centered on the realization of ethical subjects and collective economic projects of the community economy. In the process, Gibson-Graham's work has initiated an intellectual community that can equip these economic projects.[1] Gibson-Graham highlights the important role of research, and representation more generally, in activist experimentation aimed at changing the world. In *A Postcapitalist Politics,* Gibson-Graham offers several techniques with which to create change. Whereas *The End of Capitalism* focused on the discursive performation of economy, building an epistemological politics for change, *A Postcapitalist Politics* is grounded on a politics of ontology. Inspired by feminist politics, Gibson-Graham argues that politics needs to be grounded in persons. In *A Postcapitalist Politics,* she embarks on a project of "ethical self-transformation" and "(re)subjectification," presenting techniques with which to create new subjective stances and ways of relating to the world (Gibson-Graham 2006b, xxv). These techniques are premised on thinking practices of not knowing everything in advance and instead focusing on multiplicity and heterogeneity, which enables new associations and forms of emergence: of themselves, researched subjects, and the economic experiments cultivated in their PAR projects. In *Take Back the Economy,* Gibson-Graham, Jenny Cameron, and Stephen Healy (2013) continue this work, offering a range of practices premised on the well-being of people, other species, communities, and the planet. This book, *Building Dignified Worlds*, is part of this project and extends several of Gibson-Graham's concepts. In particular, I pay close attention to techniques of collectivization, techniques that both gather together diverse species and things and transform the possibilities for action.

Embodied Geographies of Performative Collective Action

Situated within the "performing diverse economies" research tradition (see Roelvink, St. Martin, and Gibson-Graham 2015), *Building Dignified Worlds* has two clear, related themes. The first is a focus on the *geography of performative action* through which new worlds come into being. There is much research on performativity, and performativity is a theme that stretches across the social sciences, picked up in particular by poststructural thinkers concerned with how the new is brought into being. Diverse economies researchers take the theory of performativity as a central starting point for economic change (see Gibson-Graham 2008). As I suggested earlier, within the diverse economies field, attention has focused on the performativity of language in projects to create a discourse of diverse economies with new subject positions for previous marginalized or absented economies subjects. Building on this work, *Building Dignified Worlds* explores theories of performativity with a more explicit geographical focus (such as the work of Michel Callon and Eve Kosofsky Sedgwick) to tease out a number of different ways in which new forms of collectivization are shaping our world. Specifically, attention to a geography of performative action gives insight into four different registers through which collectives bring about change: (1) the linguistic and discursive script; (2) the performing actor or subject and the realm of bodily dispositions; (3) the audience who witnesses, is affected by, responds to, and thereby constitutes the performance; and (4) the relational stage or space that performances constitute, that is, the way a performance gathers diverse things together. Gibson-Graham's work utilizes the discursive and subjective dimensions of performance. This book extends her thinking with an exploration of those who witness and respond to performances and the geographical and relational nature of performance. In doing so, it maps a range of performative forces enacted by hybrid collectives.

The End of Capitalism (As We Knew It) and *A Postcapitalist Politics* build on scholarship emphasizing the productive nature of language and provide us with a discourse of economic difference that might enable new economic subjects and experiments. The discourse of the diverse economy opens up the economic landscape to include all sorts of transactions, labors, and enterprises, which can then be taken into account in decision making about economic life. Yet providing a script of diverse economies does not automatically lead to economic experimentation, because the people it targets already have roles and investments aligned with the capitalist economy, most notably those associated with working-class politics. Thus, to create new subject possibilities, in *A Postcapitalist Politics,* Gibson-Graham draws on scholarship exploring nonlinguistic performance, especially recent thinking on the body and bodily experience. Here the concept of performance, especially as it has been understood in the arts and theater and in the realm of emotions and affect, has been vital to thinking about relationships between the body and forms of consciousness, that is, how we move in and how we experience the world (Massumi 2002a; 2002b). This includes thinking about how multiple bodily experiences and sensations are translated into particular emotions and meanings and the ways that these sensations might be interrupted to generate different meanings. Gibson-Graham's action research projects work to effect such changes in the subject, to open people up to unpredictable economic experimentations and hopeful futures. In the Latrobe Valley project, for example, Gibson-Graham and her team worked to generate pleasurable experiences, such as pizza making or taking a bus trip to find out about creating a community garden. Through such experiences, participants might realize their economic interdependence and come to occupy new subject positions.

Gibson-Graham's work is a good example of how the performance of diverse economies intersects with the second thematic focus of this book, namely, *embodied geographies of collective action.* The bodied nature of space, place, and geographical knowledge is a relatively recent concern within geography but one that is growing rapidly. This heightened interest in embodiment comes after feminist geographers have raised concerns about the ways that modernist dualisms, such as mind–matter, masculinity–femininity, culture–nature, and rationality–irrationality, have worked to privilege "the conceptual over the corporeal" in geographic thought (Longhurst 1995, 97; see also Longhurst 1997). Today, work on embodied geographies is diverse and extends beyond what might be considered feminist concerns to collective politics more generally, particularly as the performance of affect and emotions are held to be key forces in contemporary politics—both on the left and the right (Hardt and Negri 2000; Hynes and Sharpe, forthcoming; Massumi 2002a; Thrift 2008; Thrift and Dewsbury 2000). In this book, I am interested in both the ways in which the geography of performative collective action is embodied and the role that the embodiment of nonrepresentational forces, such as affect, plays in collective action. Thus my interest in embodied geographies of collective action directly coincides and is interrelated with my interest in geographies of performative collective action.

On the economic terrain experimentally explored by Gibson-Graham, then, this book takes off from the relational, geographical, and embodied nature of performance. In particular, I focus on the third and fourth registers of performance: the audience, the stage, and all the relations on which performances rely. Chapters 1, 2, and 4 of this book explicitly tackle the relational and geographical nature of performative collective action, including examining the role of thinking and others' participation in performative acts, who, in addition to the speaker, play a vital role in performative action but may in fact be excluded by it. Chapters 3 and 5 continue this interest, but with a more explicit focus on the embodied nature of performative collective action. The book closes with a concluding discussion on the implications of my conceptualization of a geography of collective action for researchers wishing to participate in various forms of social innovation.

Political economic research has not always been open to ideas of performativity, particularly the performativity of research itself, and, despite the huge interest in and growing practice of alternative economies and the popular uptake of Gibson-Graham's work, political economy remains an area of academic and public inquiry with a strong realist vision. Thus, to demonstrate how political economic inquiry has been opened up (and can be opened further) to new performative registers and techniques explored herein, in chapter 1, I begin with the discursive register and the actor performing research. The chapter sets the scene for the following two chapters, which explore the different ways in which hybrid collectives shape the world and how research might contribute to contemporary social movement struggles. In chapter 1, I further examine left scholarship on neoliberalism, focusing attention on the ways in which neoliberalism has been performed in intellectual thought. I am particularly interested in the ways in which political economic thinking has aligned diverse entities with neoliberalism and in other ways of thinking that facilitate the realignments that contemporary social movements are enacting. Guided by this concern, chapter 1 analyzes the different thinking techniques employed by a small and influential range of Marxist and governmentality theorists in their study of neoliberalism. I argue that some practices of thinking are more open than others to the multiplicities and diversity of the contemporary world and thus to the realignment of things, people, and representations.

Having made a case for techniques of thinking that facilitate social transformation, the next two chapters go on to offer a range of new techniques. Chapter 2 argues for a broadening of the horizons of research to include documentary film representations of peoples, things, and issues of concern. It analyzes the performative geography of two documentary films and the ways in which economic relationships might be realigned. To gain an understanding of the geographical nature of performance and performative discourse, I turn to Eve Kosofsky Sedgwick's (2003) scholarship on the linguistic utterance. Sedgwick highlights the relational nature of performance acts, such as the constitutive role of the audience or witnesses, and introduces a different type of utterance, the "periperformative," to conceptualize the ways in which the performative might be contested and radically altered. I employ Sedgwick's work to examine the spatial composition of two alternative economic representations, the documentary films *The Take* and *Les Glaneurs et al Glaneuse (The Gleaners and I)*. Through *The Take,* I explore the way in which alternative economies are performatively brought into being. I go on to argue that *The Gleaners and I* illustrates how one might go about representing and reassembling the geography of economy through the idea of the periperformative. Together, these films offer a way of spatializing and broadening the economy that has implications for the performative potential of hybrid collectives more generally. Specifically, in chapter 2 and each chapter that follows, I argue that our understandings of the discursive nature of performances and the subjects they enable need to be accompanied by attention to the geographical and relational forces shaping action.

An awareness of the different dimensions of performance is vital to how one thinks about difference and the creation of something new. Current understandings of social transformation often see performative action as something created through discursive reiteration. Yet nonlinguistic experiences, such as emotions, the movement of bodies, and connection with others, might also generate new visions and forms of being together (Massumi 2002a). Chapter 3 takes up this line of inquiry by examining another way in which hybrid collectives are changing the world: the research conducted by social movements. It begins by expanding Gibson-Graham's idea of collective action. Collective action relates to actions that fold together bodily experience and discourse, pointing more generally to the relationship between the nondiscursive and the discursive in the constitution of new worlds. In exploring this relationship, chapter 3 shows how collectivity is embodied in the subject and, in turn, shapes the kinds of experiences subjects can have. I ponder the sites, techniques, and composition of collective action undertaken by social movement groups. The WSF exemplifies this conceptualization of collective action and is a site in which diverse experiences are translated into new collective visions and knowledge of the world. Thus, in the final section of chapter 3, I examine one session at the 2005 WSF on power, paying attention to the techniques through which the experiential knowledge of diverse groups was translated into new visions and discourse. I argue that this session created new rationalities of power and an infrastructure for their transportation to other parts of the world.

Chapters 4 and 5 explore two central social movement concerns that were represented at the 2005 WSF: (1) the market and (2) achieving dignity in the face of economic and environmental injustice. Taken at face value, the market and dignity, respectively, fall into the anti- and affirmative stances associated with the social movement struggles mentioned earlier, that is, what social movements are against and what they are for. Drawing on the insights outlined in the first three chapters, chapters 4 and 5 examine this "anti-" and "for" division. In chapter 4, I argue that the market model that social movements oppose is rarely performed in day-to-day life. Rather, existing markets are better conceptualized as dynamic social networks open to intervention and occupation by social movements. I draw on Adam Smith's classical political economic thought along with more recent scholarship in the field of actor network theory to develop this conceptualization. Bringing together the themes of performativity and embodiment, I argue that markets are networks constituted through performative acts of framing and show how the sociality of market networks is embodied in the form of Smith's impartial spectator who governs market transactions. The geography of market framing reveals a range of entities gathered around the market frame and affected by market practices. A politics of the market is enacted when these entities join together to form collectives that attempt to reframe markets. I argue that the conceptualization of the market presented in chapter 4 is a valuable tool for social movement struggles. I focus, in particular, on the example of trash-pickers seeking to create markets in recycling. Viewing the market as a dynamic social network enables a variety of actors, including researchers, to participate in its performance and opens markets up to the pursuit of an array of social, environmental, cultural, and economic goals.

The ethical markets emerging through these struggles have given rise to a dignified subject. For example, dehumanized scavengers have been transformed into dignified recycling workers. Chapter 5 explores these ethical economic relationships further and the ontological possibilities they generate. The lens of dignity leads me to consider contemporary struggles that combine ecological and economic action. Dignity reflects both a mode of being human and the dignified world in which this is possible (Malpas and Lickiss 2007, 4). Struggles for dignity must thus consider human relationships with the world. In this chapter, I turn to Karl Marx's work on species-being, in which he uses the term *dignity* to refer to the kind of humanity realized in socially just economic forms. I analyze whether the theory of species-being can be reread and extended to also offer a way to understand ecologically just economic forms. My aim here is to utilize the idea of species-being to theorize social movements that are creating different ways of living with "earth others" (Plumwood 2002) in our area of anthropogenic climate change.

Throughout this book, I highlight the role of performative and embodied geographies in the constitution of our world. These geographies link diverse peoples, things, and concerns, including researchers and research technologies. This argument has important implications for researchers, who can no longer assume that they are isolated from the broader networks they study or the realities they help bring into being. In the conclusion of this book, I discuss the responsibility researchers have to those within the networks in which their research participates. This includes a responsibility to that which is made visible through research practices and also to that which is invisible. An awareness of the intertwining of research and social movement struggle is vital to ethical performances of new economies.

My conceptualization of collective associations as hybrids that create change by reformulating relationships also has important resonances for contemporary politics. In the context of concern about climate change and viruses that ignore species and geographical boundaries, we are becoming increasingly aware that action exceeds the ambit of the human. The book's conclusion, and indeed the book as a whole, suggests that representing the geography of collective action is a significant political strategy to bring about change. It contributes to understanding the co-constituting roles of humans and nonhumans in collective action and offers techniques through which the nonhuman might come to assert a stronger presence in collective responses to contemporary and future challenges.

.

1

The Discontents of Knowing Neoliberalism

Screaming Out against Neoliberalism

The photograph on the next page depicting the "vampire of neoliberalism" staked through the heart and screaming expresses a fantasy held by many social movement groups that have participated in the antiglobalization movement. This fantasy is to make the evil force of neoliberalism scream in pain. The image expresses social movement anger at the destruction caused by the neoliberal monster and takes pleasure in its demise. This fantasy is related to a particular knowledge of the world, specifically, a knowledge of how neoliberalism has systematically transformed nation-states and economies for the worse and plunged vast numbers of people into poverty. Knowing neoliberalism in this way has had mobilizing and paralyzing effects on social movement struggles. After introducing both effects, this chapter focuses on the latter.

A different scream from that of a dying neoliberalism gave rise to what, in 2001 Porto Alegre, Brazil, became the World Social Forum (WSF) movement. Cried out by people around the globe, this scream expressed the idea that something was wrong with the world. It carried with it a desire for change. John Holloway (2002, 1–2), an academic and participant at the 2005 WSF, suggests that this kind of scream can connect and mobilize people:

> Dimly perhaps, we feel that these things that anger us are not isolated phenomena, that there is a connection between them, that they are all part of a world that is flawed, a world that is wrong in some fundamental way.... Our anger is directed not just against particular happenings but against a more general wrongness, a feeling that the world is askew, that the world is in some way untrue. When we experience something particularly horrific, we hold up

Taken by the author in Porto Alegre, Brazil, during the 2005 World Social Forum, this depiction of the screaming vampire of neoliberalism staked through the heart was one of many graffiti images representing opposition to the neoliberal agenda.

our hands in horror and say "that cannot be! it cannot be true!" We know that it is true, but feel that it is the truth of an untrue world.

Holloway argues that the scream of people around the world prompts diverse groups to recognize their common oppression and to join together in opposition. The WSF has collected a considerable number of people and movements under this oppositional banner. In 2005, when I attended, the WSF gathered 155,000 participants (Keraghel and Sen 2004).

Though the scream mobilizing diverse groups around the world to participate in the WSF was initially an emotional response to a general feeling of wrongness, at subsequent WSF meetings, this emotional energy has been swept up into a specific protest against neoliberalism and into the fantasy of its demise. A central motivation of the early forums was to challenge unthinking acceptance of and thus implicit support for neoliberalism. The charter of principles, drawn up shortly after the first meeting by a group of Brazilian organizations and later revised by an international council (Sen 2004), seeks to undermine neoliberalism by exposing it as a historical manifestation of the capitalist political economic system that has been magnified by globalization. The charter depicts neoliberalism as a contemporary form of capitalist imperialism operating in the interests of multinational corporations and aligned with the policy agendas of national governments and international institutions. Principle 11 of the charter states,

> As a forum for debate, the WSF is a movement of ideas that prompts reflection, and the transparent circulation of the results of that reflection, on the mechanisms and instruments of domination by capital, on means and actions to resist and overcome that domination, and on the alternatives proposed to solve the problems of exclusion and social inequality that the process of capitalist globalisation with its racist, sexist and environmentally destructive dimensions is creating internationally and within countries.[1] (Sen et al. 2004, 71)

Possessed with this knowledge, which exposes neoliberalism for what it really is, participants of the WSF have been able to reveal and make public the agenda lying behind specific instances of destruction, dispossession, and oppression, such as the privatization of water in South Africa and factory abandonment resulting in large-scale unemployment in Argentina. Insight into the "system" of dispossession spearheaded by neoliberal policy agendas has facilitated diverse place-based groups opposed to different instances of neoliberalism to join together in common opposition.

A critical understanding of neoliberalism has also enabled social movements to explain, link, and judiciously oppose diverse and new forms of oppression. As it extends across the globe through different country hosts and, now, multiply located forums, the WSF movement facilitates further generation and collection of knowledge about the implementation of neoliberal political and economic reforms. It further highlights the changing nature of neoliberalism and the specific alignment of neoliberal policies with local forces of domination, such as hierarchies based on caste. Given such a broad ambit of knowledge, the WSF has been able to link events such as the U.S.-led invasion of Iraq with the destructive "system" underlying neoliberalism by exposing aspirations for democratization accompanied by marketization and privatization as neo-imperial forms of resource extraction and profiteering (see also Harvey 2003). Although this war was shockingly horrific, in the context of the devastation brought about through the capitalist economy, it came as little surprise to the social movement groups participating in the WSF and could be easily incorporated into the forum's oppositional framework. Such information about the different ways that neoliberalism is implemented on the ground has enabled participants of the WSF to identify specific sites and protagonists rolling out the neoliberal agenda, notably the World Economic Forum in Davos, Switzerland, and the representatives of capital, such as multinational corporations and Western nation-states, particularly the United States of America. Overall, then, a knowledge of the workings of neoliberal capitalist globalization has provided a range of social movement groups with the power to say that they really know what is happening around the world and to rally against specific institutions and events.

So far, the different ways social movement struggles can employ critical knowledge of neoliberalism suggests that this knowledge is useful. Yet, though a critical knowledge of neoliberalism has helped the WSF to oppose neoliberalism, this knowledge has been largely unhelpful and even something of a barrier when it comes to the creation of alternatives (Keraghel and Sen 2004). One concern is that this knowledge drains the emotional energy of social movement groups that have come together in their struggle for new worlds. In his discussion of the scream, Holloway (2002, 2–3) suggests that while the scream brings people together in common outrage, the scream is "smothered" by its explanation:

> There are so many ways of bouncing our scream back against us, of looking at us and asking why we scream. Is it because of our age, our social background, or just some psychological maladjustment that we are so negative? Are we hungry, did we sleep badly or is it just pre-menstrual tension? Do we know that it is unscientific to scream?

Holloway argues that explanations of the scream render it nothing more than a fetish and a projection of some other, more primary condition affecting the screamer. As a result, critical intellectual analysis of the scream depletes its embodied and emotional force, the very force through which social movements come to realize their common condition (Holloway 2002). Holloway suggests that in explaining what generates screams, "we have learnt, perhaps, how they fit together as parts of a system of social domination, but somehow our negativity has been erased from the picture" (3). Holloway is particularly concerned by the way that the explanation of the scream can depersonalize it from the screamer. He argues that this depersonalization and externalization of the scream dislocate the scream from the starting point of struggle.

I am concerned that the critical knowledge revealing neoliberalism as a manifestation of the all-encompassing, all-powerful, and adaptable "system" of capitalism renders much social movement struggle inconsequential and futile. In the context of capitalist globalization, social movement struggles and any alternatives these struggles initiate seem relatively insignificant. For alternative projects to be taken seriously by many scholars who critique neoliberalism, the projects must completely replace capitalism by a single revolution or multiplied points of struggle (see Gibson-Graham 2006a). Whereas today diverse economic initiatives are highly visible, and proliferating beyond expectation, this was not the case at the outset of the antiglobalization movement and WSF meetings, where critical elaboration of reasons for the scream against neoliberalism funneled the emotional energy joining social movements into a struggle to overthrow neoliberalism. This made it difficult for social movements participating in early WSF to move from the scream to the creation of multiple and diverse alternatives of their own and/or in concert with others. This is a problem because, though the "refusal to accept" the horrors of neoliberalism and the desire for an alternative are what prompt the scream in the first place, on its own, the scream "tells us nothing of the future, nor does it depend for its validity on one particular outcome" (Holloway 2002, 6). The scream thus needs to be accompanied by new ideas that social movement groups can use to create alternatives and initiate social innovation. This has been a challenge not only for the WSF but also for contemporary collective action more generally, as the next chapter demonstrates through the challenge to come up with an alternative put to activist and political commentator and journalist Namoi Klein. Concerned about these particular effects of the critique of neoliberalism in social movement struggle, participants of the WSF have come to challenge the forum's stance against neoliberalism, questioning the extent to which the very discussion and knowledge of neoliberalism strengthen neoliberal discourse while inhibiting the creation of alternatives (Keraghel and Sen 2004).

In light of these negative effects on social innovation, the thinking practices shaping critical knowledge about neoliberalism and thus choices open to scholars of neoliberalism require further examination to generate thinking practices to imagine new worlds. Yet this is rarely undertaken in scholarly work on neoliberalism (but see as notable exceptions Collier 2012; Weller and O'Neill 2014). Rather, the debate is largely focused on the relationship between fined-tuned analysis of neoliberalism in place and what Jamie Peck (2004) calls "neoliberalism-in-general." My concern in this chapter is thus to explore and problematize the thinking practices that generate critical knowledge about neoliberalism and, in doing so, to ask whether there are other ways of thinking that might assist social movements to create alternatives, which the rest of this book then explores. By examining the thinking practices that shape the critique of neoliberalism, I aim to provide a space for intellectual and activist reflection on the thinking that has come to shape the antiglobalization movement and social struggles that have followed. This aim is connected, perhaps somewhat implicitly, to the central themes guiding this book—the performativity of collective action and embodied collective action. When performativity is understood as involving an interconnected geography (or *agencement,* as discussed in chapter 4) of various human and nonhuman elements, the role of research in social innovation moves from reflecting the world to participating in its making (see also St. Martin, Roelvink, and Gibson-Graham 2015). In relation to the theme of embodied collective action, as I highlight in the conclusion to this chapter, the thinking practices through which we perform research are part of a stance toward the world that is difficult to shift and that shapes the choices researchers make as to how to participate in social experimentation through research practice.

This chapter investigates three different instances of research on neoliberalism: the popular and influential book *The New Imperialism* of the Marxist geographer David Harvey (2003); the influential theory of governmentality and, in particular, the work of Wendy Larner (2000; 2003); and finally, Julia Elyachar's (2005) book *Markets of Dispossession,* which is shaped both by Marxist and governmentality approaches to research and thinking. My analysis of the particular thinking moves undertaken by these scholars is directed by Eve Kosofsky Sedgwick (2003) and others' description of two forms of theorization that characterize contemporary scholarship, strong and weak theory. As with any analysis, my choice of texts is very deliberative and may seem rather selective, yet these texts enable me to clearly illustrate a range of thinking practices that differently shape scholarship on neoliberalism. Through an examination of Harvey's and Larner's respective works, I explore the strong and weak thinking techniques that represent neoliberalism in a way that inhibits and/or facilitates social movement struggles for alternatives. In the third case, my analysis of Elyachar's book demonstrates the power of strong thinking practices about neoliberalism and how they background and veil existing alternatives that might be utilized by social movements. Thus, although critical knowledge about neoliberalism has been used by social movements to mobilize global meetings such as the WSF, to join diverse groups and give social movement groups the power to say that they know the source of their oppression, I argue that there is also a need for other approaches to understanding neoliberalism that can facilitate the collective creation of alternatives.

The Thinking Techniques of Strong Theory

Sedgwick (2003) suggests that scholars have multiple choices as to how they know the world. For example, given the pervasive nature of contemporary global capitalism, many intellectuals would probably accept that some form or elements of neoliberalism can be found almost anywhere. They are thus presented with a choice of whether to develop this knowledge through further revealing, specifying, and detailing instances of neoliberalism. For Sedgwick, such choices relate to the performativity of knowledge. To some extent, most scholars would accept or be familiar with the claim that knowledge is an active force shaping the world. However, Sedgwick suggests that dominant ways of thinking, particularly critical theory, have limited the impact of this assertion and the ways in which it might be utilized by scholars wishing to contribute to social transformation (24). Sedgwick develops her argument by reflecting on the question she posed to activist scholar Cindy Patton early in the AIDS epidemic regarding the numerous sinister rumors as to the origins of HIV in the United States. Patton's response was one of disinterest: "Suppose we were sure of every element of conspiracy: that the lives of Africans and African Americans are worthless in the eyes of the United States; that gay men and drug users are held cheap where they aren't actively hated . . . supposing we were ever so sure of all those things—what would we know then that we don't already know?" (Patton, as quoted by Sedgwick 2003, 123). This response suggested to Sedgwick that:

though ethically very fraught, the choice is not self-evident; whether or not to undertake this highly compelling tracing-and-exposure project represents a strategic and local decision, not necessarily a categorical imperative. Patton's response to me seemed to open a space for moving from the rather fixed question Is a particular piece of knowledge true, and how can we know? to the further questions: What does knowledge *do*—the pursuit of it, the having and exposing of it, the receiving again of knowledge of what one already knows? *How,* in short, is knowledge performative, and how best does one move among its causes and effects? (124)

This is not a question of truth. One can accept the existence of oppression and destruction without being held to developing this knowledge through further inquiry. In fact, Sedgwick even suggests that because such knowledge has been established, one might be able step to the side of it (129).

Before the performativity of knowledge can be taken seriously and used by researchers seeking to equip social movement struggles, Sedgwick suggests that scholars must take heed of what she describes as the critical theorist's impulse toward a paranoid form of knowing the world. As she sees it, "in a world where no one need be delusional to find evidence of systemic oppression, to theorize out of anything *but* a paranoid critical stance has come to seem naïve, pious, or complaisant" (125–26). In other words, given what scholars know about neoliberal capitalist globalization, they feel morally and ethically compelled to document, analyze, and theorize this systemic force of oppression to be able to oppose it. The performative effects of Marxist and other scholarship generated through a paranoid intellectual stance have been examined in detail by J. K. Gibson-Graham (2006a) in her book *The End of Capitalism (As We Knew It)*. One effect that is especially worrying is the way that such scholarship contributes to capitalist hegemony. Similarly, as I noted earlier, understood as a description of capitalist imperialism's latest incarnation, neoliberalism has a strong hold on intellectual and activist imaginations.

Gibson-Graham (2006b, xxix) suggests that the paranoid stance is fueled by "seldom-inspected common sense" divisions like that "between thought, understood as cerebral reflection, and action, understood as embodied engagement with the world." Intertwining the questions intellectuals face about the choice of what knowledge to create with the emotional and dispositional stances affecting this decision, Gibson-Graham is interested in both what and how we act through thinking:

> Yet the kinds of choices we continually make about *what to do* and *how to act* in particular situations are also required of us as thinkers. These include the *stances* we adopt, the affective dispositions that color our thinking and impinge on consciousness as feeling—practical curiosity and openness to possibility, for example, or moral certainty and the acceptance of constraint. They also include the *techniques* we employ to actualize those stances in particular thought undertakings. (xxix)

Adding to Sedgwick's and others' work, Gibson-Graham thus directs attention to how we act as thinkers and, in particular, to the relationship between a stance toward the world and the actual thinking techniques used to generate knowledge supporting this stance. Gibson-Graham is primarily interested in the thinking techniques that scholars wishing to contribute to social innovation and transformation might employ. These techniques are discussed later in this chapter. Given that our thinking techniques are rarely investigated (Gibson-Graham 2006b), first I am interested in discussing some of the thinking techniques available in the production of knowledge about neoliberalism that promote a paranoid stance. Therefore, in what follows, I operationalize Sedgwick's description of the paranoid stance as a series of techniques of thinking about neoliberalism.

Sedgwick argues that paranoid theory has become synonymous with critical theory and has thus come to dominate intellectual inquiry. Comparing critique to conspiracy theory, Bruno Latour's (2004a) work on the orientation of critical inquiry to the task of undermining and displacing contemporary "matters of fact" supports this conclusion. Sedgwick (2003, 128) draws on Melanie Klein and Silvan Tomkin's work on paranoia to "situate it as one kind of epistemological practice among other, alternative ones," distinguishing paranoid theory as a series of practices. Through her analysis of these "differentials of practice," Sedgwick develops a picture of theory as continuously expanding to anticipate and thus negate any element of surprise (130). The theorist achieves this by putting the theorist's own self in the enemy's shoes; that is, only by performing the paranoid fear is the theorist able to anticipate surprise. And even the failure to anticipate surprise confirms that "you can never be paranoid enough" (127). As a result, paranoid practices and paranoid theory can be classified as "strong theory." Strong theory is characterized by all-encompassing theory and an affect-driven feedback loop (133). More specifically, seeking to negate the negative affects of surprise, the paranoid theorist attempts to expand the scope of theory by developing stronger associations between entities and further extending their theoretical reach, tautologically reducing chance and possibility. As Sedgwick concludes,

> this is how it happens that an explanatory structure that a reader may see as tautological, in that it can't help or can't stop or can't do anything other than prove the very same assumptions with which it began, may be experienced by the practitioner as a triumphant advance toward truth and vindication. (135)

Strong theory, however, may not only be a result of paranoid practices in social science; the philosophy of science suggests that the tradition and organization of scientific practice might also contribute to the production of strong theory. Isabelle Stengers's (2000) analysis of the scientific community's acceptance of Thomas Kuhn's famous paradigm and revolution model of science is an excellent example. Stengers's discussion of why Kuhn's theorization of "normal science" was applauded by many scientists suggests that, in addition to paranoid practices of inquiry, strong theory might also be prompted by scientific community norms that reinforce dominant ways of practicing science. Another factor in this regard is the scientific community's autonomy from political and social spheres and controversies. As Stengers puts it,

> the reading proposed by Thomas Kuhn thus justifies a radical differentiation between a scientific community, produced by its own history, endowed with instruments that inseparably integrate production (research) and reproduction (the training of those authorized to participate in this research), and a milieu that, if it wishes to benefit from the repercussions of this activity, must be content with maintaining it without making it give an account of itself. With regard to the scientist at work, no one has to benefit from a relation of force that would allow him or her to impose questions that are not the "good" questions of the community. (5)

Like Sedgwick's classification of paranoid theory as a form of strong theory, Stengers's analysis directs attention to the way the organization of science encourages scientists to reinforce and expand their theoretical ambit while excluding that which would bring the autonomy of their community into question. Some of the factors that challenge scientific autonomy that Stengers identifies are "'non-scientific' factors" like "relations of force and overtly social games of power, differences in resources and prestige between competing laboratories, possibilities of being aligned with 'impure' interests (ideological, industrial, states, etc.)" (7–8). Keeping in mind this broader context and other factors that might contribute to the production of strong theory, I will now focus on and tease out the particular techniques of thinking that prompt strong theory.

The first thinking technique of strong theory involves thinking that *looks for sameness and patterns* that will confirm that which is already known. This technique can be associated with the epistemological position of monotheism, which holds that there is a "singular nature of reality" and a "singular appropriate way to study it" (Resnick and Wolff 1987, 38). Through this thinking technique, difference that might deconstruct the monism is rendered invisible or, if visible, inconsequential to that which really matters. The theorist might also attempt to include and explain variations through their theoretical ambit, thus rendering that which is different and potentially disruptive merely another instance of what is already known. One way to establish a relationship that links different instances with a particular phenomenon is to approach that phenomenon as a general process rather than as a thing, and then use concepts like adaptation and evolution to describe that process. For example, scholarship on neoliberalism pays attention to the many different forms of neoliberalism and how they relate to the general phenomenon of neoliberalism (Peck 2004; Peck and Tickell 2002; see also Castree 2006). Theorists have established this relationship by approaching neoliberalism as a general process that is adaptable and changing. For instance, Jamie Peck and Adam Tickell (2002) identify "roll-back" and "roll-out" forms of neoliberalism.

A second thinking technique of strong theory that is related to the technique of looking for sameness might be described as a *technique of alignment.* Alignment involves formatting relationships and associations between different entities so that they are linked through a singular understanding of the world. Identifying a singular system like neoliberalism or capitalism is a key tool for making these associations and linking different instances of oppression. Socialist feminists, for instance, have developed the theory of capitalism to link patriarchal oppression with economic injustice (Gibson-Graham 2006a). Another tool is the abstraction of a process or mechanism, providing a way to relate a range of sites and changes through a singular underlying force. This thinking technique tends to foreground entities like the market as singular abstract mechanisms of dispossessing forces that, in turn, are used to link many different instances on the ground, from the rise of entrepreneurial innovation and social capital in development to the privatization of welfare (see, e.g., Elyachar 2005; Harvey 2003). Processes like marketization, privatization, and entrepreneurialism provide analytical tools with which to think about and relate a variety of social and political changes to neoliberalism. For example, the new role of community organizations in state welfare delivery has been theorized as the latest incarnation of neoliberalism, dubbed *inclusive liberalism,* in which marketization combined with new forms of social governance have transformed what were once seen as activist groups into "contractaulized service delivery NGOs" (Craig and Porter 2006, 246).

A third thinking technique involves *establishing knowledge through exposure.* Sedgwick argues that the foundations of the paranoid theoretical stance lie in knowledge itself, specifically in knowledge as exposure (138). To put it another way, the status of knowledge as truth relies on a "faith in exposure," that is, on the belief that the exposed phenomenon is the underlying essence and thus truth itself (138). The frequency with which the terms *unveil* and *expose* represent the end point or aim of critical inquiry demonstrates the commonality of such practice (Sedgwick 2003, 138). Bruno Latour (2004a) is similarly concerned by critical theory that rests on knowledge as the exposure of underlying forces. Comparing critique to conspiracy theory, he remarks,

> Of course, we in the academy like to use more elevated causes—society, discourse, knowledge-slash-power, fields of forces, empires, capitalism—while conspiracists like to portray a miserable bunch of greedy people with dark intents, but I find something troublingly similar in the structure of the explanation, in the first movement of disbelief and, then, in the wheeling of casual explanations coming out of the deep dark below. (229)

Sedgwick (2003, 140) goes on to suggest that the exposure of oppressive hidden forces is often unnecessary at a time when so much oppression and violence are visible and can be taken as exemplary. Like the effects of visibility, research that is premised on unveiling something that is present but hidden needs to be understood as performative and thus constitutive of particular effects. In assuming the exposed phenomenon is knowledge itself, the paranoid theorist is in danger of missing the performative force of representation. Latour's analysis of critique helps to distinguish two moves involved in this technique of establishing knowledge through exposure. The first relates to Latour's (2004a, 237) description of "criticism as anti-fetishism." Undertaking criticism as anti-fetishism, the theorist inscribes people's relationships with objects and things, from fashion to music, as projections of their wants and desires, such as a desire for a particular identity. In doing so, loved things are robbed of a social life and rendered nothing but projected desires. Second, the theorist translates these fetishes into forces of power, domination, and/or oppression, which, thus exposed, can be used to explain the original behavior:

> When naïve believers are clinging forcefully to their objects, claiming that they are made to do things because of their gods, their poetry, their cherished objects, you can turn all of those attachments into so many fetishes and humiliate all the believers by showing that it is nothing but their own projection, that you, yes you alone, can see. But as soon as naïve believers are thus inflated by some belief in their own importance, in their own projective capacity, you strike them by a second uppercut and humiliate them again, this time by showing that, whatever they think, their behaviour is entirely determined by the action of powerful causalities coming from objective reality they don't see, but that you, yes you, the never sleeping critic, alone can see. (239)

This circular process of critique ensures that the critic will always be right (239). In light of Latour's analysis, it is easy to see how exposure directly translates into a technique of thinking. In the first step of this technique, the theorist identifies things as desires. This is best illustrated by returning to the issues raised in the beginning of this chapter in regard to the application of Holloway's discussion of the scream to the WSF. Rather than viewing the forum as an active thing in and of itself, the first step in this technique directs attention to the participants of the forum and explains their participation as a manifestation of the scream and as a desire for change. Bringing together the other thinking techniques of strong theory, looking for sameness and alignment that relate to the analysis of systematic associations, the second step in this thinking technique involves establishing a primary force that can explain the forum participants' anger and their desire for change that generates their scream. Such a force needs to be abstract enough not to be visible, and thus already exposed in its entirety, and a force that can be seen to align multiple relations between people and things. Indeed, Holloway notes that the scream can be explained as a symptom of common oppression under capitalism. He laments the way that such explanation has excluded from the picture the emotional force mobilizing screamers to come together. Thus these thinking techniques help to explain how a theorist can render the WSF as little more than a protest against neoliberalism and, ultimately, capitalism. To demonstrate these thinking techniques further, I now turn to David Harvey's (2003) influential work *The New Imperialism.*

A Strong Theory of Neoliberalism

Marxist scholarship is one of the most vocal and theoretical engagements with the topic of neoliberalism and oppositional collective action. Scholarship in this general field of inquiry ranges from the regulation approach to capitalism and associated institutional arrangements (see, e.g., Amin 1994; more recently, see Brenner, Peck, and Theodore 2010; Peck 2004; Peck and Tickell 2002) to Michael Hardt and Antonio Negri's (2000) manifesto *Empire.* Though perhaps less sophisticated than his earlier work, David Harvey's (2003) book *The New Imperialism* crosses disciplinary boundaries, different Marxist approaches; has been widely utilized by social movements; and is clearly, in many ways, a strong statement against neoliberalism:

> If . . . we find that the WTO proclaims free trade but actually delivers unfair trade in which the richer countries maintain their collective advantage over the poorer, *then we should not be surprised.* (133, emphasis added)

The New Imperialism thus deserves serious attention.

In what follows, I draw on *The New Imperialism* to exemplify a strong theory of neoliberalism. It is rare today to find such a strong theory of neoliberalism in geographical scholarship and other cognate disciplines, even though the various thinking practices forming strong theory pervade the scholarship on neoliberalism and neoliberal discourse more generally, as I demonstrate later in this chapter. One might thus criticize my analysis as evoking a "straw man" of neoliberalism or, as J. K. Gibson-Graham (2006a,

9–10) describes such an exaggerated image, "a bizarre and monstrous being that will never be found in pure form in any other text." Indeed, when Jamie Peck (2004, 403) describes "neoliberalism-in-general," he notes that "neoliberalism does not, and cannot, exist in pure form, but only manifests itself in hybrid formations" and goes on to warn that scholars should be weary of "succumbing to the fallacies of monolithism, functionalism or convergence thinking." My reading of *The New Imperialism* is, however, purposeful and strategic and, of course, one of many possible readings. Not only can *The New Imperialism* be used to exemplify the thinking practices that generate a strong theory of neoliberalism but it also raises the question of how one might approach a straw man of neoliberalism. One approach that arguably characterizes much scholarship on neoliberalism parallels a Marxian approach to capitalism: "our usual strategy is not to banish or slay it, but rather to tame it: hedge it with qualifications, rive it with contradictions, discipline it with contingencies of politics or culture; make it more 'realistic' and reasonable, more complex, less embarrassing, less outrageous" (Gibson-Graham 2006a, 10–11). A good example of this approach is Jamie Peck's (2004, 403) writing on "neoliberalism-in-general," which he suggests is "a loose and contradiction laden ideological framework that is evolving not only through conflict with the 'external' social worlds that it encounters but also through vacillating tensions between its *own* authoritarian and libertarian moments and constituencies. . . . Its much-less-than-ideal type if you like, is being conjointly and socially reproduced on a continuing basis." This approach to "taming" neoliberalism, as Gibson-Graham (2006a, 11) notes of scholarship on capitalism, does not address the powerful discourse of neoliberalism and its hold over the imagination and critical space. Nor does it draw attention to the role of thinking habits in this discourse, which, once examined, might enable experimentation with other thinking strategies more generative of alternatives. Thus, with this caveat in mind, I now turn to Harvey's *The New Imperialism*.

In chapter 1, "All about Oil," Harvey (2003, 1) lays out his intentions in writing the book:

> My aim is to look at the current condition of global capitalism and the role that a "new" imperialism might be playing within it. I do so from the perspective of the long durée and through the lens of what I call historical-geographical materialism. I seek to uncover some of the deeper transformations occurring

beneath all the surface turbulence and volatility, and so open up a terrain of debate as to how we might best interpret and react to our present situation.

As this passage suggests, in *The New Imperialism,* Harvey aims to think about neoliberalism and other contemporary political economic manifestations in relation to and as a form of global capitalism. In doing so, he hopes to facilitate collective resistance that might lead to the creation of an alternative. In this work, Harvey provides a way to think about and connect a diverse range of social movement groups. More specifically, by exposing the underlying dynamic of contemporary capitalism, he offers social movements a "generalized political goal" to gather around (179). He does so by producing a strong theory of neoliberalism. Although his account facilitates collective mobilization against neoliberalism and provides a general and widely accessible understanding of global capitalism, Harvey gives little attention to the choices researchers have in their knowledge production and the performative effects of their work. This limitation not only compels Harvey to leave the creation of alternatives to others but leads him to neglect the effects of his work on these other projects.

Building on his earlier work, in *The New Imperialism,* Harvey theorizes capitalism as the underlying force of contemporary imperialism. For Harvey and other Marxists, capitalism is understood as a continually expanding system based on the accumulation of capital. Capital cannot stand idle but must be continually reinvested to generate further surplus capital. Harvey draws on Karl Marx's formulation of "the tendency for the profit rate to fall" to suggest that, to varying degrees, capitalism is a largely unsustainable system (88). He extends Marx's theory of overaccumulation as a means to think about and explain systemic crises and their resolutions. A crisis of overaccumulation occurs when there is a "lack of opportunities for profitable investment" and capital lies idle rather than being reinvested to generate further profit (139). To explore how capitalism might be changing in response to the problem of overaccumulation, Harvey returns to the analysis of primitive accumulation, the forceful dispossession of people from their land as a precondition and continual accompaniment to capitalist development. Current acts of dispossession resolve the crisis of overaccumulation by opening up new or expanding old markets through commodification and privatization. Harvey suggests that the proponents of contemporary dispossession employ the ideology of neoliberalism to justify and legitimate their actions.

Harvey's analysis of the ways in which the crisis of accumulation is re-solved rests on his thinking about the relationship between capitalism and its "outside," noncapitalism. He employs the first thinking technique of strong theory outlined earlier, looking for sameness in his analysis of this relationship. In contrast to poststructural scholarship, which attempts to depict a "radical" outside or alterity that escapes the binary of capitalism—noncapitalism—Harvey reads capitalism and noncapitalism through the logic of the capitalist system as sameness. Harvey demonstrates and devel-ops this relationship by considering Marx's analysis of the reserve army of labor as a function of capitalism (141). The reserve army of labor is thought to serve the interests of capitalism by keeping wages down and increasing the opportunities for capital investment. The ranks of the reserve army are swelled through processes like colonization, which transforms peasants into landless laborers forced to sell their labor as workers or through the un-employment of current workers. In both cases, the reserve army of labor is an "outside" that is actually inside capitalism when understood through Harvey's theory of capitalism. Harvey writes,

> Now in all of these instances capitalism does indeed require something "out-side of itself" in order to accumulate, but in the last case it actually throws workers out of the system at one point in time in order to have them to hand for purposes of accumulation at a later point in time. Put in the language of contemporary postmodern political theory, we might say that capitalism necessarily and always creates its own "other." The idea that some sort of "out-side" is necessary for the stabilization of capitalism therefore has relevance. But capitalism can either make use of some pre-existing outside (non-capitalist social formations or some sector within capitalism—such as education—that has not yet been proletarianized) or it can actively manufacture it. I propose to take this "inside-outside" dialectic seriously in what follows. I shall examine how the "organic relation" between expanded reproduction on the one hand and the often violent processes of dispossession on the other have shaped the historical geography of capitalism. (141–42)

To think about the relationship between different territories, states, and con-flicts throughout history as the historical geography of capitalism, Harvey elaborates on this dialectic of accumulation noted in the preceding quotation, paying particular attention to the idea of accumulation through expanded reproduction and dispossession. Expanded reproduction involves reducing production costs to increase capital surplus. Dispossession aims to increase opportunities for the investment and further generation of capital surplus through the incorporation of new capitalist territories, industries, and commodities. Employing the thinking technique of seeking sameness, Harvey identifies abstract mechanisms such as the market to theorize these processes across space and time. More specifically, he focuses on markets, privatization, and the commodification of public or common assets as mechanisms through which capitalism's outside is incorporated.

In this context in which global capitalism is understood as the primary political economic force, Harvey views neoliberalism as an ideology of capitalist dispossession: "Put in another way, if capitalism has been experiencing a chronic difficulty of overaccumulation since 1973, then the neo-liberal project of privatization of everything makes a lot of sense as one way to solve the problem" (149–50). In Harvey's analysis, the concept of neoliberalism functions in a way that is indicative of the second thinking technique of strong theory outlined earlier: alignment. Harvey uses the concept of neoliberalism to associate a wide variety of political economic processes and entities, such as privatization and markets, with accumulation by dispossession and ultimately capitalist dynamics. He summarizes:

Accumulation by dispossession became increasingly more salient after 1973, in part as a compensation for the chronic problems of overaccumulation arising within expanded reproduction. The primary vehicle for this development was financialization and the orchestration, largely at the behest of the United States, of an international financial system that could, from time to time, visit anything from mild to savage bouts of devaluation and accumulation by dispossession on certain sectors or even whole territories. But the opening up of new territories to capitalist development and to capitalistic forms of market behaviour also played a role, as did the primitive accumulations accomplished in those countries (such as South Korea, Taiwan, and now, even more dramatically, China) that sought to insert themselves into global capitalism as active players. For all of this to occur required not only financialization and freer trade, but a radically different approach to how state power, always a major player in accumulation by dispossession, should be deployed. The rise of neo-liberal theory and its associated politics of privatization symbolized much of what this shift was about. (156)

Harvey sees neoliberalism as a narrative that aligns different moments and events in history and uses this narrative as a way to associate the 1970s crisis of overaccumulation with different instances of accumulation through dispossession. He employs the narrative of neoliberalism to link the privatization of public assets in welfare states such as the United Kingdom (e.g., the privatization of housing estates that led to housing speculation and gentrification) with the modernization-modeled industrialization of countries such as Argentina, which resulted in social destruction after an enormous amount of capital inflow then withdrawal (158–60). The privatization of common indigenous land in Mexico is another example of neoliberalism, one that Harvey suggests in part explains the Zapatista uprising. In each case, then, different instances are linked not only through the symbolic lens of neoliberalism but also through different forms of social destruction, oppression, and resistance.

Following Marx's narrative of progressive development, Harvey suggests that despite the many social improvements created through modernization, accumulation by dispossession always entails social struggle. He goes on to suggest the dialectic of accumulation as a way to explain and link social movements across space. Harvey is concerned that divisions between social movements, such as the division between labor union politics and newer social movements arising from the struggle "against the encroachment of capitalist imperialism," like the Zapatistas, veil the common force behind contemporary accumulation through reproduction and dispossession:

> But in the same way that dismissal of the "organic link" between accumulation by dispossession and expanded reproduction disempowered and limited the vision of the traditional left, so resort to the conception of postmodern struggle has the same impact upon the newly emerging movements against accumulation by dispossession. (175)

Harvey argues that social movements need to be able to collectively address this underlying common hegemonic force. In this way, he draws together labor struggles against expanded reproduction and the often dubbed postmodern social movements against dispossession into a single trajectory. Harvey employs the third thinking technique of strong theory outlined earlier, exposure, as a way to join these diverse social movements. In exposing different forms of capitalist accumulation, Harvey aims to bring diverse social movements into conversation and ultimately unite them in collective political struggle. He highlights Arundhati Roy's critique of "dam construction in the Narmada valley in India" as a way for the traditional left and postmodern social movements to work together (177–78). Harvey suggests that Roy's critique connects class struggle with struggles over localized instances of dispossession by arguing that such dam projects are an inefficient means of creating energy, creating environmental degradation, financially benefitting foreign investors rather than local people, and creating large-scale displacement, and are a great risk for the state that "guarantees a rate of return" to investors (177–78). In light of this, Harvey writes, "the reconciliation depends crucially on recognizing the fundamental political role of accumulation by dispossession as a fulcrum of what class struggle is and should be about" (178). While critical of sweeping concepts like the "multitude," Harvey offers this technique of exposure to social movements as a way to collectively oppose and destroy the sites, protagonists, and force of capitalist accumulation. He points to the antiglobalization movement as an example of the form this struggle might take. From this perspective, it seems that in resisting institutions of capitalism like the World Economic Forum, the WSF was on the right path:

> Above all, the connectivity between struggles within expanded reproduction and against accumulation by dispossession must assiduously be cultivated. Fortunately, in this, the umbilical cord between the two forms of struggle that lies in financial institutional arrangements backed by state powers (as embedded in and symbolized by the IMF and the WTO) has been clearly recognized. They have quite rightly become the main focus of the protest movements. With the core of the political problem so clearly recognized, it should be possible to build outwards into a broader politics of creative destruction mobilized against the dominant regime of neo-liberal imperialism foisted upon the world by the hegemonic capitalist powers. (179–80)

At the start of this chapter, I discussed several ways in which a strong theory of neoliberalism has facilitated social movement struggles. Harvey's exposure of the relationship between accumulation by dispossession and expanded reproduction offers social movements a way to distinguish between different forms of accumulation, particularly the forms that might be tolerated (he suggests land reform as an example) and the forms that must be collectively rallied against, such as "financial institutional arrangements" (179). But despite the recognition of the diversity of social movements coming together to create new worlds, a strong theory of neoliberalism centered on a singular force and explanation of oppression orientates social movements to one alternative. That is, it directs them to the destruction of the global capitalist system and the politics of revolution. I now want to turn to scholarship on neoliberalism that might better equip social movements to actually create diverse and multiple alternatives.

The Thinking Techniques of Weak Theory

In light of contemporary oppression and the related ethical impulse of theorists toward strong theory, it may seem complacent and naïve to suggest that there are alternative ways of knowing the world. Rather than complacent, however, the weak theory outlined here is no less concerned about contemporary realities and is motivated by a desire for alternatives (Sedgwick 2003). In contrast to strong theory, weak theory provides social movement collectives with an understanding of neoliberalism conducive to alternative projects and social change. Despite its name, then, weak theory can have strong effects. As with strong theory, Sedgwick links weak theory to an affective stance toward the world. The weak theorist might be concerned to the extent of being depressed by contemporary oppression and as equally pessimistic as the paranoid thinker. But unlike the strong theorist, who adopts a coping strategy of anticipating negative affect, from a depressed affective state, the weak theorist seeks out positive affect, which orientates the weak theorist toward a reparative stance (136–37). Drawing on the work of Klein and Tomkins, Sedgwick argues that a weak thinking stance orientates the theorist toward a "seeking of pleasure" rather than the anticipation of pain (137). As a result, the thinker looks beyond the negation of bad affect to positive, joyful possibilities. This evokes ethical compassion for the self:

> It's probably more usual for discussions of the depressive position in Klein to emphasize that that position inaugurates ethical possibility—in the form of a guilty, empathetic view of the other as at once good, damaged, integral, and requiring and eliciting love and care. Such ethical possibility, however, is founded on and coextensive with the subject's movement towards what Foucault calls "care of the self," the often very fragile concern to provide the self with pleasure and nourishment in an environment that is perceived as not particularly offering them. (137)

Weak theory also evokes an ethical compassion for unknown others and different possibilities of being. It does so by abandoning the project of acquiring an all-encompassing knowledge structured around a primary destructive force, like capitalism, and instead attempts "little better than a description of the phenomena which it purports to explain" (145). The weak theorist's description is open to difference and unthought possibilities both of the present and the past:

> Hope, often a fracturing, even a traumatic thing to experience, is among the energies by which the reparatively positioned reader tries to organize the fragments and part-objects she encounters or creates. Because the reader has room to realize that the future may be different from the present, it is also possible for her to entertain such profoundly painful, profoundly relieving, ethically crucial possibilities as that the past, in turn, could have happened differently from the way it actually did. (146)

The weak theorist has ethical compassion not only for the self but also for the world more generally and thus offers a different kind of intellectual engagement with history, one that might be more suited to facing contemporary challenges, such as climate change, that raise questions about our evolution as a species (Chakrabarty 2008).

Investigating the body–mind relationship, William Connolly (2002) argues that the translation of affective impulses into thought tends to become habitual. Theorists who seek pleasure are therefore at risk from the habits of strong thinking techniques. Connolly's work highlights the need for techniques of thinking that might accompany a weak stance. Responding to this challenge, Gibson-Graham (2006b) has operationalized Sedgwick's analysis of weak theory in terms of several thinking practices that perform economic diversity. Gibson-Graham employs these techniques to "prompt the affective orientations of openness/freedom, interest/curiosity, and joy/excitement" (xxix). In turn, this orientation compels the theorist toward the production of weak theory. For instance, instead of confirming what we already know, the researcher can read for difference or even what is absent (xxxi–xxxii).

In the introduction to *A Postcapitalist Politics,* Gibson-Graham (2006b) outlines three thinking techniques with which to translate a weak affective stance toward the world into weak theory. The first of these techniques, ontological reframing, works to shift thinking toward openness, possibility, diversity, and connection. Gibson-Graham suggests that the concept of over-determination can play an important role in this technique in that it "pre-sumes that each site and process is constituted at the intersection of all others, and is thus fundamentally an emptiness, complexly constituted by what it is not, without an enduring core or essence" (xxx). The idea of over-determination offers an alternative to determinist thinking practices like monotheism by directing the theorist's attention to multiple interrelated forces shaping social life. Another aspect of ontological reframing high-lighted by Gibson-Graham is thinking that privileges "difference and differ-entiation as a generative ontological centripetal force" (xxxi). This technique prompts descriptions of multiplicity, of both possibilities and challenges. Ontological reframing relates to the second technique described by Gibson-Graham, rereading, involving rereading texts for difference and contingency (xxxi). In contrast to looking for sameness by relating various instances of oppression to a single system, a theorist rereading for difference emphasizes historical and geographical specificity and thus coexisting multiplicity. A similar technique is offered by Doreen Massey (2005) in her book *For Space*. Specifically, Massey argues for an approach to space as multiple coexisting trajectories that are thrown together in, and overdetermine, place. The third thinking technique discussed by Gibson-Graham, creativity, offers an alter-native to the strong thinking technique of alignment, which operates by asso-ciating different entities through a singular system. In contrast, creativity works by gathering different things together to generate something new. For example, creative thinking might involve a theorist transferring a theoretical approach used in one area of research into another area, as Gibson-Graham (2006a) has done in "queering" the economy to disassociate economic diver-sity from capitalism.

Weak theory is experimental and risky. The weak theorist does not set out to anticipate further instances of oppression and is thus open to further trauma (Sedgwick 2003, 146). But importantly, the weak thinker is also open to another world, one that offers pleasure. Sedgwick thus characterizes the weak theorist's engagement with the world as one of hope. I now want to explore the possibility of a weak theory of neoliberalism.

A Weak Theory of Neoliberalism

Academic debate on the study of neoliberalism in economic geography pro-vides a lens on the different forms of, and relationships between, strong and weak techniques of thinking. Noel Castree (2006), for instance, is concerned that scholars "want to have their cake and eat it." That is, they want to hold on to the idea of a generic neoliberalism while calling for the study of different kinds of neoliberalisms or neoliberalizations. Castree suggests that there cannot be a generic theory of neoliberalism, for neoliberalism can only be judged against "real world" instances and is context dependent (3). Commentary like Castree's also brings into question attempts by Marxist political economists, such as scholars of the regulation school, to account for the implementation of macro-level regimes of neoliberalism in day-to-day life (Barnett 2005; but see also Castree 2006; Sparke 2006; Jessop 1995). To do so, neo-Marxists have incorporated Michel Foucault's ([1978] 1991) governmentality approach to the study of rule and power. Clive Barnett (2005, 9) argues that neo-Marxist scholarship has employed Foucauldian concepts such as subjectivity and technology to show how hegemonic regimes like neoliberalism are "anchored" in everyday practice. He argues that the result has been a neglect of analysis of intermediary levels that translate the macro into the micro (9). Barnett's criticism draws attention to the difficulty and never-ending task of a strong theorization of neoliberalism, and he calls for the project to be abandoned. But in response to this criticism, those committed to a theory of neoliberalism will most likely try to strengthen it further. Castree's and Barnett's concerns also raise questions about the relationship between strong and weak theory and the extent to which scholars can use both types of thinking techniques to study neoliberalism. In one sense, this does seem possible. For instance, a strong theory of neoliberalism might give the theorist confidence to leave theorizing neoliberalism to one side while the theorist explores weak thinking techniques, as reflected in the WSF's shift in stance from critique of neoliberalism to the creation of alternatives. However, as I show later, when adopted together, strong theory interacts with weak theory in a way that foregrounds a singular force structuring the world and backgrounds other existing and potentially pleasurable possibilities. I will now examine the work of one author, Wendy Larner, whose call for theoretical engagement with neoliberalism through practices of inquiry that destabilize its discursive power prompted Castree's and Barnett's critiques. In examining Larner's work on neoliberalism, I argue that, rather than analyzing difference in a manner that consolidates a strong understanding of neoliberalism, she employs the governmentality approach in a way that generates a valuable weaker theorization of neoliberalism.

Foucauldian political economic scholarship moves away from Marxist analysis of the way the regime of accumulation is politically secured, rolled out, or instituted to examine the conditions of the government of the state, population, economy, and other entities. As Barry Hindess (1996) explains, Foucault distinguished between several types of power: the first is "power in general," which refers to the ability to act on the actions of others or oneself and which may be reversible in practice; the second is "domination"; and the third is "government." Hindess writes, "Government lies between domination and those relationships of power which are reversible; it is the conduct of conduct, aiming to affect the actions of individuals by working on their conduct—that is, on the ways in which they regulate their own behaviour" (97). Governmentality theory turns away from the examination of "systems of rule" toward empirical and diagnostic investigation into the knowledge and technologies that direct governance, the conduct of conduct (Rose 1999, 19). Governmentality theorists view neoliberalism as a particular framework of knowledge about the society that has come to define certain problems and their solutions. For example, Nikolas Rose (1999, 27) describes neoliberalism as a rationality of government. Initially a mixture of "thought and action" responding to the "problems of governing," for Rose, neoliberalism "came to provide a way of linking up these various tactics, integrating them *in thought* so that they appeared to partake a coherent logic" (27). Governmentality scholars have examined the application of neoliberal rationality to a number of areas of life (such as the welfare state), paying particular attention to market-oriented practices, such as accounting and technologies of subjectification.

In response to strong theoretical engagements with neoliberalism and globalization, scholars such as Larner (2003; see also Larner and Walters 2004; see, more recently, Higgins 2014) have emphasized the importance of the governmentality approach. Larner calls for theorists of neoliberalism to pay greater attention to the diversity that has been displaced by strong readings of neoliberalism. As she states it, "in these accounts of neoliberalism, for all their geographical and scalar diversity, little attention is paid to the *different variants* of neoliberalism, to the *hybrid nature* of contemporary policies and programmes, or to the *multiple and contradictory aspects* of neoliberal spaces, techniques, and subjects" (Larner 2003, 509). Larner's commentary can be seen as a call for a weak theory of neoliberalism. She emphasizes the need for attention to difference (through the second technique of weak thinking, rereading) and, in particular, consideration of the different versions of neoliberalism that have arisen out of interaction with other political rationalities (such as neoconservatism) (510). She also seeks to draw attention to the mutation of neoliberalism in different contexts and the evolution and different phases of neoliberalism (510). Focus on contingency, messiness, and failure is vital to this theoretical stance. As Thomas Lemke (2002, 56) describes it, the governmentality approach leads to an examination of the complex intermeshing of rationalities with those on which they seek to operate:

> The relations between the envisioned aims of a program and its actual effects does not refer to the purity of the program and the impurity of reality, but to different realities and heterogeneous strategies. History is not the achievement of a plan but what lies "in between" these levels. Thus, Foucault sees rationalities as part of a reality that is characterized by the permanent "failure" of programs.

Though this might suggest further analysis of the role of failure in governmental projects, such as whether failure provides a rationale for further reform, Larner (2003) is particularly interested in messiness and failure in relation to the performativity of knowledge. More specifically, reflecting on the performativity of knowledge, Larner proposes the governmentality approach as a way "to give neoliberalism an identity crisis" (510). In addition, in taking a reparative stance, one of Larner's aims is to remain hopeful of change:

> What would highlighting complexity and contradiction in analyses of neoliberalism mean politically? Most immediately, it would overcome the fear and hopelessness generated by monolithic accounts of the "neoliberal project." It would allow us to think about the multiple forms that political strategies, techniques, and subjects take. Indeed, it may be more useful to see the current moment as involving profound experimentation rather than the rolling out of a coherent programme. (512)

Motivated by this stance, Larner's work on one failed project in particular provides a lens with which to further explore weak thinking about neoliberalism.

Larner's (2000) agenda to destabilize neoliberalism's hegemonic identity by detailing the "messiness" of specific neoliberal projects has led her to think about "failed" projects. One example of this broader research project is Larner's (2000) analysis of the New Zealand government's public discussion document "Towards a Code of Social and Family Responsibility," which was produced in response to the social destruction brought about by early neoliberal policy. The code aimed to establish a consensus on the social governing roles of the family and the community in response to increasing social inequalities produced by a period of market restructuring that aimed at reducing the role of the state in social provisioning. As Larner describes it, the code "represents an explicit attempt to generate a post-welfare state consensus around social institutions" (244). The document was posted to households and encouraged discussion and feedback on a range of social issues, from parenting to health care (252). Larner is interested in the new forms of social governance the code describes (254). Her analysis highlights the intertwining of neoliberal and neoconservative rationalities and technologies of subjectification in the code as well as the partial incorporation of liberal feminist and other political agendas. Larner shows that the code attempts to constitute active "self-responsible and autonomous" citizens, while disciplining those unable to govern themselves through authoritarian forms of rule (251). For example, the code reformulates social issues in terms of subnational arenas like family and community in a hands-off way that constitutes them as self-governing spheres characteristic of the neoliberal project. At the same time, the code suggests that these arenas should be monitored hands-on through neoconservative measures to ensure that particular responsibilities are met.

Larner explores these new forms of governance in a way that is indicative of the weak thinking technique of creativity. She draws on feminist scholarship on the gendered nature of liberalism and the sexual division of labor to gender the governmentality approach. More specifically, she uses gender as a way to analyze the family, work, and community spheres of governance. For instance, Larner describes the gender neutrality of the code, which can be related to liberal modes of governance, while also highlighting representations of the punitive measures facing families that resist highly gendered, traditional roles. For instance, the code represents women's role in the family as a matter of choice and lifestyle but also as a natural obligation, while suggesting that failure to provide adequate child care and other familial responsibilities will be met with state monitoring and the assumption of custody over children (256, 260). Larner writes:

However, the code is also ambiguous on the concept of family. . . . Rather than portraying family units as self-governing, the code implies that state monitoring of familial relationships is required to ensure that family members fulfil their responsibilities to each other. . . . Moreover, whereas in much of the document the family is degendered, the color photograph on the cover shows an exemplary heterosexual, nuclear family made up of a Maori man and a Pakeha women hand in hand with two happy children. These observations suggest that the family is not a straightforward category of neoliberal governance in the code. (256)

She thus goes on to suggest:

It can be argued that family provides a nexus for the articulation of neoliberal and neoconservative formulations in the code. Yet while both neoliberalism and neoconservatism are hostile to social welfarism and mobilize the family as a solution to "state dependency," each is premised on a different understanding of the concept. In turn, these differences generate significant contradictions within the code. (256)

Larner counters top-down, monolithic and programmatic accounts of neoliberalism through the detailed description of a document full of contradictions and the complex intertwining of rationalities and technologies designed to govern conduct through "new forms of social governance" (26). Her analysis is guided by the weak theory technique of rereading for difference. She employs a feminist reading of the gendering of different social arenas to tease out the contradictions of the code, showing many cracks and opportunities for contestation. The cracks in neoliberal governance provide space for different kinds of governmentality to emerge, such as an economy centered on ethical decision making about social and individual needs (Gibson-Graham 2008).

From the outset, the code was plagued with methodological problems, and public response was limited. The code could thus be viewed as an "abject failure as a policy initiative" (254). It failed because it was largely ignored by New Zealanders. It was also overtly resisted by particular groups, for instance, both Māori and women's groups saw it as an attack and exercise in blame (253). While Larner suggests that one of the reasons why the code was rejected might lie in the "significant tensions between the new formulations, and the legacy of welfare-centred views of society," she leaves to the side the issue of resistance and the diverse governmentalities any resistance might be indicative of (261). This possible blind spot relates more generally to the governmentality approach and, in particular, to the focus of governmentality scholarship on the instalment of power regimes and "forms of rule" rather than on the forms of power continuing to enable and constitute everyday life on the ground. Thus Larner is interested in the "productive forms of power," even failed technologies, that in this case, are "premised on particular forms of social governance and political identities" (254). The governmentality approach has been criticized for this focus on "official discourses" because it neglects to take into account the ways in which resistance shapes rule (O'Malley 1998). While the governmentality approach does in fact lend itself to analysis of the manner in which governmental programs clash with "reality," Pat O'Malley argues that the way this is translated into analysis of failed programs continues to focus attention on the program itself rather than on the constitutive force of other "external" factors like resistance. As O'Malley states, "one of the consequences is that what is missing from the literature is a sense of "government from below" and, more generally, a rather pronounced silence about the ways in which resistance and rule relate to each other in positive and productive ways" (157). In response, O'Malley suggests that "this implies an approach in which politics is a far more open-ended process of contest and engagement than readily emerges from viewing it as 'a mentality of rule'" (158).

The first thinking technique of weak theory outlined earlier, ontological reframing, is helpful in addressing the programmatic focus of governmentality scholarship. Ontological reframing is a means for scholars to foreground preexisting and diverse forms of governance, knowledge, and practice that shape life in particular places (Gibson-Graham 2006b, xxxi). To recall Gibson-Graham, the perspective of ontological reframing "tolerates 'not knowing' and allows for contingent connection and the hiddenness of unfolding; one that at the same time foregrounds specificity, divergence, incoherence, surplus possibilities, the requisite conditions of a less predictable and more productive politics" (xxxi). Ontological reframing, however, does not guide Larner's analysis. For all its weakness and openness, existing governmentalities operating from below or at the grass roots are notably absent from Larner's analysis of the code and its failures. This suggests that weak theories of neoliberalism that highlight diversity and contradiction within governmental rule, and thereby create openings for alternatives, also need to be attentive to existing alternatives. I turn now to Elyachar's *Markets of Dispossession,* a work that represents the continuing existence of such "grassroots" governmentalities, despite the implementation of neoliberal rationalities and technologies.

Strong Theory, Weak Theory, and a Glimmer of Other Worlds

Julia Elyachar's (2005) book *Markets of Dispossession* is a curious achievement in that it has made contributions to two fields of research that are generally thought of as epistemologically opposed (Roelvink 2007). As the title suggests, *Markets of Dispossession* extends Harvey's (2003) work on accumulation by dispossession that, as I argued earlier, is committed to the critical documenting and thereby consolidating of neoliberalism. At the same time, Elyachar's research is cited by Michel Callon and Koray Caliskan (2005) as exemplary of research that shows how the enactment of the networks that we call "markets" produces particular subjects and agencies. The book demonstrates how strong thinking about neoliberalism can dominate analysis by the backgrounding of existing diversity on the ground. Elyachar's research explores markets in one particular setting—the Cairo neighborhood of el-Hirafiyeen in Egypt. El-Hirafiyeen is of particular interest because it was purposely built as a marketplace to house and support both relocated "traditional" workshops and new microenterprises funded by the World Bank as part of its neoliberal agenda. Though small enterprises represent a large part of Egypt's economy, there is substantial diversity within this sector. Reading for diversity, Elyachar thus distinguishes between the workshops run by master craftsmen, which account for most small enterprises, and microenterprises established through neoliberally modeled development loans and run by "microentrepreneurs." *Markets of Dispossession* traces the practices that constitute these two markets, with particular interest given to the many actors that come together in this site, including the World Bank, international organizations, nongovernmental organizations (NGOs), and the masters of workshops.

The story foregrounded by this book is one of shifting regimes of neoliberalism in which the market continues to be represented as *the* central mechanism of economic development and social progress. *Markets of Dispossession* shows how, in the name of poverty reduction and improved wellbeing, the World Bank, through its Social Fund and other international,

national, and local actors, has enrolled what was once seen as the informal economy and social networks of the poor into the market. Thus small enterprises in the informal economy are now viewed by development professionals as sites where cultural and social value can be transformed and extracted by entrepreneurial individuals, in turn generating economic growth (9, 189). In the scheme that Elyachar studies, "youths" in Cairo gain funds through NGOs for market-oriented microenterprises. The idea is that they will become entrepreneurial individuals who, by following their own interests, will create a society of plenty and stability.

To understand and think about this attempt to install neoliberalism in Cairo, Elyachar employs Harvey's powerful narrative of capitalist development and, in particular, his theorization of the solution to the crisis of over-accumulation, accumulation by dispossession. She also draws on Annette Weiner's (1992) work on the commodification of the commons to emphasize that accumulation by dispossession is a process of politicoeconomic *and* cultural dispossession. This involves thinking about how neoliberalism affects both economic and cultural spheres, not only in a similarly destructive way, but to advance the same capitalist agenda. In doing so, Elyachar employs the thinking techniques of strong theory, namely, looking for sameness, alignment, and exposure. Elyachar employs these thinking techniques to represent microenterprise interventions as a contemporary form of dispossession. She reveals that Cairo is being dispossessed of the same informal market networks that World Bank interventions aim to harness for development. As Elyachar explains, by transforming existing social networks into realms of individual pursuit, attempts to implement this neoliberal version of the market threaten the very characteristics required for all market performances in the first place, namely, the social networks represented through the discourse of social capital. Thus Elyachar argues that through the neoliberal market, diverse existing markets that are highly social, cultural, and moral have become sources of capital accumulation within a global capitalist system.

Elyachar pushes this analysis beyond what she sees as Harvey's restricted focus on the state as the vehicle of dispossession to a range of agents of dispossession involved in markets, especially international organizations and NGOs. As such, Elyachar is suspicious of research that posits NGOs as part of "grassroots globalization" or "globalization from below," in which democratic social mobilization and alternative knowledge are generated from diverse localities (Appadurai 2002, 3). Against this argument, she writes that

"NGOs need to be analysed as part of—rather than as something lying outside—the dominant model of political economy in the world today" (169). In a strong theoretical fashion, then, Elyachar sees everything not only as part of capitalist political economy but also necessarily aligned with and therefore tainted through that connection. Thus, in contrast to other representations of NGOs as clueless radicals, ineffectual humanitarians (Chandhoke 2002), or sources of progressive transformation and grassroots democracy (Appadurai 2002), Elyachar reveals that they are in fact vital for the enrollment of the poor into the process of dispossession. Using the lens of governmentality, she shows that NGOs channel the funds, technologies, and concepts through which microenterprises and their markets are installed.

There are many parallels between Larner's work and Elyachar's analysis of the actual processes of dispossession, especially in the way that she shows how development agencies use markets, and in particular entrepreneurs pursuing their individual interests, as vehicles for political empowerment. Responsibility for poverty is shifted away from development agencies to poor individuals and communities themselves, where, as Elyachar notes, these actors come to claim ownership not simply of their own poverty but of increasing debt. As a technology of neoliberal governance and resource extraction, "empowerment debt" is a means by which the excluded poor are to be "included" in, or, more accurately, subjected to, wider political economic systems and thus constituted as self-governing subjects. *Markets of Dispossession* also moves beyond descriptions of governmental rationalities, such as microenterprise and social capital, to the subjects and practices that they seek to install. This leads Elyachar to explore what happens to neoliberal programs of rule on the ground, that is, when they come up against other realities. And it is these realities that not only threaten neoliberal modes of governance but also lead Elyachar to consider countergovernmentalities and the way they intermesh with neoliberal governance.

Importantly, Elyachar suggests that neoliberal microenterprise schemes have largely failed to create markets, contributing to Larner's project to perform the messiness and failures of neoliberalism. But even more interesting are the reasons why the neoliberal market has not led to the dispossession of all markets in el-Hirafiyeen. Of particular interest is Elyachar's description of the continued existence of other forms of governmentality and markets made up of craftsmen. *Markets of Dispossession* examines these craftsmen's markets and the forms of value they produce in some detail. In doing so

Elyachar develops a narrative about long-standing "traditional" market networks. Her lens on the workshop market practices and networks is the craftsman. The craftsman is master of his workshop, his trade, or both. The craftsman who is master of his workshop embodies the network through which this mastery is constituted—the community that supports the market and the master's "good will" that has gone into building and maintaining this community. *Markets of Dispossession* shows that markets are crafted through relational networks that are at once economic, social, cultural, and moral.

In this representation of markets of "diverse possessions," Elyachar has moved far from a monolithic view of the market as solely a means of commodity exchange and capitalist development. Instead, she has thought about difference and how it might be something more than just an outside on which capitalism draws. One example is Elyachar's description of the complex intermeshing of neoliberal governmentality and existing forms of governance in everyday life. For instance, in el-Hirafiyeen, the failure to value relationships has serious social and economic consequences. In particular, Elyachar discusses interest, or, more correctly, "vested interest," a negative value arising from practices through which individuals pursue personal interests without regard to the broader community that legitimates economic activity. Moving away from capitalist dispossession, *Markets of Dispossession* shows how a different form of dispossession can arise from negative value produced in craftsmen's market networks. Elyachar shows that pursuing vested interests attracts the "evil eye," which targets the individual for bad times. These might include an unfortunate accident or a loss of market and possible separation from the community. In this discussion, Elyachar demonstrates how market intervention of the kind espoused by the World Bank interacts with existing relations and, in particular, with the evil eye that threatens the very market networks these schemes attempt to capture. The evil eye can thus operate positively as part of a countergovernmentality, protecting market networks from technologies of entrepreneurial subjectification that privilege individually oriented economic behavior. *Markets of Dispossession* reveals a long history of existing and continually shifting market networks. This suggests that the lens of "accumulation by dispossession" is somewhat more peripheral to this analysis than Elyachar argues. Rather, the background of the book opens up diverse existing market practices that can be utilized in terms of countergovernmentality and social innovations of the kind I discuss in later chapters.

Utopias

Today, an awful lot is known about neoliberalism, and research continues to develop an appreciation of neoliberalism's capacity to change, diversify, and combine with other political economic orientations and oppositions. Knowledge of neoliberalism has performative effects, contributing to social movement struggles in various ways. Strong theoretical accounts of neoliberalism have facilitated the mobilization of social movement struggles and provided the knowledge with which to expose and undermine support for neoliberalism. But social movements like those gathered at WSF now call for other ways of knowing political economy that might facilitate the creation of alternatives. One important aspect of Occupy Wall Street, for example, was daily free classes and lectures on popular economics, one of which was taught by a community economies scholar who works closely with J. K. Gibson-Graham (Safri 2012). Before new visions of political economy can be constituted and taken up, however, habits of thinking (Connolly 2002) and ways to shift these habits require attention. Habits of thinking are difficult to shift and often linger. For example, although, in her later work, Julia Elyachar (2011) aims to foreground and thereby help cement a commons of bodily gesture in Cairo, she concludes that this commons could become a tragedy of the commons as the forces of dispossession and structural adjustment policies take their toll on communities that practice such bodily gestures. Likewise, in his consideration of urban social movements and the recent emergence of Occupy Wall Street, David Harvey (2012, 162) continues to urge that the "movement . . . reach out to the 99 percent," that is, connect to all the other groups, "students, immigrants, the underemployed, and all those threatened by the totally unnecessary and draconian austerity politics being inflicted upon the nation and the world" and oppressed by Wall Street, which he sees as ultimately part of a systemic drive for capital accumulation. This chapter has aimed to draw attention to a range of habits of thinking with the hope that conscious and strategic decisions can be made in how we think about neoliberalism. These decisions, and indeed our research politics, can then be made explicit to audiences.

Both strong and weak techniques of thinking have largely succeeded in disrupting the "conservative utopia" of neoliberalism. This is a type of utopia that Boaventura de Sousa Santos (2004, 236) describes as promising the end of history through the full realization of the perfectly functioning "market":

> What distinguishes conservative utopias such as the market from critical
> utopias is the fact that they identify themselves with present-day reality and
> discover their utopian dimension in the radicalisation or complete fulfilment
> of the present. Moreover, if there is unemployment and social exclusion, if
> there is starvation and death in the periphery of the world system, that is not
> the consequence of the deficiencies or limits of the laws of the market; it results
> rather from the fact that such laws have not yet been fully applied. The horizon
> of conservative utopias is thus a closed horizon, an end to history. (236)

Santos contrasts conservative utopia with "critical utopia," that is, intellectual understandings critical of neoliberal realities and that also desire an
alternative world. Though valuable, like Santos's reflection on the early WSF's
utopian aim to overthrow neoliberalism, when critical utopias focus on
opposing conservative utopias like the "market," they remain negative in
stance and attached to what they oppose. As Santos writes,

> this is the context in which the utopian dimension of the WSF must be under-
> stood. The WSF signifies the re-emergence of critical utopia, that is, of a radi-
> cal critique of present-day reality and the aspiration to a better society. This
> occurs, however, when the anti-utopian utopia of neoliberalism is dominant.
> The utopian dimension of the WSF consists in affirming the possibility of a
> counter-hegemonic globalisation; it is a radically democratic utopia. In this
> sense, the utopia of the WSF asserts itself more as negativity (the definition of
> what it critiques) than as positivity (the definition of that to which it aspires).
> (236–37)

Both strong and weak theories of neoliberalism offer ways to critique current realities. However, whereas the critical utopia of strong theory remains
fixated on the conservative utopia of neoliberalism, the utopia offered by
weak theory is more open to difference in and changes to existing neoliberalisms and other forms of everyday power and rule. Recent work on hope
"as a philosophical and political concept" offers another form of utopia, one
more applicable to weak theory, oriented toward the experience and vision
of joy, happiness, and change (Zournazi 2002, 14). Mary Zournazi's conver-
sations with intellectuals show what a dialogue of hope might look like. Her
conversation with Isabelle Stengers (2002), for instance, highlights the distinction between probability, which, like the paranoid stance, is oriented

toward anticipating what we already know, and the possibility of that which escapes pregiven descriptions of the world. In contrast to probability, possibility is centered on the belief that the world itself is constantly changing and thus cannot be fixed or calculated once and for all (246). As Zournazi and Stengers describe it, a utopia of hope aims to slow down the process of question and answer to promote dialogue and the production of collective knowledge (see esp. 251). Hope also emphasizes the process of convergence in which diversity is privileged in the making of alternative visions (254). For Zournazi and Stengers, this is not a future-oriented utopia but one that is for the everyday and all of the histories, futures, and current problems the everyday contains. This is what weak theory strives for.

Wendy Larner's (2014) work on the U.K. radical social enterprise Coexist is an excellent example of such hopeful scholarship responding to neoliberalism. In this work, she explicitly challenges strong theories of neoliberalism, which she suggests take the postpolitical neoliberal environment as a "matter of fact" rather than a "matter of concern" (192) (see also Latour 2004a and chapter 4 in this book). In contrast, Larner is interested in "begin[ing her research] from the recognition that radical social movements have shaped neoliberalism itself" (194–95). This orientation, missing from her early work on the Code of Social Responsibility, draws attention to forms of counter-governmentality from the outset and their effects on governmental initiatives. She offers a detailed and diverse yet loose and at times seemingly contradictory and challenging account of Coexist and the way it potentially activates ethical economic subjects of a radical social enterprise. Interestingly, Larner notes the strategic political choice taken by Coexist to "move past the moment of critique," a choice that Larner has also taken in her recent work with this enterprise, and she concludes that "we need to think harder about the kinds of worlds we, as critical scientists, want to make" (204).

2

Spatializing Economic Concerns

Representing Economic Concerns

We have recently been flooded with an array of representations of economic concerns. Books such as Paul Kingsnorth's (2003) *One No, Many Yeses* and films like *The Corporation* (Achbar, Abbott, and Bakan 2003) have emerged in steady succession to capture and make real a broad political terrain of concern. They represent a vast range of people and things gathered around contemporary economic issues, such as the power of corporations and alternative economic futures. These diverse books and films can be seen as an attempt to bring social movements like that of antiglobalization and the World Social Forum to places and peoples they might otherwise not reach, such as those far removed from protest meetings and website networks. But more than that, these representations have begun to map out and spatialize what Bruno Latour (2004a; 2005a; 2005b) sees as a new agent of social transformation: groups gathered around issues of concern. This idea of concern groups departs from conceptualizations of social movements or collectives as people joined through a clear political identity. Instead, concern groups are centered on an issue that relates to a diverse array of humans and nonhumans, including animals, the natural environment, machines, and objects. These groups seek new ways to bring about change without the continuity, closure, and exclusions on which social movements based on a clear political identity rely (Latour 2005a, 15). This chapter explores some of the ways in which this politics of concern might bring about social change.

Just as maps are often observed as complete and inactive truths (Massey 2005), representations of contemporary concerns and the groups gathered around them often give the impression of doing nothing more than reflecting, and thus opposing by exposing, an external terrain of concern about which we can do little; neoliberalism, globalization, capitalism, or all three together are the usual candidates. The previous chapter explored the thinking practices generating such "strong" and politically limiting representations. The political limitations of such a strong approach to contemporary forms of domination have also been discussed at length elsewhere (Gibson-Graham 2006a; 2006b). Gibson-Graham's work in particular has shown how critical representations of the "economy" and capitalism have inhibited the imagination and enactment of alternative economic projects. How, then, might the representations of concerns and Latour's concern groups bring about social change, and by what means? In her work, Gibson-Graham argues that understanding economic representations as performatively constitutive of current realities is a vital part of political struggle. In light of such work, this chapter takes the performative force of contemporary representations of economic concern seriously. It does so by exploring the spatiality of representation when understood as an economic terrain in which concern groups and concerns are gathered.

Representing concern is no simple thing, as highlighted by Latour and Peter Weibel's (2005) experimental collection *Making Things Public: Atmospheres of Democracy*. This book is an experiment in relating and thereby assembling and disassembling concerns, people, and things in political space. The collection offers a democracy-centered terrain that brings together two aspects of representation often held apart: first, the way in which the public is gathered, and thus politically represented, around things of concern, and second, the way that issues of concern are themselves discursively represented (Latour 2005a, 15–16). Thus there are two senses of representation to consider here. In his introduction, Latour (2005a, 15–16) argues that political theory has given much more attention to the political and democratic representation of the different parties gathered around political issues over the discursive representation of the matter of concern. In contrast, in subsets of political theory, such as feminist, cultural, and geographical studies, the opposite seems to be the case. Through the concept of performativity, the latter have paid much attention to how objects of concern, from women to the "economy," have been discursively represented and thereby brought into being as subjects and spheres, while less attention has been given to the way people and things are gathered around this performance or, in other worlds, the broader geography of performative action.

Making Things Public is an experiment in putting these two aspects of representation together and, in doing so, introduces a third sense of representation that relates to the composition of the "body politik" (Latour 2005a, 16). For Latour, the body politik is a site in which the first two senses of representation come together, representatives of concern groups and discourses of concern (16). In contrast to the view of a unified and stabilized political body or identity, this reading of the body politik offers a political space in which diverse and shifting concerns and concern groups assemble. Taking inspiration from Latour, this chapter tackles the way in which concerns and concern groups are discursively and politically represented and gathered together through experimental assemblies like *Making Things Public*. I ask how this body politik might operate to bring about social transformation. I explore this question through the theoretical field of the performative, aiming to extend our understanding of the performative to appreciate the productive force of new forms of collectivity. I further aim to provide a technique with which to bring about alternative economies. I draw on recent developments in the theory of performativity, including Judith Butler's (1988; 1990; 1997) influential work and Eve Kosofsky Sedgwick's (2003) more recent idea of the periperformative, to open up the geography of peoples and things gathered around concerns to generate new economic possibilities.

With reference to these three understandings of representation and theories of performativity, this chapter looks at a number of films that represent economic concerns and concern groups as experimental assemblies or bodies politik. These films represent gatherings around concerns, but they also constitute different economic realities—from passionately reperforming what we have while demanding intervention to bringing into being alternative economic realities to reassembling the terrain of political economy. The first film I examine is Avi Lewis and Naomi Klein's (2004) *The Take,* which focuses on an alternative to neoliberal political economy by tracing the action of a concern group that occupies Argentinean factories. I go on to discuss the periperformative nature of Agnes Varda's (2000) film *The Gleaners and I,* probing the extent to which its exploration of the topic of gleaning reassembles the economic landscape. These two films suggest an economic broadening in two important senses: first, in the nature of economy brought into being, and second, in the way that these representations open, reassemble, and compose economy. This process of broadening widens the economy to encompass not only central yet diverse issues of concern but also all those things that are gathered around and in various ways related to this nucleus. Through this analysis, I offer a new technique with which to broaden the economy. In doing so, I add to discursive politics a political space with which to join discursive concerns and concern groups made up of diverse people and things.

Theorizing the Performative: Performative Acts and Their Surrounds

Contemporary understandings of the performative stem from J. L. Austin's ([1955] 1962) seminal work on a specific type of utterance. In his 1955 William James Lectures at Harvard University, published as *How to Do Things with Words,* Austin famously described a type of utterance that performs actions, employing his now well-known example of "I do" as the act constituting marriage during a marriage ceremony. He wrote, "In these examples it seems clear that to utter the sentence (in, of course, the appropriate circumstance) is not to *describe* my doing . . . or to state that I am doing it: it is to do it" (6). Other utterances of this kind include "I promise" and "I dare you" (Sedgwick 2003). Austin named this the performative utterance to indicate its active rather than descriptive nature. Since then, intellectual work on the constitutive force of the performative has taken several directions and has been picked up in two strands of thought important to this chapter (Sedgwick 2003). One of these extends the idea of the performative to develop an antiessentialist understanding of the constitution of social life. Another develops Austin's work on the speech utterance to understand the performative's linguistic and spatial configuration, particularly through the idea of the periperformative (Sedgwick 2003).

The performative has come to provide a powerful explanation of how social phenomena like subject identity, understood as an effect of power, come into being. This antiessentialist thinking draws on Austin and others' emphasis on the "productive aspect of language" to argue against claims that language merely describes facts or a reality outside of it (Sedgwick 2003, 5). Discourse, rather than some natural predeterminant like biology or the environment, thus explains our social realities. And as social life is performed, it is materialized in bodies, practices, networks, and other manifestations (Gibson-Graham 2006b; Mitchell 1998). Judith Butler's (1988; 1990) early work on the discursive and dramatic embodiment of gender and queer performativity is a notable example. In this work, Butler (1990, 33) challenges foundationalist premises of the subject by showing that, rather than an internal, fixed, stable essence, gender is a "process, a becoming." Gender is a historical act based on an existing script that is repeated in time to give the appearance of a continued stable identity. While appearing stable, the fact that identity must be repeatedly performed introduces room for slippage and excess, that is, a means for alteration, difference, and the creation of the new (Butler 1988, 520). In her later work on subjection (the process whereby power constitutes the subject), Butler (1997, 11) explores the relationship between the constitution of the subject and the subject's agency, including agency to resist or oppose that subjection and subordination on which the very existence of the subject relies. Tackling the question "how, then, is subjection to be thought and how can it become a site of alteration?" (11), Butler suggests that the power constituting the subject is temporally different when taken up by the subject:

> Consider that in the very act by which the subject reproduces the conditions of its own subordination, the subject exemplifies a temporally based vulnerability that belongs to those conditions, specifically, to the exigencies of their renewal. Power considered as a condition of the subject is necessarily not the same as power considered as what the subject is said to wield. (12)

Understood as a "site of . . . reiteration" in the complex process of assuming power, subject agency introduces slippage and contingency into the constitution of social life and, just as importantly, the possibility of the new (16).

The performative has thus succeeded a narrow understanding of the linguistic utterance to encompass all language and creation of meaning (Sedgwick 2003, 6). And, as Butler's work highlights, it also provides a means to think about social transformation. The performative has not been restricted to analysis of gender and subject identity; it has also been employed to challenge the essentialist foundations of a number of different entities, especially the economy. For instance, marking out an "anthropology of (the) econom(y) ics," Michel Callon and Koray Caliskan (2005) have drawn attention to the way "economics performs the economy," whereby, as others have shown, particular economic subjectivities are brought into being (Gibson 2001). Timothy Mitchell's (1998) examination of the Egyptian economy is exemplary of research in this field. Mitchell traces the construction of our modern understanding of economy through the intellectual imaginary of political economy, physics, and economics, highlighting, for example, the vital roles played by the concept of energy, mathematical formulae, and mechanical models. Going on to disrupt this representation of economy, Mitchell's close examination of the agricultural sector shows how previously invisible and noneconomic forms of subsistence and political governance might be included in the economy. The economy can therefore be reframed and reconstituted through the performative act of research, as has been noted by Gibson-Graham (2006a) in her examination of the way that feminist research has included domestic labor in the "economy." In light of such reframing, more recent work in this area has moved beyond challenging essentialist thought to instead use the idea of the performative to actively construct alternative realities. This is exemplified in Gibson-Graham's (2006b) book *A Postcapitalist Politics,* in which she retheorizes the economy to bring into being a new economic politics, new economic subjects, and an intellectual community that can equip alternative economic projects. To reiterate an earlier passage,

> successful theory "performs" a world; categories, concepts, theorems, and other technologies of theory are inscribed in worlds they presuppose and help to bring into being. . . . Thus the ability of theory to describe and predict is not an outcome of accurate observations/calculations, but a measure of the success of its "performation." With this understanding of the performativity of theory, we have engaged in theorizing and researching diverse and community economies, hoping to help bring these into being by providing technologies for their conceptualization and enactment. (Gibson-Graham 2006a, xx–xxi)

This understanding of the performative suggests an important role for research, and representation more generally, in activist experimentation aimed at changing the world. Yet this is not a simple intervention; not only does "doing thinking" have varied success, but the success of performing theory can limit rather than open the way for alternatives. As Latour (2005b, 226) explains in relation to sociology, because sociologists are so successful at "*performing,*" "*formatting,*" and, consequently, fixing relationships that form the social sphere, they encounter difficulty when faced with the task of examining and reassembling it. This is because social scientists tend to enact the social in a way that extends and strengthens rather than opens up the associations through which the social is constituted. In other words, social science gives substance to the sphere of the social by associating different entities and, in doing so, risks producing what might be called "Christmas effects" (Sedgwick 1993, 5–9). As Sedgwick explains, Christmas effects are the result of practices that associate entities so that *"everything means the same thing"* (6). Sedgwick demonstrates this idea with the social site of the family, a site in which sexual relationships, lineage, home, care, and so on are gathered and gain meaning (6). Timothy Mitchell's (1998) work provides a good example of the way that the economy has been fixed through the application of scientific ideas and imagery to economic relations and processes, with the recent inclusion of the informal economy into the "economy" exemplifying this process. By employing these and other ideas, economics has formatted relationships between diverse aspects of economic life and thereby constituted a totalized field of the "economy." Consequently, both existing and new associations of terrains like the social and the economy have to be examined carefully: "If the social sciences per-form the social, then those forms have to be followed with just as much care as the controversies" (Latour 2005b, 227).

A performative approach to research should thus be attentive to the ways in which research assembles, fixes, gives form to, and makes true spheres like the social and the economy. Moreover, the project of reassembling or creating alternatives needs to consider the performativity of concern in terms of how this performance is achieved, not only through reiteration but also in terms of all the entities it involves and all of the associations made. In a move to examine how the performative is achieved, geographical research has revealed the instability, relationality, and spatially constitutive nature of performative acts (Gregson and Rose 2000). But to make visible and create room for all of the other things that make performative acts possible—that is, to move from the performative's temporal force to also consider its spatial force—we need to reconsider the linguistic utterance. Sedgwick (2003) returns to Austin's performative theory of speech to offer another line of inquiry into political, economic, and social association. It is one that suggests a way around the performative, that is, to speak about and spatialize the performative act and thus open it up for reassembly. Sedgwick's work indicates a move away from the consideration of how objects of concern are represented, and thus performed, to consider the groups gathered around that performative act and the way those groups are represented. Thus she suggests another way to think about social transformation and the creation of the new.

To respond to contemporary uses of performativity theory and the questions these raise, like the difference between linguistic and nonlinguistic acts and temporal and spatial registers, Sedgwick attempts to clarify Austin's per-formative utterance. Sedgwick aims to spatialize the performative utterance, to map out the relationship between different forms of utterances and utter-ers and, in particular, the relationships on which its constitutive force relies:

> If, as Austin himself says, there is finally no yes/no distinction between perfor-mative and nonperformative utterances, then it could be more helpful to imag-ine a maplike set of relations: a map that might feature *explicit performative utterances* . . . and a multitude of other utterances scattered or clustered near and far, depending on the various ways they might resemble or differ from those examples. (5)

Sedgwick begins by exploring the ideal form of the performative utterance (e.g., performatives that take the first person singular and are active in tense), the exemplary "I do." She notes that not all performatives take the ideal grammatical shape but are "scattered or clustered near and far" (5). For example, "you're out" is not in the first person singular but is nevertheless a performative in the Austinian sense (4). Extending from the exemplary of marriage, Sedgwick goes on to show that performatives rely on "the tacit demarcation of the space of a third-person plural, a 'they' of witness—whether or not literally present" (69). The "I do" of marriage, for instance, requires the presence of a state authority as well as witnesses (71). Similarly, in the case of "I dare you," the darer evokes consenting witnesses through which the dared person will be judged (69). These witnesses on which the performative utterance depend are not inactive stand-ins; rather, they sug-gest that the force and authority of the performative is relational and open to challenge through further performative utterances by those witnesses, such as "count me out" in the case of a performative utterance that responds to "I dare you" (70).

Recognizing that antiessentialist thought tends to privilege the perfor-mative's temporal character and force, which is illustrated by the importance scholars place on reiteration, Sedgwick develops her understanding of the spatial nature of the performative further by introducing another type of utterance, the periperformative. Periperformative utterances speak about and "*allude to* explicit performative utterances" (68). Sedgwick demonstrates this distinction through the case of the performative "I dare you" that is responded to by the periperformative "don't accept the dare on our account"

(70). As this example shows, the periperformative is not only about the performative "I dare you" but includes challenges that potentially reorganize the relationships on which the performative force of the dare depends, especially the authority and agency of the darer:

> For in daring you, in undertaking through any given iteration to reinscribe a framework of presumptive relations more deeply, and thereby to establish more firmly my own authority to manipulate them, I place under stress the consensual nature both of those valuations and of my own authority. To have my dare greeted with a periperformative witnesses' chorus of "Don't accept the dare on our account" would radically alter the social, the political, the interlocutory (I-you-they) space of our encounter. So, in a different way, would your calmly accomplishing the dare and coming back to me, in the space demarcated by the presence of the same witnesses, with the expectation of my accomplishing it in turn. (70)

Whereas the performative utterance brings with it a crisis of agency in that it can be responded to and challenged by others implicated in its utterance (such as witnesses), periperformatives "dramatize . . . the pathos of uncertain agency, rather than occluding it as the explicit performative almost must" (76). The periperformative achieves this because it avoids the active and first person "I" and instead makes a dramatic statement about the performative act by, for instance, naming the utterer in third person (76). Unlike the performative utterance, where action is performed through the speech act, the periperformative can refer to several speech acts and place them in the context of other acts. The periperformative can therefore "invoke . . . the force of more than one illocutionary act" (78). And it can register several meanings at once as well as historical change. Sedgwick's analysis of George Eliot's *Daniel Deronda* is an excellent example, especially her reading of the utterance "these diamonds, which were once given with ardent love to Lydia Glasher, she passes on to you" (Eliot, as cited in Sedgwick 2003, 76). Discussing the periperformative force of this utterance, Sedgwick draws attention to the way that the third person and "inversion in the word order of subject and object" displaces the agency of the utterer, Lydia Glasher, while giving the diamonds "an oscillating and uncanny agency" (77). This utterance also refers to more than one act, namely, a gift and the act of passing on the diamonds, in a way that Sedgwick suggests evokes "the material and legal problematics of how a woman may be said either to own or transmit property" (77). The periperformative utterance thus not only enables the discussion of performatives but also offers a way to represent and move between the dramatic and linguistic senses of the performative. This makes the periperformative particularly potent, mapping the force of the performative:

> Periperformative utterances aren't just about performative utterances in a referential sense: they cluster around them, they are near them or next to them or crowding against them; they are in the neighborhood of the performative. Like the neighborhoods in real estate ads, periperformative neighborhoods have prestigious centers (the explicit performative utterance) but no very fixed circumferences; yet the prestige of the center extends unevenly, even unpredictably through the rest of the neighborhood. (68)

Revealing a vast relational geography around the performative, Sedgwick's work opens up the space through which entities like the economy are performed and assembled as well as the ways in which they can be can be contested, reassembled, and connected differently. In this respect, the periperformative speaks directly to Latour's (2005a; 2005b) inquiry into the way that groups gathered around discursive concerns might be represented, making explicit the relationships and the people and the things clustered around and enabling the performative acts of concern. In other words, different people and different things have different relationships to the matter of concern; some explicitly perform it, others witness and enable it, while others speak about, convey, or contest it. Mapping this relational geography through the periperformative offers a way to represent gatherings around concerns, which relates to Latour's third sense of representation as a composition of political space. The periperformative also offers a means for those related to the performative to contest and undermine its constitutive power.

Mapping this relational geography involves several moves. Specifically, naming the utterer displaces the performative agent and the singular location of agency, opening up the assembly of the economic to the other, always already implicated, human and nonhuman witnesses. In addition, the periperformative shows how several meanings are generated through one act and how this act relates to different contexts and times. It provides a vehicle for others to respond to and thereby contest the force of the performative.

This technique not only reveals a broader geography of relations, circuits, and abilities but the territory of the performative is opened to a variety of entities and ways to displace the performative. It thus presents a means to assemble the world differently, enabling particular kinds of links and associations between things that might otherwise have been held apart or not even seen. In sum, this approach offers a new technique with which to shift the terrain of the economy and to open it to alternative economic performances. It offers theorists of performativity who follow in the tradition of Butler's work another means for thinking about how the new arises. Butler suggests that the new is created through a temporal register and is linked to subject agency and the "assumption" of power. Sedgwick, conversely, shows how the new can be created through the spatial register and is linked to relationships and associations.

Broadening the Economy through Film Bodies Politik

The documentary films *The Take* and *The Gleaners and I* are unlike many of their political economic contemporaries that critique larger underlying forces while giving little attention to the various concerned groups and/or alternatives already within their topic's ambit. Joseph G. Ramsey (2005) criticizes Mike Moore's 2004 film *Fahrenheit 9/11*, for instance, for its limited focus on the lies wielded as fact by the Bush administration after the September 11, 2001, terrorist attacks on the United States. He further criticizes the film for the exclusion of a huge range of concern groups and alternative politics across the globe. Thus, Ramsey states, "Having erased the anti-war movement as an option, *Fahrenheit 9/11*'s select examples of people undergoing political transformation have no place to go" (172). In contrast, the film *The Corporation,* also released in 2004 and based on the book by the legal scholar Joel Bakan (2004),[1] shows a fuller spectrum of concerned groups gathered around the powerful institution of the corporation, from activists, academics, and managers to brokers and beyond (although, as Ramsey notes, excluding some groups, such as workers, within the corporation). The representation of concerns about the "corporation" is also more diverse than the concerns canvassed in *Fahrenheit 9/11,* including, for example, the corporation's history, psychology, and effects beyond the market. The effect of this gathering is to perform a truly terrifying monster. Although *The Corporation* does include social and economic movements struggling against this beast, they are represented as mostly external to the corporation rather than transformative of it. Consequently, *The Corporation* is vulnerable to Mitch Rose's (2002) criticism of resistance studies. He contends that such studies performatively reaffirm and indeed rely on the preexistence of the systems they seek to resist. In a similar vein, Ramsey observes,

> Still, while this remarkable film depicts plenty of local resistance . . . one would have liked to see *The Corporation* (and one *would still like* to see its viewers) move beyond its extensive discussion of the way that corporations routinely violate the (moral as well as juridical) law to a consideration of political strategy. (178)

In contrast to their contemporaries, *The Take* and *The Gleaners and I,* released in 2004 and 2000, respectively, represent alternative forms and ways of organizing economic life. Unlike other films, *The Take* and *The Gleaners and I* achieve this by both performing alternatives to capitalism and reflecting on the performance of the capitalist economy through the periperformative. *The Take* and *The Gleaners and I* are performed in settings of marked inequality, a time of extreme wealth, consumption, and waste and one of equally extreme poverty and need. In highlighting the interconnected nature of these extremes, both films point to the constitution and maintenance of the capitalist economy. In the context of a wide range of literature and forms of film analysis, what especially interests me and guides this chapter are questions concerning the nature and political force of the media in response to the capitalist economy (Hynes, Sharpe, and Fagan 2007). In the analysis that follows, I argue that the performative force of *The Take* lies in the assertion of an alternative to the capitalist economy—the cooperative owner-worker-led recuperation of abandoned factories in Argentina. Moreover, *The Take* strongly illustrates the way in which performative statements made in response to assertions supporting the capitalist economy can contribute to social change. In contrast, *The Gleaners and I* best illustrates the force of the periperformative and, in particular, the way that witnesses can undermine the force of performative statements constituting the capitalist economy while reconfiguring who and what is associated with economy. *The Gleaners and I* assembles economic alternatives by building associations through and around the central theme of gleaning, here loosely defined as the collection of materials discarded by the capitalist economy.

Performing Alternative Economies: *The Take*

The Take is the product of a partnership between Canadian media person-alities Avi Lewis and Naomi Klein.[2] It was directed by Lewis, his first feature-length documentary, and written by Klein, who is perhaps best known for her 2001 book *No Logo*. Both are outspoken political commentators, as demonstrated by Lewis's short film on police repression in Argentina titled *Gustavo Benedetto: Presente!* (2002), and Klein's commentaries on globaliza-tion for leading news media. Early on in the film, we learn that Lewis and Klein's motivation for making *The Take* is to address critics' negative assess-ments of their past work and activism. As one television interviewer com-ments about Klein in the beginning of the film, "apart from protests, what has she got to offer?" In her voice-over, Klein responds, "He had a good point. There is only so much protesting can accomplish. At a certain point you have to talk about what you are fighting for." Reading this exchange through the lens of the performative utterance, the interviewer's question sets up the dare of TINA—There Is No Alternative—which goes something like, "After all your criticism of the capitalist economy, I dare you to come up with an alternative." Lewis and Klein take up this dare and, as I argue, accomplish it. In doing so, they challenge the performative force of the utter-ance "there is no alternative to capitalism." Furthermore, this reflection on their past work in relation to what the film is doing establishes from the outset a periperformative position, setting up Lewis and Klein's role in the film through the third person and thereby making room for the presence of all the other agents that perform the alternative that Lewis and Klein find in Argentina, the worker-occupied factory movement. Specifically, *The Take* follows a group of former workers in their recuperation of an Argentinean auto parts factory, Forja.

The Take is backgrounded by the "Model" of neoliberalism and its fallout. As elections in Argentina get under way during filming, the documentary also grapples with the model of national politics and political economy more generally. Although protest and resistance in Argentina are set against the Model in general, the film singles out ex-president Carlos Menem as its chief protagonist, highlighting his implementation of the entire "IMF [Interna-tional Monetary Fund] rulebook" in one go, including "downsizing, corpo-rate handouts and selling off every public asset he could find." These policies are shown to have had devastating effects on a once prosperous and quickly industrializing country, creating a "wild west" characterized by vast poverty with little hope left in government solutions. Lewis and Klein go on to suggest that capitalism itself has been plunged into disarray, showing us "abandoned factories, cracked cement, rusting machines"—all the signs of industrial production in tatters. But unlike much left-leaning critique (see Roelvink 2007), the narrative of capitalism is not what this film is about; rather, it is the context of the dare to which Lewis and Klein respond by stating "jobs are being taken back" through a strategy of "occupy, resist, produce."

The film employs this discourse, "occupy, resist, produce," strategically to bring into being an alternative to the Model. With the "power to create the effects it names" (Gibson-Graham 2006b, 2), *The Take* forcefully gives presence to an alternative economy through an economic discourse that is already well known and, ironically, has been made powerful through capitalist representations: the discourse of factory production. The title of the film is presented in steel, placed on top of images of industrial production, including steel being crafted into cogs, mass production assembly lines, workers in overalls, and protective eyewear and a vast array of machines operated with skill and speed—all accompanied by the sounds of factory production. These symbols could be from any film on industry and industrialization. This is, however, factory production with a twist, with the typical images of industrial processes juxtaposed with cooperative worker meetings, the absence of bosses, male workers overcome with emotion, and worker-driven battles with the authorities to gain access to and stay in their workplace. Thus, though one might expect images of factory production to be used to represent capitalist class divisions, the alienation of labor, and the justification for working-class struggle, these images represent a victorious end result of a struggle to gain the right to occupy an abandoned factory. They represent the early stages of production by the group of Forja workers followed in the film. This dramatization of factory production, so strongly associated with the capitalist economy, is full of slippage and excess, not adding up to or contained by capitalist discourse. In sum, *The Take* acquires its performative force from the powerful discourse of large-scale capitalist economic production. At the same time, it transforms this discourse through the performance of resist, occupy, produce, that is, resistance to the Model, collective occupation, and cooperative production.

In contrast to these bustling images of industrial production, the film's heroes begin their struggle in a mostly empty factory that even the pigeons have deserted. As the workers stroll around the abandoned factory, they reflect on this space of absence and silence. Viewing these scenes, it is tempting to suggest that the struggle by the Forja workers, at least in part, nostalgically performs a common working-class identity or working-class politics and is therefore comparable to Gibson-Graham's (2006b) analysis of the film *Brassed Off*. In *Brassed Off*, the about-to-be-unemployed mine workers remain "fixated on a bygone capitalist order"; they are focused "on keeping the mines open; on being employed (and thus exploited by capital); on solidarity based on shared male experience, including that of capitalist exploitation; on keeping alive communities built on exploitation as well as life-destroying work" (Gibson-Graham 2006b, 13). Indeed, there are representations of remnants from the Forja workers' former working-class selves throughout the factory, in lockers, a recovered cup, and other items. But *The Take* moves quickly over these objects to the men themselves, who perform their undignified existence as men and human beings, as they weep openly about their state of unemployment and their inability to provide for their families. This moment of shame can be read as a moment of vulnerability in the process of subjectification that Butler (1997) writes of. These men are no longer able to maintain their working-class identity and, in particular, the strongly associated identity of the masculine breadwinner.

The film's dramatization of the workers' breakdown compels witnesses to see and feel shame for the workers. For Sedgwick (2003), shame is performative and potentially transformative. This is because shame is a moment in which the onlooker fails to recognize the one who the onlooker once knew, which has the effect of interrupting the process of identification (35–36). At this moment, the witness not only feels shame for the other (in this case the Forja worker) but is also keenly aware of both the witness's own individuality and his or her relationship to the shamed other (37). To demonstrate this, Sedgwick imagines the experience of witnessing a misbehaving man, which, while creating a desire to be elsewhere, results in an extreme sensation of presence and "identification with the misbehaving man" (37). Drawing on the psychology of Silvan Tomkins, Sedgwick thus argues that shame is a moment that raises questions about one's identity and relationship to others. Consequently, the shame experienced by witnesses of these workers breaking down—wives, coworkers, viewers, and so on—can also be seen as a moment of interruption in their own identities and relationship to the workers. Shame felt by the witnesses of the Forja workers heightens the presence of these witnesses and their relationship to the workers in a way that gestures toward a geography or spatiality of subject formation. In sum, in making a dramatic statement about their failure to perform a common working-class identity and appearing strange to witnesses of this statement, these workers break with past associations between their identity and work *and* create an opportunity for new relations with others. Thus a different form of worker identification and wider economic organization is able to emerge.

To develop their case for worker occupation, then production, the Forja workers collectively calculate their owed wages and assess the factory for things that have been sold off or stolen by its former owners. As they assess these absences and occupy the factory, a new form of worker organization is reiterated. "In the cooperative, we'll all be administrators," one man states.

> I'll check on what he does and he'll check on me. Of course we're going to have to be more conscientious. And not be too bourgeois like before under the boss, when you would duck into a corner for a break whenever you could. Now, no. If a light is on, turn it off, if it's not necessary. The salaries will all be equal. There won't be exaggerated salaries like there were before, which was one of the things that caused all of this.

As the Forja workers develop a business plan, they build on this sense of cooperation by making links with other occupied factories with which they can trade. For instance, we see representatives from the Forja cooperative visiting the tractor factory, Zanello, operated through a partnership between workers, former managers, and the dealers who sell tractors. This enterprise is organized differently from the Forja worker cooperative, and in Zanello, workers do not receive equal pay. It is, however, part of the broader concern movement gathered around recovered companies and economic justice, and Forja will easily be able to sell forged pieces of metal to Zanello. This is an important feature of the economic alternative performed by *The Take*. Recuperated factories are reiterated as an alternative throughout the film; however, as it moves back and forth to the ongoing struggle of longer established factories and that of the Forja workers, the film highlights the many differences between recuperated factories. Indeed, Lewis and Klein state that they are not proposing a single one-size-fits-all model. Thus this alternative economy remains open to different forms of organization and to the involvement of different concern groups. For instance, in the case of Zanello, a concerned group of managers is included in the organization and management of the factory, just as, similarly, other factories gather a range of different concern groups. All these groups are collected around the concern of recuperated factory production, and *The Take* provides a glimpse of this expanding network of companies that goes beyond factories to education, health, and other service providers. The movement draws much support from communities, who turn out in great numbers when the companies are threatened with eviction.

The Take represents resistance to the Model and those attempting to enforce it in a number of ways, from workers protecting their factories with marbles and slingshots to enormous protests outside the Brukman suit factory after its workers were evicted during the night to citizens refusing to participate in national politics. One instance in which the film explores this broad scope of political struggle is by looking at the family of a new worker at Zanon, a ceramics factory that has been occupied for two years. Zanon employs three hundred equally paid workers and, because of its success, has been able to employ new workers, including the young woman in question. Her mother and extended family are, however, supporters of the Perón pro-labor party in national elections and strong believers in national politics. These women from two different generations illustrate the contrast between the politics from an era of prosperity and strong government and the newer politics based on direct action and grassroots democracy. The coexistence of these strategies asserts that an alternative economy based around factory recuperation is not one that must overthrow existing political economic formations, such as socialist formations in which large-scale, statecontrolled factory production played an important role. Rather, following the second-wave feminist movement (Gibson-Graham 2006b, xxiii–xxiv), the alternative offered by this film is performed through, and transforms, different "subjects" and "places" in various and partial ways and, in this case, is lived through household politics.

The Take traces and brings into being a network of people and things that have gathered around the recovered companies' movement after the devastation of neoliberal reform. In doing so, the film includes a variety of different groups all concerned about economy and, in particular, the livelihoods centered on the abandoned factories. This alternative economy is performed through a discourse that has become conflated with capitalist development, but in a way that de-links the two to join factory production with political struggle and cooperatively organized relations of production. Through this strategic reiteration, *The Take* makes alternatives recognizable, viable, and necessary, compelling us to open our eyes and hearts to them. More than this, the film accomplishes the dare "after all your criticism of the capitalist economy, I dare you to come up with an alternative." In doing so, *The Take* works to undermine the performative force of capitalist discourse.

Reassembling Economy: *The Gleaners and I*

Coming at the end of a long and successful, but perhaps under-recognized, filmmaking career, Agnes Varda's 2000 documentary *The Gleaners and I* is widely acclaimed (Carter 2002). *The Gleaners and I* can be viewed as a political commentary about capitalist discourse. In particular, the film is about claims that the capitalist economy is efficient, provides for all, and discards only undesirable waste. As Varda describes it,

> it's like a jazz concert. They take a theme, a famous theme. They play it all together as a chorus. And then the trumpet starts with a theme and does a number. And then, at the end of his solo, the theme comes back, and they go back to the chorus. And then the piano takes the theme again. The other one goes crazy, you know, then comes back to the theme and back to the chorus. I had the feeling my digressions were like this—a little fantasy; a little freedom of playing the music of things I feel, things I love. And come back to the theme: People live off of our leftovers. People feed themselves with what we throw (away). And I say "we" because it's you, it's me—it's everybody. (Varda, interviewed by Meyer 2001)

In contrast to *The Take,* which focuses on performing an alternative to capitalism, as the preceding quotation suggests, *The Gleaners and I* enlists the periperformative to dwell on and undermine capitalist claims and, in doing so, illustrates another way to transform the economy. Varda's *The Gleaners and I* takes the viewer on a journey through France, tracing the diverse activities of gleaners across the country and through history and exploring the representation of gleaners in a range of mediums (such as art, music, film, and interviews). The film pays particular attention to both the excesses of capitalist production and, despite such excess, the needs and desires that are unmet by the capitalist economy.

Varda is very much a part of her films, and the way she incorporates herself into *The Gleaners and I* enables Varda to make many periperformative utterances. *The Gleaners and I,* or literally "the gleaners and the feminine gleaner," immediately positions Varda as one of the film's subjects, from the outset establishing a relationship between herself as a performer in the film and as the creator of the film. This enables Varda to relate to her performance in making the film through the lens of the third person. The nature of gleaning is also vital to Varda's periperformative moves, and, using voice-over, Varda describes her relationship to the film and indeed herself through its content. Varda builds this relationship to herself in many ways during the film, including by filming her hands, graying hair, and other parts of her body. She further develops this relationship through her voice-over, which reflects on the texture of her body and compares it to the objects she has gleaned, such as the heart-shaped, now rotting potatoes. These images in which Varda refers to her body in the third person can thus be seen to take the form of the periperformative, dramatizing Varda's performative act of making the film through which the reality of gleaning is constituted. Applying Sedgwick's (2003) analysis to this and many other instances in the film, there is a sense that Varda is stating, "These images, which Varda has gleaned, she gives to you." Such periperformative statements displace Varda as the agent of the film, in this case giving the gleaned images a life and circulation of their own. Throughout the film, Varda avoids making performative statements about the nature of the economy gathered around the discards of the capitalist economy. This has the effect of delinking agency from herself and spreading it to all others constituting the film. In other words, by problematizing the agency of the utterer, Varda herself, to reveal others implicated in the utterance, Varda lays bare the space of agency–authorship constituting the film. She shows the other actants on which the film depends and how they transform the film's performance, such as those discussed in what follows, that take the film in unpredictable directions. These agents are not restricted to human actors; rather, this film is enlivened by circulating objects. The film in fact relies on things—particularly their ability to enter into new relationships, to be transferred, and thus to be gleaned.

As I noted earlier, the periperformative utterances shaping *The Gleaners and I* are about performative statements of the capitalist economy. For example, as the film traverses France, it maps out agricultural production for the capitalist economy, revealing multiple people and things gathered around this sector and providing a site from which concerned groups can respond to claims that constitute and support this economy. Varda and the other subjects of the film gather around, indeed, they glean waste and leftovers of production for, capitalist markets, such as produce left behind from a harvest, produce discarded on the ground after a fruit and vegetable market, or produce left in bins and on the street to be taken away. People glean these things for diverse reasons; some have no other way to support themselves, others are activists, some are collectors, and others are artists gleaning "materials," just as Varda describes her own gleaning of images in creating the film. Exploring agricultural and other forms of production in this way, *The Gleaners and I* challenges the efficiency of the capitalist economy. Reflecting on the "waste" produced by the capitalist economy, the film shows that it can be used in multiple ways, challenging the categorization of waste itself and opening up the possibilities of what can be achieved through gleaning, including art—where waste becomes material for sculpture or painting. Somewhat more obscurely, the discards from fruit and vegetable markets support free French language classes for refugees—their teacher's voluntary labor physically sustained by these edible leftovers. Read as a periperformative utterance, to the effect of "this waste, which you have produced and discarded, the gleaners take as a gift," the film also conveys many meanings. In particular, it problematizes relationships to, and ownership of, waste. We get a stronger sense of this when Varda explores the legal rights over waste and shows that waste can be taken as a "gift" to gleaners from the capitalist economy. Waste is thus framed as a gift while at the same time damning the capitalist economy, revealing both its excess and its inability to provide for all.

Gleaning reaches out further to a range of people and things, from lawyers and refugees to oil-slickened birds and paintings. Varda intuitively traces this vast ensemble collected, as in her earlier description of jazz, around the theme of gleaning. We meet artists gleaning pieces for their work, wine makers happy for people to glean the second harvest of grapes, and oyster gleaners at low tide. We are also presented with images of perfectly sized potatoes sold to markets and oddly shaped potatoes that are dumped; images of Rembrandt paintings gleaned from Varda's trip to Japan; and, last, blowing in a concrete alleyway, a painting dug out from storage of women gleaning in a field. Like this parting shot, Varda brings gleaning out from its historical consignment to assert its presence everywhere and in everyone—in trash-picking, in art, in the viewing of this film, and elsewhere. Comparable to the alternative performed by *The Take,* through repeated representations of such diverse instances of gleaning, *The Gleaners and I* constitutes gleaning as a generalized category, broadening what it is to glean and who is included in its realm.

Going beyond this reiteration of gleaning, *The Gleaners and I* employs the periperformative to map out relationships clustering around that which is discarded from the capitalist economy. In the film, Varda follows those who, through gleaning, can be seen to respond directly to acts that constitute that which is discarded as waste, and also others who are only tangentially related to gleaning and the economy. In seeking out vineyard owner Jérôme Noël-Bouton, who "cares for his gleaners," for instance, Varda finds a link to Étienne-Jules Marey, an engineer and erudite physiologist who invented chronophotography. Coincidentally, Marey is an absolutely vital figure in the development of film. Staying with the gleaning of grapes, Varda's trip to Burgundy includes a visit to Van der Weyden's painting *The Last Judgement*, which is filmed in great detail. She pays particular attention to the torturous images of people sent to hell. Varda then films wine growers who tell us that they have "always protected themselves" from gleaners by leaving the surplus grapes on the ground to rot, thereby "protect[ing] our profession and capital." In contrast to this position, Varda interviews another grower, Jean Laplanche, who loves to see gleaners in the fields and also happens to be a psychotherapist. Laplanche tells us about his contribution to the philosophy of therapy, stating that he has "tried to integrate into a man's psyche the Other above the Ego, that is, I have developed an anti-ego philosophy, a philosophy which shows how a man first originates in the Other." Gleaning is thus an open territory for formatting relations between diverse things. These relationships are not fixed a priori but rather are assembled through Varda's unpredictable journey across France, which in turn creates a path through which objects circulate, including Varda's gleaned images.

In the opening of the film, Varda states, "In times past only women gleaned. Millet's *Gleaneuses* were in all the dictionaries." In his review of *The Gleaners and I,* Jake Wilson (2002) draws attention to Varda's feminist political stance, the film's feminist character, and its implicit associations with other contemporary political movements. In doing so, he highlights the collective and open-ended nature of Varda's gleaning of images. Indeed, Varda's approach to filmmaking is comparable to Sadie Plant's (1998) book *Zeros + Ones,* which reassembles the domain of cybertechnology by collecting and linking the margins, footnotes, and feminine elements from which it emerged and continues to evolve. For instance, the story of mathematician Ada Lovelace's role in the development of computing through footnotes and margins is interwoven with science fiction, the virtual world of cyberspace, computer viruses, the shifting position of women in the paid workforce, and the emergence of life itself on earth. Plant traces these connections, reassembling the terrain of cybertechnology by associating these various elements in explicitly feminist and feminine ways. *The Gleaners and I* similarly associates things in a particular way to reassemble the landscape of economy, radically altering the pregiven content of this terrain and undermining capitalist exclusions of waste and people from the economy. It is gleaning that gathers these diverse things and issues together and builds social and economic relationships between them. Like *The Take,* the performance of gleaning relates things in a particular way, giving dignity to the once undignified practices of trash-picking in contemporary societies. Through these proliferating associations, waste is made beautiful, and living off waste becomes a dignified way of being. This is not due to the performance of shame or a transformation brought about through the acting subject; rather, it comes about through a geography of interdependence in which things circulate. In viewing this film, one is implicated in this geography if only by simply gleaning its imagery.

Broadening the Horizons of Economy

For some time now, economic issues have been represented through a range of media, with concerns about industrialization being a well-established example (see, e.g., Carter 2001). The growing number of documentary films accompanying left intellectual critique suggests that the current era is no exception. While there is no doubt about the importance of critical intellectual thought in the constitution of the economy, the performative force of these diverse representations also needs to be taken seriously. All forms of representation do more than simply expose current realities to resist them. They also forcefully participate in the constitution of the realities that they represent. To bring new realities into being, we need to move beyond the practice of exposure (Sedgwick 2003). This chapter has attended to and thereby spatialized or mapped the geography of the performative to offer a new political strategy for economic change.

I have operationalized theories of performativity to understand the constitutive force of contemporary representative assemblies of Latour's politics of concern. I have shown that documentary films can play an important role in the politics of economies, representing disparate groups of people and things gathered around contemporary concerns. *The Take* and *The Gleaners and I* are distinctive in the economic alternatives they bring into being and in their effect on the networks and associations that constitute economies. Their success is premised on the knowledge that things and categories are performed, must be constantly reiterated, and, thus, are open to change. Responding to the dare of claims that there is no alternative to the capitalist economy, *The Take* performs economic life with a difference, placing factory production in a larger cooperative movement to make alternatives real and, in the process, transforming workers' identities, communities, and politics more generally. In accomplishing this dare, *The Take* shows that the economy is not a fixed external reality but a political field that is, in part, constituted through the realm of film. However, to accept the performative force of the representation of concerns does not automatically lead to the reassembly of the relationships that are possible and the things that can circulate through them. As Latour's (2005b) work suggests, the social sciences, and especially their radical wing, have been particularly powerful in making associations stronger and more fixed, whether social or economic. Offering a response to this, Sedgwick's discussion of the periperformative shows a vast geography filled with many things and relations that constitute the performative act. The periperformative brings about a broadening of the nature of economy in terms of the associations and relations that are possible. Enlisting the periperformative to comment on that which is discarded by the capitalist economy, *The Gleaners and I* navigates the geography of gleaning and, in the process, builds new associations between people and things.

I have shown how we can broaden the media through which economy is made true. Knowledge of the performativity of research has already moved beyond the discursive to encompass research practices and technologies, such as those used in economics, mathematics, and cartography (Callon and Caliskan 2005; MacKenzie, Muniesa, and Siu 2007; Mitchell 1998; St. Martin, Roelvink, and Gibson-Graham 2015). Performative representations attempting to assemble gatherings around concern require a much wider awareness of representative media, one that can include issues and objects as well as groups of people and things in an "aesthetic of matters-of-concern" (Latour 2005a, 23). *The Take* and *The Gleaners and I* are two powerful representations of the shifting geography of economy and are vehicles for its transformation. Such an open topography of research is receptive to many lines of inquiry, some of which are addressed in the following chapters. This includes inquiry into the ways people and things are included or excluded in the process of framing markets and inquiry into the character and types of relationships performing the economy (chapter 4). In light of the techniques of theory and of broadening the economy offered in this and the preceding chapter, an immediate question addressed in the next chapter is how thinking techniques, and research more generally, can utilize the emotions that bring social movements together in the creation of new discourses of economy.

3

Affective Collective Action

"It's Air Force One!" someone shouts. *A roar ripples through the crowd; a cheer, a jeer and a yell of defiance rolled into one.* Hundreds of middle fingers shoot upwards in a mass salute. "Hey, fuckwit!" a voice rings out. "Welcome to Genoa!"

The world woke up. Something was happening, and it was something different. This wasn't just another show of the disgruntled old left—the slogans, the tactics, the organisational principles showed that. The demands of this new and untested coalition were many and diverse, and sometimes contradictory, but were couched, like those of the Zapatistas, in a *new language*. The Seattle protests were organised by no single group, had no leaders, no one ideology. They were impolite, they were novel, they were radical, they were determined. And they were spectacularly successful.

—Kingsnorth, *One No, Many Yeses*

The Politics of Antiglobalizaon

Many of the contemporary forms of political economic collective action that we see today stem from what was, and still is, widely known as the antiglobalization movement. The antiglobalization movement is a contested banner for the range of new collectives that gather together diverse participants around common concerns that I discussed in the previous chapter (see also Callon and Rabeharisoa 2008; Latour 2005a). What interests me about these collectives today is that, over time, despite their label, they have explicitly shifted away from a politics, highlighted in chapter 1, that aims to uncover and resist neoliberal ideology. As I mentioned in the introduction to this book, the World Social Forum (WSF) movement is exemplary in this regard. The WSF began in 2001 in opposition to neoliberalism:

The World Social Forum is an open meeting place where social movements, networks, NGOs and other civil society organisations opposed to neo-liberalism and a world dominated by capital or by any form of imperialism come together to pursue their thinking, to debate ideas democratically, for [*sic*] formulate proposals, share their experiences freely and network for effective action.[1]

As the WSF has grown from 25,000–30,000 attendees at its inception to 155,000 in 2005[2] (Keraghel and Sen 2004), participants have become aware that, while mobilizing participation, the discourse of neoliberalism does not necessarily prompt the creation of alternatives. Rather, as proposed in chapter 1, the discussion and generation of knowledge about neoliberalism can stymie participants' hopes for other worlds and strengthen neoliberal discourse.

Several scholars have investigated this shift in the antiglobalization movement from a politics focused on ideology to one that bypasses and potentially disrupts habits of thinking about neoliberalism. Focusing on mass gatherings, such as the Seattle demonstrations in 1999, Brian Massumi (2002a) and Maria Hynes and Scott Sharpe (2009) suggest that the antiglobalization movement has embraced a politics of affect. Working in the tradition of Spinoza and Deleuze, Massumi and Hynes and Sharpe view the antiglobalization collectives as shifting compositions of multiple interacting bodies, where "bodies are reciprocally distinguished with respect to motion or rest, quickness or slowness, and not with respect to substance" (Spinoza, as quoted in Hynes and Sharpe 2009, 7). Affect relates to an increase or decrease in the collective body's capacity to act (Hynes and Sharpe 2009). Though affect is not the same as emotions felt by an individual, Massumi (2002a, 213) suggests that it can be felt: "every transition is accompanied by a *feeling* of the change in capacity" (see also Massumi 2002b). This feeling of change also has affects; it increases the intensity of affect, "[giving] the body's movements a kind of depth that stays with it across all its transitions—accumulating in memory, in habit, in reflex, in desire, in *tendency*" (213). As Ben Anderson (2006, 736) sees it, feelings assess and express an "affecting body," whereas emotions relate to the personal, qualified, and named experience of affect. Feelings thus provide a way to "gauge affect" (Hynes and Sharpe 2008). As a politics, affect can create feelings of possibility in the context of hegemonic ideology and hopelessness (Anderson 2006; Gibson-Graham 2006b). Thus Anderson (2006, 738) suggests that affect expands the political field because it introduces awareness of endless possibilities in every moment and brings attention to practices that might capture some of these possibilities to create change.

Affect, and its modulation, has become an important form of political power, one that can create "ideological effects through non-ideological means" in that it does not rely on cognitive persuasion or "identification" (Massumi 2002b, 40). Indeed, in the context of affective forms of power, political strategies based on rational communication appear to have little force (Massumi 2002a, 234). Thus contemporary political power frequently operates through media-propagated affect rather than through moral rationalization (Massumi 2002a). One example of the political force of affect modulation explored by Massumi (2002b) is Ronald Reagan's political success in the United States. Considered separately, Reagan's body and verbal languages "[failed] to persuade" the public (41). However, for all his incoherence, together this "double dysfunction" wielded great affective power (41). Massumi argues that Reagan's remarkable success was achieved in part through his interruptive style of communication whereby breaks in communication created moments in which affect could be actualized. These moments of interruption, which I discuss in more detail later, also enabled audiences to give their own meanings to different components of the speech, so that Reagan could mean "many things to so many people" (41). Massumi suggests that Reagan held together these jerky moments through his appealing voice.

What this new form of power characterized by affect means for a politics of the left calls for ongoing thought, experimentation, and debate (on the recent debate about affect and politics, see Hynes and Sharpe 2015). Massumi (2002a) argues that the kind of affective power wielded today requires an equally affective form of political action to generate change. That is, it requires "a performative, theatrical or aesthetic approach to politics" (234). He also suggests that those on the political right are much better than those on the left at establishing the arrangements (such as media arrangements) through which affect can be performatively produced and actualized. In among the many examples of the use of affective power by the right, the anti-globalization movement provides an excellent example of a left politics of affective collective action. Massumi argues that the power of the antiglobalization movement rests in political performances that include violence and anger, like that of the Seattle demonstration in 1999 (234). The "theatrical and performative" violence of the Seattle demonstrations enabled otherwise unheard and marginalized groups to expand their networks and get a message out via the media about economic inequalities produced by global financial institutions and arrangements (234). As Massumi puts it, "it was able to shake the situation enough that people took notice. It was like everything was thrown up in the air for a moment and people came down after the shock in a slightly different order, and some were interconnected in ways that they hadn't been before" (234).

A detailed examination of the politics of affect practiced in the antiglobalization movement is provided by Hynes and Sharpe's (2009) analysis of the shifting bodily relationships in mass protests. Hynes and Sharpe are interested in shifts in the capacity for action of the collective body constituted by protesters at the 1999 Seattle demonstrations. They focus on the protesters' response to violence waged by police and the passage from bodies paralyzed by tear gas to bodies joining together in resistance. In this passage, Hynes and Sharpe detect a shift in the protesters' collective capacity for action: "There is a transition from the state of being 'asphyxiated and blinded' [by tear gas] to the state of having 'arms locked more tightly,' which seems to represent an increase in the power of acting" (8). Hynes and Sharpe therefore argue that violence can increase the possibilities of affecting and being affected. Drawing on Spinoza, they suggest joy and sad passions as a way to "gauge affect" (8) and note the joy tinged with sadness in protesters' accounts of Seattle.

Reflecting on the Seattle demonstrations, Massumi is concerned that, in addition to potentially making new connections between people, violent performances also often produce fear that heightens existing divisions between people. And Hynes and Sharpe suggest that mass demonstrations can decrease the possibilities of action for those gathered around them, such as the police, whose "forceful movements" generate a weakness, a limit in their ability for affecting and being affected (9).[3] They suggest joyous and sad passions as a way to judge whether actions increase or decrease the possibility of bodily experience. Given the limitations of Seattle, Massumi asks, "are [there] ways of practising a politics that takes stock of the affective way power operates now, but doesn't rely on violence and the hardening of divisions along identity lines that it usually brings[?]" (235). In response to Massumi's question, this chapter explores the kind of politics to which the WSF moved. In 2003, the WSF shifted in stance from saying *no* to neoliberalism to the *many yeses,* that is, to the affirmation of diverse alternative movements and projects currently under way (Keraghel and Sen 2004, 483; Kingsnorth 2003). The WSF joined other "antiglobalization" movements to practice a politics centered on affirmation rather than resistance (Hynes, Sharpe, and Fagan 2007). While attention has been given to the force of affect in the experience of and resistance to "capitalism" (Hynes and Sharpe 2009; Massumi 2002a; Stewart 2007), I am interested in exploring how affect might be operationalized in a politics of affirmation that aims to generate economic possibility. This interest directly connects to the overarching concern of this book with the embodied nature of collective action and, in particular, the role of embodied processes and forces, such as affect, in collective action aiming to bring into being new economies.

In this chapter, I investigate the force of affect in an alternative form of collective body to that of mass protests. After discussing a politics of collective action more generally, I begin this exploration of affect by extending Bruno Latour's (2004a) account of how bodies learn to be affected in collectives to consider how thinking is moved by the play of affect (Connolly 2002). William E. Connolly's (2002) neuropolitics of affect helps me to consider the role of affect in the production of new knowledge. I then turn to Michel Callon and Vololona Rabeharisoa's (2003) work to begin my exploration of the operation of affect in collective action. I am particularly interested in how affect can be utilized by antiglobalization collectives as a pedagogy for imagining new economies, and in the third section of this chapter, I bring a politics of affect to bear on Paulo Freire's pedagogy. Freire's work draws attention to the importance of testimony as a collective affective technique for prompting new thinking. In the next section, I discuss one session of the 2005 WSF to illustrate how my understanding of a politics of affect might be practiced. Affect is not a force that can be directly observed or documented, and it operates in "a zone of indiscernibility" (Connolly 2002, 64). Rather than documenting the force of affect, then, this chapter draws attention to the WSF to gesture toward what a politics of affect might look like.[4] I adopt the description of the WSF as a "pedagogical space" for social movements to analyze current realities and create new ways of reimagining the future (Andreotti and Dowling 2004, 605). As receivers of testimony, researchers can be caught up in a politics of affect. The chapter thus concludes by briefly commenting on the role of researchers in collective action. First, though, I discuss a politics of collective action in which my exploration of affect is located.

A Politics of Collective Action

There are vast numbers and forms of social movements struggling with the material realities that mark bodily existence (Gibson-Graham 2006b). These include, for example, struggles to overcome the drudgery of exploitative and degrading work conditions, struggles against the violence and oppression maintaining conditions of contemporary slavery, struggles against the denial of livelihood to marginalized peoples, and struggles for access to privatized commons, such as water and land. The combination of such experiences and the alterative economic experiments that social movements seek to install with discursive projects to re-present the economy can be understood through Gibson-Graham's (2006b) notion of "a politics of collective action." This politics attempts to fold "'matter' and thought, experience and concept," or the material and the discursive in new ways (xxxvi). As Gibson-Graham describes it,

> a *politics of collective action* involves conscious and combined efforts to build a new kind of economic reality. It can be engaged with here and now, in any place or context. It requires an expansive vision of what is possible, a careful analysis of what can be drawn upon to begin the building process, the courage to make a realistic assessment of what might stand in the way of success, and the decision to go forward with a mixture of creative disrespect and protective caution. (xxxvi)

A politics of collective action involves an engagement with material experiences and being able to visualize alternative futures. Through this engagement, a politics of collective action can be understood to translate bodily experiences of "affecting and being affected" into new visions and discourse. Understood in this way, collective action is an ideal place to start exploring a politics of affect.

For Gibson-Graham, the creation of new collective visions starts in place. This "suggests that there is no privileged social location from which to embark on building a community economy. For us this means that our academic location is no less or more suitable as a starting place than our other social locations as women, citizens, middle-aged adults, yoginis, local residents, workers, and bearers of racial privilege" (195–96). Collective action connects multiple experiences and knowledges, often occupied by the same person but also just as often by many different people, in the making of collective visions. Similarly, Arjun Appadurai (2000, 6) has argued that collective knowledge generation "informs the daily lives of ordinary people in myriad ways." He is concerned with the gap between knowledge produced by social movements and that produced by intellectuals within the academy. He goes on to note that the former "have barely been named by current social science, and even when named their dynamic qualities are frequently lost" (6). Appadurai suggests that diverse research practices through which knowledge is produced are often marginalized by the cultural ethic of research developed in the academy, research that, though also a collective endeavor, has evolved through codified bodies of knowledge and particular cultural practices through which knowledge is valued (12). Given that a politics of collective action is centered on collaboration between diverse knowledge producers, this division poses a challenge to both intellectuals and activists. There is a need to ask how these different forms of research and knowledge generation might join in conversation to build new worlds.

Alongside Appadurai's critique of academic practices of knowledge generation, there is increasing academic interest in diverse forms of knowledge production. Attention is directed to the role of expertise housed outside traditional academic confines in economic and political decision making (Callon and Rabeharisoa 2003). Callon and Rabeharisoa relate this intellectual interest in diverse forms of knowledge production to two developments (194). The first draws attention to the expert role of the consumer in production and the definition of demand. For example, one area of concern is the role of the consumer in the organization and shape of markets (see also Carrier 1998). In the following chapter, I expand on this area of concern by looking at the role of social movements in the performance of markets. The second development highlights the increasing role of the public in politics and policy development and a broader trend toward participation. Although the power of these groups is often debated (Roelvink and Craig 2005; Craig and Porter 2006), publics are increasingly seen as stakeholders in areas ranging from the governance of welfare and poverty to the implementation of scientific technologies (Callon and Rabeharisoa 2003; see also Larner and Butler 2005).

One could add to this diversity of knowledge producers the nongovernmental organizations and social movement activist research networks that have emerged to contest and inform development bodies. The WSF is one example of such a network in which diverse knowledge and experience is gathered and new ideas and visions are generated. Appadurai (2000, 3) describes these research networks that emphasize diverse activist knowledge in place as "grassroots globalization":

> A series of social forms has emerged to contest, interrogate, and reverse these developments and to create forms of knowledge transfer and social mobilization that proceed independently of the actions of corporate capital and the nation-state system (and its international affiliates and guarantors). These social forms rely on strategies, visions, and horizons for globalization on behalf of the poor that can be characterised as "grassroots globalization" or, put in a slightly different way, as "globalization from below."

These networks privilege the role of knowledge production in social struggle and the capacity of people to learn and create their own strategies and visions for the future.

Picking up on the participation of nonacademic knowledge producers in economic political decision making, actor network theorists have turned their attention to the way in which diverse knowledge producers come together in the "co-production of scientific knowledge" (Callon and Rabeharisoa 2003, 196). Callon and Rabeharisoa show how marginalized groups join with other experts in "hybrid collectives." In another work, Callon and John Law (1995) use the French term hybrid *collectif* to understand the collective production agency. They emphasize interdependence and interaction over the independent agents massed together, as is often invoked by the term *collective*. From this perspective, it is the network as a whole and the relationships through which it is constituted that enable performative action, including collective vision making. The hybrid collective, to which I return in the next section, can be understood as a site and an assemblage for the process whereby diverse experiences are translated into new collective visions that, in turn, shape what is possible. To understand how this process might work in practice, I now turn to the operation of affect in collective knowledge making.

Collective Politics and the Force of Affect

The Spinozan approach to a politics of affect focuses on the shifting relationships that constitute the collective body's affect or "force of existence" and capacities for action (Hynes and Sharpe 2009, 7). To explore how affect shapes thinking and the production of new knowledge, I need a theory that shows the impact of affect on individual bodies in the collective. I am interested in the way that changes in the collective's capacity for action are embodied. Latour's (2004a) work directs attention to the relationship be-tween the individual and collective bodies. Latour's work on affect suggests that for a body to be alive in the world, it must be able to be moved by its relationships with the wider body-world or collective body. Latour calls this "learning to be affected" (see also Hinchliffe 2003; Gibson-Graham and Roelvink 2010). He illustrates learning to be affected with the perfume industry and the training sessions through which a pupil becomes a "nose":

> It is not by accident that a person is called "a nose" as if, through practice, she had *acquired* an organ that defined her ability to detect chemical and other differences. Through the training sessions, she learned to have a nose that allowed her to inhabit a (richly differentiated odoriferous) world. Thus body parts are progressively acquired at the same time as "world counter-parts" are being registered in a new way. Acquiring a body is thus a progressive enter-prise that produces at once a sensory medium *and* a sensitive world. (207)

The capacity of a nose to be moved by the world, to detect different odors in this case, is achieved through the training session made up of a teacher, a pupil, and an odor kit. Without these elements in relationship to each other, the body would be static, and odors would smell the same. Latour thus suggests that the kit, teacher, and pupil can be viewed as a collective body that enables the differentiation of an "odoriferous world" (207). Learning to be affected is thus cotransformative, increasing the collective's capacity for action in a more highly differentiated world. Latour's work also shows how this capacity is embodied (in this case through the nose) as individual bod-ies learn to be affected in collectives or body-worlds.

Whereas Latour's concept of learning to be affected demonstrates embod-ied learning in collectives, Connolly's work provides a way to explore in detail how *thinking* is moved by living bodies. Connolly is interested in a "neuropolitics" of affect, which he describes as "the politics through which cultural life mixes into the composition of body/brain processes" (xiii). This mix of culture and bodies occurs in "a zone of indiscernibility because within this zone we are still unclear exactly how the mixing occurs, how complex each layer of capacity is, and how much room there is for mobility and creativity once a set of initial capacities and dispositions has become organized" (64). Although it is indiscernible, Connolly argues that this zone is vital to creativity, and he goes on to thematize body–brain–world interactions to develop an appreciation of affect as a source of creative thinking. His work is particularly instructive for exploring the role of thinking, language, and ideas in a politics that utilizes the force of affect.

For Connolly, affect relates to "body/brain systems" interacting with the world and "traces of past experiences" (62). More specifically, affect operates in the encounter between the different layers of thinking that are triggered by one's engagement in the world. "Thought embodies" this thinking process (65). Performances, such as film and the example of Ronald Regan discussed earlier, structured through "'irrational cuts' between scenes," are especially effective at producing the "movement of affect" (67). The breaking up of a narrative "opens a new round of intrasubjective communication between your virtual register and a conscious line of reflection" (67); "it allows new thoughts to stroll or run onto stage, now and then setting an internal dialogue into motion that brings something new or exciting into being" (71). Outlining this "multidimensional process of thinking," Connolly explains,

> First, there is the dissonant conjunction between the scene and the distinctive thoughts it might rapidly mobilize in people with different, affectively imbued memory banks. Second, the initial encounter may later spur more disciplined thinking about the fugitive relation between the virtual register and consciousness in thought. And third, the conjunction of the first two moments might later yet encourage a disciplined train of thought about the relations among affect, discipline, and technique in fomenting new thoughts and enabling a disciplined train of thought. For discipline and logic are both essential to a sustained train of thought. (71)

Expression and language, such as bodily posture and words, have a role in articulating the play of affect. Connolly in fact suggests that language and linguistic distinctions operate throughout the process of affects, "even if they do not exhaust them and even if many thoughts move too fast to render the linguistic element explicit" (71). Expressions will also be shaped by the "public context" and transformed through the process of putting affects into language (71–72). Yet new expressions have the potential to intervene in discourse and, importantly, to generate alternatives to restrictive discourses and binary thinking (73). I am interested in exploring how this process of affect might be utilized as a politics to create new knowledge and a more highly differentiated world with greater possibilities for action.

How might a neuropolitics of affect be enacted by contemporary collectives gathered around common concerns? Callon and Rabeharisoa's (2003) case study of a muscular dystrophy collective is useful for extending Connolly's work to collective action that creates new possibilities. Callon and Rabeharisoa's case study investigates the Association Française contre les Myopathies (AFM), a French muscular dystrophy association formed to create new knowledge. They describe this association as a "hybrid collective" to reflect the "mixing [of] humans and non-humans" (195) in the constitution of knowledge, identities, and spaces for political intervention (198). Hybrid collectives are engaged in processes of learning to be affected by the collective body-world (Callon and Rabeharisoa 2003; Gibson-Graham and Roelvink 2010). The AFM collective developed in response to the dehumanization of patients with muscular dystrophy and the medical community's lack of interest in the disease. The AFM gathered together patients and families to create new possibilities for living with muscular dystrophy. They took photos, collected testimonies, and employed other research methods to collect and convey patients' experiences of life with muscular dystrophy. Just as the odor kit enables the nose to differentiate odors, through their research, patients and families developed a kit of representations that differentiated life with muscular dystrophy. Through their initial research, the AFM made bodily experiences available for dialogue with medical researchers. This research disrupted the discourse representing patients with muscular dystrophy as a single homogeneous terminal case. It created a discursive interruption in which the play of affect and creative thinking about the disease could occur in the emerging collective.

The AFM embarked on fund-raising to continue research into life with muscular dystrophy and partnered with the medical community. The broader collective that formed through this partnership launched a range of new research projects to build knowledge of the disease. This research has had important effects and demonstrates the possibilities for action potentially generated through processes of learning to be affected. It has created different therapeutic options for patients and personalized and humanized them in the eyes of scientists, constituting them "as individuals caught up in a peculiar network of social relations" (199). Patients, in turn, learned to experience their bodies in relation to others in the collective, including scientists, prostheses, and genes, and they have come to see these others as "part of themselves" (199). The research has also created opportunities for new alliances between a range of experts to conduct research and further differentiate the picture of muscular dystrophy:

> The more knowledge about . . . the disease advances, the more complex the picture becomes. The number of actants involved (all kinds of proteins, antibodies, enzymes, etc.) multiplies and causal links proliferate. As a result, differences between individual patients intensify, and the number of specialists that can be mobilized increases. This opens the way for strategic options. (199)

From my perspective, this case highlights that learning to be affected can be undertaken by collectives to create knowledge that increases the possibilities for action. Callon and Rabeharisoa describe this knowledge in terms of a "discourse [that] combines the biological and the social to produce what Paul Rabinow has suggested calling a 'bio-sociality'" (198–99). More specifically, this discourse "[links] individual behaviour or social relations to biological data in a constantly revisable way" (198). The possibilities for action Callon and Rabeharisoa highlight are a range of scientific research options each with "a different set of alliances" (199). This approach to the politics of affect opens up the possibility that the antiglobalization movement might create a new econosociality, connecting economic information with social relations to create new economic identities, experiments, alliances, and options for ethical decision making (see Gibson-Graham and Roelvink 2010).

Operationalizing Affect through Freirean Pedagogy

The pedagogy of social movement collective action builds on a long tradition in Latin American politics, instigated by the influential work of Paulo Freire and his well-known book *Pedagogy of the Oppressed* ([1968] 1996). Beginning in the 1940s, Freire developed a pedagogy through which the masses could come to identify oppressive ideologies of the present and begin a dialogue for utopian futures (Gaudiano and Alba 1994). For Freire, the struggle for utopia involves acquiring the knowledge to name and oppose the present and, in doing so, to create new worlds (Weiler 1994, 15). His work suggests that social change arises through spaces that generate other ways of knowing and being in the world.

Freire's vision of social transformation was developed in a context in which the discourse of capitalist imperialism was dominant and Marxist understandings of the peasant and working classes as agents of transformation prevailed. Freire's politics is grounded in modernist Marxist ideas about revolution, the unitary singular subject, and an instrumental view of political action. Consequently, there has been much debate on the applicability of Freire's work to the diverse agents of social transformation found today. Peter McLaren and Colin Lankshear (1994), for instance, have questioned the importation of Freire's ideas to the Global North and to postcolonial contexts. They also ask whether Freire's work can be applied to contemporary forms of capitalist power. Despite this questioning, they argue that two central remaining ingredients in Freire's pedagogy are the experience of diverse forms of oppression and the desire for change.

Freire's pedagogy offers a way of thinking about the practices whereby hybrid collectives come to express affecting body-worlds through collective knowledge and discourse. As I discussed in the previous section, Connolly (2002) shows how, in the play of affect that triggers multiple lines of thought, some thoughts are captured and expressed. He further differentiates this process in which affect is expressed and translated into discourse and provides a guide to reading Freire's pedagogy (73–74). The first step involves the creation of a "new word or phrase" and its introduction into the public (73). This new word or phrase has an effect on the public discourse it enters, for instance, it could express "an absence retrospectively where none had been experienced before" (73). Second, this new word or phrase offers others a way to capture and express similar feelings or sensibilities. Third, if the word or phrase comes to express a common experience, it can be translated into discursive representation. As the new word or phrase becomes "an object of thought," it might be used to think about and act on the world (73). These steps correspond to Freirean thinking on generative themes and dialogue, through which an awareness of other possibilities of being in the world is generated and expressed in language.

Social movement groups gather together around common concerns. For Freirean scholars, common concern is achieved through *generative themes*. Generative themes are centered on everyday experience and arise from the "thematic [or discursive] universe" in which people see themselves (Freire 1996, 77). Freirean scholars further suggest that gathering around and discussing generative themes, such as neoliberalism or capitalism, can have a creative effect, generating a space of hope and possibility (Johnston and Goodman 2006). Freire distinguishes the difference between one's discursive universe and alternative possibilities as the difference between the "is" and the "ought" (see also Johnston and Goodman 2006). Naming the "is" is the initial task for those gathered around generative themes. For Freire (1996, 68), to name something is to problematize it and thus to begin to change the world. Naming the "ought" relates to Connolly's (2002, 73) first step of the creative force of affect, "revealing an absence"—an alternative to the "is"—"retrospectively where none had been experienced by most before." Josee Johnston and James Goodman (2006, 20) highlight the WSF as exemplary of a gathering around generative themes and write that the movement "establishes frameworks for living and acting together that provide fertile soil for growing paradigmatic alternatives—for connecting critiques of 'what is,' to the many different visions of 'what ought to be.'" In 2005, the WSF was organized into thematic spaces in which participants gathered around a range of generative themes. "Espaco F, Social Struggles and Democratic Alternatives—Against Neoliberal Domination," for example, included sessions called "Knowledge, Democracy, and Revolutions," "SCHOOL: Against Education Commodification," "Global Apartheid, Global Alternatives," "Reform or Revolution," and "Women and Trade Unions—Towards a Wider Working Class Politics." All of this is just a taste of what the program had to offer on January 27, the first full day of sessions (Forum Social Mundial 2005). These thematic spaces reflect participants' concerns about the world. For example, some sessions named and thereby problematized existing forms of oppression or the "is" of generative themes, such as "Global Apartheid," while at the same time gesturing toward an "ought," such as "Global Alternatives." This "ought" reveals an absence and a space of possibility (Johnston and Goodman 2006).

Yet the pitfalls—such as the squelching rather than prompting of creativity—of critical discussion of one's discursive universe have been well documented (see chapter 1; also Gibson-Graham 2006a; Latour 2004b; Sedgwick 2003). As I discussed in chapter 1, Sedgwick's (2003) work suggests that critical analysis has become analogous with, and even indistinguishable from, paranoid thinking. Drawing on Melanie Klein and Silvan Tomkin's thinking on paranoia, Sedgwick develops a picture of the critical thinker who, taking a "depressive" "anxiety-mitigating" stance, is continuously expanding the thinker's existing discursive universe to anticipate and thus negate any element of surprise (128, 130). The critical thinker achieves this by putting the thinker's own self in the enemy's shoes; that is, only by performing the paranoid fear is the critical thinker able to anticipate surprise. And even the failure to anticipate surprise confirms that "you can never be paranoid enough" (127). Connolly (2002, 76) similarly suggests that "habits of feeling and judgment" capture affect in familiar moralistic, reactive, and depressive stances that limit alternative visions of the world and possibilities of being. And looking directly at Freire's pedagogy, Peter Findlay (1994) notes that consciousness raising is a very difficult task for social movements today because their subjective experience often works against new ways of knowing the world. More specifically, he argues that, because it deals with experience, consciousness raising is easily turned "into personal growth techniques" and, in doing so, loses focus on collective struggle for social change (118). The sense of possibility and hope, and even the ability to name the alternative "oughts" following discussion of the "is" in Freirean pedagogy is, then, not automatic and needs to be thought through in relation to affecting bodies in dialogue.

For Freire, knowledge and agency are fundamentally connected (Gaudiano and Alba 1994). Indeed, he writes that "to speak a true word is to transform the world" (Freire 1996, 68). Such transformative knowledge is collectively constituted through dialogue. In Freire's pedagogy, "individuals, subjects, groups, social sectors, and nations play simultaneously the roles of educator and student" (Gaudiano and Alba 1994, 136). Freire emphasizes the co-production of learning and knowledge in *Pedagogy of the Oppressed* and writes, "Authentic education is not carried out by 'A' for 'B' or by 'A' about 'B,' but rather by 'A' with 'B,' mediated by the world—a world which impresses and challenges both parties, giving rise to views or opinions about it" (74; see also Gaudiano and Alba 1994, 136). This resonates with Buddhist pedagogy, in which one recognizes the knowledge one holds rather than learning it from someone else (Sedgwick 2003). Gaudiano and Alba's (1994) research demonstrates how this idea has been taken up in the education of Guatemalan refugees in southeast Mexico. This large group of refugees consists of many different ethnic groups with different linguistic backgrounds. Following Freirean principles, education in Spanish has enabled these refugees to share experiences, and, especially for children, Spanish education has provided a means with which to construct new identities and visions for the future. Central to this process is testimony:

For me, teaching is the form or the act of knowing, which the professor or educator exercises; it takes as its witness the student. This act of knowing is given to the student as testimony, so that the student will not merely act as a learner. In other words, teaching is the form that the teacher or educator possesses to bear witness to the student about what knowing is, so that the student will also know instead of simply learning. (Torres and Freire 1994, 103)

In social movement struggles, witnesses of an event narrate and give testimony to their experience for judgment by others (Routledge 2003). Testimony calls on the recipient to believe what they say. In Freirean dialogue, testimonies are centered on personal experience infused with love for the world and hope for the future (Freire 1996). In testifying to an experience, one conveys memories of that experience as it was lived, bearing witness to elements of that experience that are not governed by dominant discourses linked to oppression (Laub 1992; Oliver 2004). Testimonies are conveyed in words and through bodies (Sharpe 1999), in other words, through cognitive and affective registers. Theorists of affect argue that these two registers need not be consistent with one another, and as Massumi's analysis of Ronald Reagan's performances mentioned earlier shows, they may be more powerful at producing moments of creativity when they are not. In fact, this is one way in which the affective register can prompt new trains of thought. Gibson-Graham's (2006b) and Anderson's (2006) research shows how experiences of surprise, delight, hope, and desire that break with existing habits of thought can open thinking to other possibilities. Scott Sharpe (1999, 99), drawing on Julia Kristeva's work on the effects of bodily drives or the "semiotic" on symbolic communication, shows how bodily posture, the rhythm of speech, laughter, and other expressions of the semiotic can "disrupt or destabilise the symbolic and thus the social order."[5] In Sharpe's case study, semiotic expressions are seen to disrupt the dualistic discourse of natural and medicalized childbirth, "[enabling] an appreciation of a multiplicity of experiences" (100). Testimonial accounts of social movement struggles expressing hope, like those recounted at the WSF, are often at odds with prevailing cognitive understandings of the oppressive hegemonic powers expressed in the "is" of generative themes, such as neoliberalism. This disjuncture is an important part of creating a new stance toward the world. Although a testimony might discursively document the penetration of capitalism into yet another part of the globe, through other affective registers, it can also relay hope for the future that conflicts with this discourse.

Testimonies with affective force can also create connections between people in ways that bypass cognition (Connolly 2002). Described by Connolly as the "contagion of affect," affect is carried through multiple channels, such as public gatherings, and flows, such as through voice, bodily movement, touch, and texture:

> The contagion of affect flows across bodies as well as across conversations, as when anger, revenge, or inspiration is communicated across individuals or constituencies by the timbre of our voices, looks, hits, caresses, gestures, the bunching of muscles in the neck, and flushes of the skin. Such contagion flows through face-to-face meetings, academic classes, family dinners, public assemblies, TV speeches, sitcoms, soaps operas, and films. (75)

Testimonies can operate in this way, creating connections between the person testifying and the recipient. As Freire notes in a preceding passage, to be a recipient of a testimony is to experience the knowledge conveyed through that testimony. Experiencing what it feels like to know something can have affective and cognitive force on the recipient, prompting a relationship to the other and expanding the collective's capacity for affecting and being affected, prompting joy.

Through dialogue that follows testimonies at the WSF, social movement groups can begin to develop a new discourse corresponding to their hopes and desires of how the world "ought" to be. Connolly suggests that this sense of possibility, what I have read as Freire's "ought," can be expressed in a word or phrase, although always with an excess of affect. Theorists of brain–body connections argue that the translation of bodily experience into thought and language is vital to the actualization of the creative force of affect (Connolly 2002). Once the play of affect is captured in thought, it might be creatively expressed in language (67). Through collective dialogue, this language can become an object of thought and communication—through bodies and words—creating "the practical opportunity that the coining, expression, and representation of the new phase creates for you and others to work on yourselves to render your actual sensibilities more congruent with the self-representation you advance" (74). In Callon and Rabeharisoa's (2003, 199) muscular dystrophy case study, for example, "the patient's identity and that of the group of patients, of which he or she becomes a member, are simultaneously shaped" by the new biosocial discourse, and they came to consider themselves as part of a hybrid collective. Transformations in identity that are brought about when one becomes part of a collective in this way resonate with the Foucauldian idea of "self-cultivation," the "care of the self" that can lead to new ways of "being in the world" (Gibson-Graham 2006b, 6). Connolly draws on Nietzsche to describe this as a "self 'artistry'" process whereby "consciousness enables humans to devise experimental practices and arts by which to work on affect-imbued thoughts below its direct regulation but pertinent to its conscious deliberations" (77). The WSF can be viewed as a collective experiment enabling self-cultivation.

The World Social Forum:
Putting This Pedagogy into Practice

Closer examination of the thematic spaces of the WSF suggests how affect might be utilized in pedagogical practice. Particular sessions brought many different groups together. The sessions were mostly self-organized by groups coming together around a particular issue, including picking up from discussions begun at previous forums and affiliated events. Sessions typically took the form of individuals testifying to groups gathered in tents about the struggles and interventions they were part of, closely followed by discussion and debate. The session "Change the World without Taking Power: Intercontinental Dialogue on Theory and Praxis of Social Movements against-in-and-beyond State and Capital" is of particular interest here because it focused on new forms of power, such as "affect modulation" (Massumi 2002a). The generative theme of this session might be described as "oppression is installed through diffuse channels and transforms relationships" (the "is") and "alternatives are constituted through material struggles in everyday life" (the "ought"). This session involved many different participants, from academics, such as sociologist John Holloway, to social movement representatives, such as representatives from the Argentina Movement of the Unemployed, the Occupied Factory Movement of Argentina, and from a number of different countries, such as Germany, the Philippines, Italy, Brazil, South Africa, Thailand, and India. These participants shared their experiences through testimonies to struggle, such as the testimony of the representative from the Coalition against Water Privatisation in South Africa.

The Coalition against Water Privatisation was formed in 2003 by the Anti-Privatisation Forum, the Anti-Eviction Campaign, and many other social movements and activists. The work of the coalition has been documented in a research report written by Prishani Naidoo (2005a) and published by the Centre for Civil Society at the University of KwaZulu-Natal. The Centre for Civil Society is a research center committed to supporting nonprofit and community organizations and collaboration more generally.[6] The coalition was initiated by residents of Phiri in Johannesburg in response to the privatization of the commons, in particular public services like water and electricity. Previously, residents of Phiri and other areas had free access to water and saw this access as "essential for meeting their basic needs for survival" (Naidoo 2005a, 156). As Naidoo explains, water was viewed as a common and shared source of life and thus, in Stephen Gudeman's (2001, 157) terms, as a foundation for community. In South Africa, the provision of common resources to all sectors of society was offered by the South African government in 1994 as a response to the social divisions and exclusions created through apartheid (Naidoo 2005a, 159). At the 2005 WSF, Naidoo's testimony placed the coalition's intervention within this longer history of struggle and shifting regimes of governance in South Africa, from collective struggle and strategies of "ungovernability" during apartheid (such as mass boycotts, strikes, and armed struggle) to the struggle to create alternatives as the new regime of postapartheid governance shifted to a politics of "inclusion."

I was a recipient of this testimony, and what I initially heard was a sophisticated, confidently delivered narrative of the development and adaptation of neoliberal governmentality. For instance, I heard how the new postapartheid regime of governance has linked the idea of "responsible citizenship" with the privatization and commodification of public services and has sought to implement this neoliberal rationality through prepaid meters and other user-pays systems. In the broader historical context of South Africa, Naidoo's testimony and report suggested that after the period of ungovernability, it has been difficult for the South African government to shift the responsibility for public services to citizens as consumers, because consumers simply do not pay and use debt as a form of resistance (160). The prepaid meter is seen by the government as a technology to eliminate the "option" of debt altogether. That is, the meter is viewed as a technology of neoliberal governance implemented to transform how people relate to and use common resources. The prepaid water meter not only threatens the commons but

also, by powerfully "individualising the relationship of people to the resources necessary for life,"[7] shifts government responsibility for public pro-
visions to individuals. This technology is linked by the coalition to practices
like budgetary advice, planning, and other technologies to reveal a broad
network of neoliberal governance. Together these technologies aim to reshape
community life. This testimony fitted nicely with my thinking at the time
(Roelvink and Craig 2005), which was highly attuned to intellectual debates
about neoliberalism, and my written comments show how I used these habits of thinking about neoliberalism to digest these accounts. My notes included,
for example, statements such as "sounds like 'roll-out neoliberalism' (Peck
and Tickell 2002) and reflects the adaption of neoliberal policy."

In her testimony, Naidoo also bore witness to the coalition's struggle.
In doing so, her narrative of neoliberalism was punctured by something
different—an intervention centered on "reclaiming of our common":

> It is in the struggles of people against these attacks on life, that our move-
> ments, such as the Anti-Privatisation Forum and the Anti-Eviction Campaign,
> have emerged. One of our key strategies in these struggles has been that of
> reclaiming our common—reconnecting water and electricity that [have] been
> disconnected, and putting people back into the homes from which they have
> been evicted, denying the commodification of resources that are basic neces-
> sities for life and insisting on their common ownership by us all. Against the
> language of "responsibility to pay," campaigns such as "Operation Khanyisa"
> ("Operation Switch On/Light Up") and "Operation Vula 'manzi" ("Operation
> Open the Water") have allowed for people to come together again in refusal of
> a logic that speaks against life and the common, and to institute in the imme-
> diate an alternative to this logic—freely connected water and electricity.[8]

Naidoo described the coalition's enormously challenging and constantly
shifting struggle to reconnect people with resources while assisting them to
reassert common ownership. Following this description, she went on to tes-
tify to the government's response to the coalition's efforts, such as the crimi-
nalization of the coalition's actions and attempts to convert the struggle
through concessions, including reducing electricity debt and providing a certain quantity of free water. Naidoo was again picking up the narrative of neoliberalism, noting "that these measures are but partial solutions to problems
that persist, replicate, and change their form, with an unchallenged overall

framework of neoliberalism."[9] Yet the interruption in Naidoo's testimony—her recollection of the coalition's inventions—had produced a break through which affect could play. Her testimony to this invention or alternative was by no means clearly formed—it was a gesture to other possibilities conveyed largely by her physical presence; on stage she looked small, while her voice was powerful, confident, and energized. The stories about the struggle to truck water to people, the dangers of reconnecting electricity illegally, and the risks of contesting state power expressed strength, hope, and a will that could affect participant witnesses in the session. Naidoo's description of "freely connected water and electricity" provided words from which a discourse of the commons and the collective subject could be developed in dialogue with other participants in the session.

The session "Change the World without Taking Power" included many other testimonies. In one moving example, a woman conveyed her experience of the precarious yet hopeful life shared among a group that occupy a forest in Germany. There were also testimonies from agricultural plantation workers from the Philippines and from a movement in northern Italy that utilizes squatting as a form of social provisioning, especially for migrants. As with that of the coalition, these testimonies included experiences of social movement struggle and intervention. Yet each testimony was very different. The representatives spoke of radically different interventions in a variety of languages, and their testimonies were more or less formed with some narratives delivered confidently and others in stuttering, less confident ways. Each representative and a range of other participants were recipients of these testimonies. Interrupting my notes on and thinking about neoliberalism, I recorded these grueling stories of experimental interventions, including the German woman's life in the occupied forest, which she described as "dodgy." Not captured in my notes, but recalled through the excitement I experienced, which in turn has driven this research, was the physical presence of these representatives in Porto Alegre, their strength to get up and tell their stories, the performance of their interventions as existing alternatives, their calls for others to join them, and the sense of possibility that energized the participants in dialogue. This sense of possibility, I think, was related to the affecting bodies gathered in the session and the increased opportunities of being affected generated by the testimonies.

Following the simultaneously translated testimonies of the participants, the session divided into small groups to discuss specific themes arising from the testimonies. This framework for discussion developed by the organizers gave each group a specific question that required the proposal of an intervention as an answer. The questions included, How do we refuse and live? How do we defend ourselves against state oppression? How can we develop alternative social relations? What is our relation to the state-centered struggle against capitalism? How do we multiply and expand our fissures? What other questions should we be asking? Whereas the testimonies performed particular experiences from around the globe, dialogue in the small group discussions that followed aimed to articulate common visions to feed back to the larger group.

The small group discussions brought together representatives who had given testimony and recipients of that testimony. Having both experienced and been affected by the preceding testimonies, the dialogue between participants that followed aimed to capture and magnify this affect to generate new thoughts and build a collective language. The action-directed questions were important in guiding participants' dialogue to explore absences and possibilities rather than focusing only on the constraining discourses at odds with the hope felt by participants yet penetrating each testimony, such as the logic of neoliberalism. Through collective investigation of the testimonies and discussion questions, participants were able to form relationships with one another and together, through dialogue, to discover new possibilities of being. These exchanges enabled participants to capture and magnify moments of affect generated in the words of the testimonies, and this was reflected in a shift in discourse. The suggestions put forward were notably stripped of concern about neoliberalism and instead proposed diverse alternatives such as traditional medicine, new technologies, systems of reciprocity, the formation of cooperatives, and ideas about how to maintain and build the connections initiated in the session. The co-constitution of proposals and the ideas that emerged for future intervention further connected these participants and the projects they represented through a common language that could be used for self-cultivation. In the session "Change the World without Taking Power," this language concerned the multiple and diverse registers of being shaping social movement struggle. As Naidoo reflected after the session,

> without seeking to derive any consensus out of the discussions, activists were
> able to share and engage in a discussion about the creation of alternatives to

capitalism through new, shared understandings of power to understand the ways in which capitalism controls us as individuals and ways in which we are able to live outside of it. . . . In the words of a comrade from the MTD-Matanzas [the occupied factory movement in Argentina], "Before, our slogans were for freeing the prisoners, fighting neoliberalism; today, our struggle is on a different terrain—it is in our heads; in how we live; in our family structures; it is in creating new forms of family and love; it is in rethinking life." (Naidoo 2005b)

This vision was accompanied by an orientation to self-cultivation, with participants drawing attention to the relationships between thought, language, and the way in which the world is lived and experienced. This was demonstrated by the debate over how workers might redefine themselves in accordance with their vision of alternative economies rather than as unemployed, as in the occupied factory movement in Argentina and the Argentina Movement of the Unemployed (Naidoo 2005b).

Following the small group sessions, the subsequent forum regrouped all participants to share ideas, generate e-mail lists, and proclaim a collective. In addition to the more traditional sense of a collective organization, the session had performed a collective of interacting body-worlds akin to a hybrid collective. The Freirean pedagogical techniques of the WSF can be seen as enabling Latour's (2004a, 205) "learning to be affected," "meaning 'effectuated,' moved, put into motion by other entities, humans or non-humans." The session, a hybrid collective involving diverse representatives, translators, speakers and microphones, tents and chairs, and so on, differentiated and transformed body-worlds into a range of possibilities for action and experience. In bringing together diverse participants and, through dialogue, developing a collective knowledge of the world, the session "Change the World without Taking Power" can be understood as enacting a new econosociality.

Performing New Worlds through Hybrid Collectives

As it has grown and shifted from a stance of opposition to one of affirmation, the WSF has reoriented itself toward the creation of new knowledge. It shows little concern, however, with the creation of a singular prescription for action or manifesto. Rather, like other social movement performances (Hynes et al. 2007), its force lies in the act of participation and the arousal of hope for new worlds. This is not just a hope for the future, although it is that, too, but an experience of new possibilities in the present—the experience of learning to be affected in collectives and thereby contributing to the differentiation and proliferation of alternative economic possibilities for action. In this chapter, I reread Freire's pedagogy through Connolly's *Neuropolitics* to show how such an experience of possibility can be generated through learning centered on dialogue. The 2005 WSF session "Change the World without Taking Power" juxtaposed a range of narratives about neoliberalism punctured with accounts of experimental economic interventions. Together these testimonies triggered moments of "affective energy" for creative thinking (Connolly 2002, 76). In collective dialogue, this energy was harnessed, and new thoughts were captured and expressed through a language of the multiple and diverse forces that shape social movement struggle. This session can be seen as a first step in the generation of an alternative economic discourse to guide experiments in self-world cultivation.

When I arrived at the 2005 WSF, I believed that my role as a researcher was to document the mutations of neoliberalism and to analyze how shifts in neoliberal governance were co-opting social movements. In doing so, I hoped to help social movements resist neoliberalism. Participating in the WSF sessions, however, and receiving social movement testimonies to experimental interventions and economic alternatives shifted my thinking from neoliberalism to the alternative economic experimentations currently under way. I also began to see myself as part of a hybrid collective creating new worlds. This collective includes all that made the WSF possible (such as technologies required for dialogue, tents, and food markets), participants of the WSF and the collectives they represent and more. Taking this point further, the hybrid collective in which I have learned to be affected reaches out to touch and involve a broader assemblage, including debates in the research fields of social movement studies, actor network theory, neuroscience and pedagogy, and the academic infrastructure through which this knowledge travels. This idea of an assemblage is taken up and extended in the following chapter through the case of markets.

In among this broader assemblage, one could focus on and explore further the infrastructure through which the alternative knowledges produced at the WSF are traveling. Gibson-Graham (2008), for example, finds inspiration in Michael Piore and Charles Sabel (1984) and the research collective created through intellectual networks centered on the book *The Second Industrial Divide*. In this case, research on capitalist industrialization in Italy generated knowledge of flexible specialization that was packaged and transported around the globe, "transforming industrial planning and creating industrial clusters worldwide" (Gibson-Graham 2008, 14). What could be described as a hybrid "research" collective of flexible specialization thus provided an infrastructure of transportation to mobilize and proliferate knowledge. In light of this, in her work, Gibson-Graham (2006a, xvii) aims to engage a diverse range of participants "in theorizing and analyzing individual projects, thereby making them available and transportable as models or inspirations; and the action involved is the effectivity and extension (in time and space) of the heterogeneous collectivity, including the performativity of the often tacit knowledge that it generates and brings to bear in world-changing experiments."

Importantly, the 2005 WSF hybrid collective created a different role for me than that of a critical observer; it has produced openings in my habits of thinking and trained me to appreciate the diverse economic interventions and alternatives around the world. Ultimately, this hybrid collective has enabled me to engage in this line of thinking. In turn, by elaborating a technique for creative thinking that can be used to increase the options for economic action, this chapter can be seen to contribute to the performance of a new econosociality (see also Gibson-Graham and Roelvink 2010). This research thus joins others aiming to perform diverse economic experimentation around the world and to open up the economy as a site of decision making, ethical debate, and possibility (Gibson-Graham 2008). The politics to which I have gestured in this chapter embraces a utopia of hope, that is, a utopia centered on the possibilities contained in the present (Stengers 2002, 254).

4

Transforming Markets

Social Movements and Markets

Markets are of central concern in contemporary social movement struggles. The antiglobalization movement is well known for gathering people together in protest against the "market." Understood through a strong theoretical lens, the "market" is viewed as a mechanism of neoliberalism. Thus being against neoliberalism necessarily means being against the market through which it is instituted. Many antiglobalization movements oppose consumer freedom, the alienation and purchasability of all things, the idea that markets can efficiently meet needs like hunger and can provide for all, the idea that freeing up land creates efficient production, and so on. Politically, these social movements attempt to move completely outside of the market's reach, arguing that markets cannot be applied to particular areas of life (Carrier 1997). In doing so, as Michel Callon (2015, 324) argues, such an approach denies markets a politics in and of themselves, as "it is because markets are instruments of domination that they become political issues" rather than because of the politics of their organization and role that they play in collective life. In contrast to the resistance view of the "market," at the 2005 World Social Forum (WSF), I participated in many discussions about "alternative markets." In and around the Porto Alegre forum, all manner of markets could be seen in operation—helping to organize rubbish collection and recycling and the selling of food, crafts, and other goods. The Economy of Solidarity movement, which integrates collective and self-managed economic initiatives, played a large role in the 2005 WSF, including a solidarity exchange market that used alternative forms of money based on social relationships, "social money," to exchange goods. It seems that there is actually much diversity among social movement concerns about markets, ranging from outright rejection of neoliberal marketization to exploration of the ways in which markets might be employed in the creation of alternative worlds.

Fair trade exemplifies the kind of market embraced at the WSF. This is an international trading network that seeks to change the way that markets operate to benefit small producers largely in developing nations (Nicholls and Opal 2005). It has two main branches, the Fairtrade Labelling Organizations International (FLO, now Fairtrade International) and the World Fair Trade Organization (WFTO; previously called the International Fair Trade Association and, before that, the International Federation of Alternative Trade), an association of alternative trade organizations (ATOs). FLO encapsulates a range of labeling and certification initiatives to assist producers in entering markets. Through an "innovative supply chain model" and the provision of market information, FLO aims to ensure that producers receive a fair price for their products (Nicholls and Opal 2005). FLO also implements labor and environmental standards in the production of goods like bananas (Tallontire 2006). WFTO, which includes both labeled and nonlabeled fair trade goods, has broader ambitions. It aims to enable consumers to discriminate between different traders (such as between Oxfam and Nestle) and, by highlighting the relationship between producers and consumers, seeks to ensure that the least well-off producers are privileged in trade (Bezencon and Blili 2006). In general, fair trade is about making trade fair, that is, ensuring that ethical principles and practices shape markets. Fair trade offers a vision of markets as a means to address social justice concerns.

Particularly in respect to the ways in which they gather a diverse range of people and things, these kinds of markets have strikingly different characteristics to those that social movements rally against. In the fair trade networks, for instance, multiple actors are gathered through ethical decision making to ensure certain production and trade standards are adhered to. Fair trade relies on an awareness of a broad network including collectivized producers, certification and regulation experts, nongovernmental organizations (NGOs), a range of labeling procedures, retail outlets, and information distributors, among others (Bezencon and Blili 2006; Nicholls and Opal 2005). Consumption is shaped by a genuine concern for distant producers. Fair trade also points to another common characteristic of socially oriented markets: the vision that markets are open to reinvention. This suggests that the people and things taken into consideration in market transactions can be challenged and changed. Farmer's markets are another example of markets reorienting produce markets away from supermarkets to increase producers' surplus and hence maintain local farms, while also providing consumers with fresh produce. Such markets are governed by moral values and shaped by ethical decision making. Markets centered on craftsmen in Egypt, for example, are governed by moral relations that maintain the broader community and ensure that masters do not act with only a view to individual gain (Elyachar 2005). Because of this, these markets are viewed as irrational from the perspective of neoliberal policy (Nicholls and Opal 2005, 13). But how are these markets to be conceptualized? Is the very discourse of neoliberal marketization preventing us from seeing the potential of existing markets for creating alternative economies? In this chapter, I ask how these "alternative" markets might be conceptualized in a way that contributes to the new worlds that social movements are fighting for. I explore how these markets are constituted in a way that contributes to an ethical performance of markets.

My approach to understanding markets draws on research in the field of science and technology studies (see, e.g., Callon 1998c; 2015; Mitchell 2007; 2008). Researchers in this area view markets as actor networks or hybrid *agencements* (Callon and Law 1995; Mitchell 2008). Discussed in more detail later, the term *agencement* refers to a network made up of human and nonhuman elements that collectively enable action (Callon 2005). Markets are constituted by all sorts of things, including economics. Science and technology researchers see markets as performative achievements whereby an *agencement,* including a statement and all that it refers to, brings something into being (see Callon 2007). This perspective on the performativity of markets provides a framework with which to further explore the geography of market performance, a central focus of this book. Michel Callon and Kory Caliskan (2005) and Timothy Mitchell (2008, 455) have highlighted the success that classical and neoclassical economic theory has had in performing markets and in shaping the constitution of markets as networks in which the field of economics and the world it describes can prosper. Explaining the *agencement* approach to the study of these markets, Mitchell writes, "The goal is to study how economists are actively engaged in the co-construction of socio-technical worlds that enable this narrow, calculating rationality to thrive" (455). Classical and neoclassical economics and "homo economicus" (the individual rational actor) thrive in markets that contemporary social movements fundamentally oppose.

A hybrid *agencement* approach to markets suggests that while economic theory and abstraction have played a central role in their performance, economic theory is not immune from contestation, nor is it the only factor shaping the networks we call markets. Mitchell (2008, 462) highlights the importance of alliances and contestation between a range of market actors and concepts. For example, in the United States, a cellular phone license market was developed by auctioning frequency rights. Contestation during the development of this market revealed "rivalries among different theorists recruited by different corporations, short comings in theoretical models . . . and tiny errors in the design of the auction procedure that triggered much larger failures" (Mitchell 2008, 462).

The market of homo economicus has received much attention by social movements and academic researchers. It seems as if we have been flooded with both strong and weak theories of this kind of market (see, e.g., Barry 2002; Carrier 1998; Elyachar 2005; Miller 2005; Mitchell 2008). While this market might often be taken for granted as the "market" or the "market model," a hybrid *agencement* approach suggests that the constitution of any market involves contestation, political struggle, and much slippage. Market performances are thus open to transformation. Given this body of work, in this chapter, I happily leave the "market" to one side to focus on, in the hope to contribute to, the performance of ethical markets by social movements. I argue that markets are, potentially, one contemporary form of collective action that brings new worlds into being. To do so, I explore geographies of market performance in which social movements play a key role. I focus in particular on one performative act enabling markets, the act of framing. Framing relates to the kinds of relationships that are taken into account in market action (Callon 1998a). I argue that the framing in "alternative" markets such as fair trade is governed by an ethical awareness of the multiple relationships constituting *agencements*. I draw on the work of Adam Smith to think about the way in which this awareness is embodied and shapes market actions. In doing so, this chapter further develops the second thematic focus of this book, namely, embodied geographies of collective action. In particular, Smith's work leads me to consider the role of embodied geographies in ethical awareness and ethical actions. Like other performative acts, the act of framing is enabled and surrounded by other relationships and can be responded to by concern groups. Throughout this analysis, I discuss a range of different social movement struggles coalescing around and transforming market frames. In the final section, I focus on the case of trash-picking to demonstrate this approach to markets.

Performative Geographies of Markets

Alongside individually oriented, abstract, apolitical, and amoral markets, there are many different kinds of markets and market practices linked with social movement struggles. These markets gather together a diverse range of concerned people and things that constitute what Callon (2005) refers to as *agencement.* The notion of *agencement,* related to the idea of *collectif* discussed earlier, is an extension of new understandings of agency that shift attention away from the human actor toward a performance that is enabled and gains meaning through networks or collectives made up of humans, nonhumans, technologies, machines, and so on (4). From this perspective, agency is seen as "collective," as "multiple and diverse," constituted through *agencements* and interwoven with other agencies (4–5). These multiple constituted *agencements* interact to perform markets and market transactions. This understanding of the constitution of markets displaces the calculating human subject from the center of market transactions (50). The constitutive power of an *agencement* rests, instead, on multiple factors. For instance, a performative act constituting a market might involve calculative practices that value goods, forms of marketing that attract buyers, and or legal institutions that guarantee the transfer of property. The collective force of *agencements* that bring markets into being invokes the relational character of performativity and the gathering together of different agents, institutions, and utterances in a geography of performative action (Sedgwick 2003).

Agencements perform markets through an act of framing (Callon 1998a). In Callon's words:

> Framing is an operation used to define agents (an individual person or a group of persons) who are clearly distinct and dissociated from one another. It also allows for the definition of objects, goods and merchandise which are perfectly identifiable and can be separated not only from other goods, but also from the actors involved, for example in their conception, production and circulation or use. It is owing to this framing that the market can exist and that distinct agents and distinct goods can be brought into play. Without this framing the states of the world can not be described and listed and, consequently, the effects of the different conceivable actions can not be anticipated. (17)

Framing enables market transactions in which multiple *agencements* inter-act to exchange goods. Framing performs and differentiates between calcu-lated economic transactions and noncalculated acts such as gift giving (15). A transaction is performed as a gift when a countergift is excluded from the market frame and thus is not taken into account in the transaction. In con-trast, a calculated transaction is performed when framing takes into account a return, this is, an exchange for the gift (15). Callon's now well-known exam-ple of this performance of framing is the purchase of a car:

> The transaction is possible because rigorous framing has been performed. This framing has reduced the market transaction to three distinct compo-nents: the buyer, the producer-seller, and the car. The buyer and the seller are identified without any ambiguity, so that property rights can be exchanged. As for the car, it is because it is free from any ties with other objects or human agents, that it can change ownership. (18)

For Callon, calculation (and market actions more generally) is only possible when the entities involved in the transaction and the nature of their relation-ship are identified and framed.

Much debate surrounds just which relationships are framed and the extent to which they can be isolated and identified, particularly in relation to more recent work on how objects are valued in economic transactions and how various relationships are taken into account and shape the valuing process (see Lee 2006; Miller 2005; Slater 2002). Attention to the geography of the performative act of framing suggests that there are multiple relationships surrounding and connected with acts of framing, some of which are included into frames and others of which are excluded. For instance, today some rela-tionships between car use and the environment are taken into account in market frames and influence consumer action. Yet other relationships are excluded, such as the relationship between car use and road deaths (Callon 2005, 7). Callon suggests that often, more relationships included in the frame will make the transaction more difficult. Taking into account a range of fac-tors, such as "global warming, traffic congestion, problems of urban road tolls or safety," will greatly slow the process of transaction (7).

Callon focuses on the relationships that enable a thing to be transferred from one *agencement* into another, and he describes these relationships in terms of a process of entanglement–disentanglement–entanglement. As a thing moves from one *agencement* into another, it is transformed or revalued by the exchange (Appadurai 1986; Callon 2005, 5). Entanglement refers to the relationships that connect different agencies, for instance, between a consumer and all the work (such as marketing) that goes into entangling them with the purchasable object (Callon 2005, 6). Entanglement therefore enables the transaction: the more relations that connect them, the more likely it is that the seller, product, and buyer will be brought together and the product will be exchanged. The disentanglement that follows enables the thing to be transferred and these agencies to be broken free of one another following the transaction. Disentanglement rarely completely frees the exchanged item from other *agencements* because the thing that is exchanged continues to be attached in some way to the previous *agencement,* such as by embodying the knowledge that went into its creation (Callon 1998a, 18).

Research plays an important role in the performance of framing and the processes of entanglement–disentanglement (Callon 1998b), as demonstrated by the case of greenhouse gas emissions trading. Greenhouse gases comprise several different gases, including carbon dioxide, nitrous oxide, methane, and tropospheric ozone. The greenhouse gas market trading schemes developed thus far typically involve gas emissions permits that are awarded to emitters based on emissions targets, such as those set by individual countries (Victor 1991). Emitters can then trade these permits with other emitters, and their emissions levels are evaluated according to their permits (Victor 1991). In addition, greenhouse gas–reducing activities (such as tree planting) receive credits that can also be traded. Early research by David Victor (1991) on the applicability of this type of market provides great insight into the extent that different kinds of emissions can be calculated, how emitters can be identified and awarded permits, and how market transactions can be framed. In other words, he provides insight into whether a market transaction can be enacted or if an emissions trading scheme is even feasible. Victor's research identifies the enormous difficulty in calculating emissions of nitrous oxide, methane, and tropospheric ozone and, thus, whether it is possible to use a market mechanism to regulate emissions. For example, there is considerable uncertainty about the sources and sinks that sequester tropospheric ozone. And what is known is complicated by the fact that tropospheric ozone varies "annually, seasonally, diurnally, and spatially" (212). Tropospheric ozone is also produced from other pollutants, such as methane, making emitters difficult to pinpoint. In contrast, there is much more agreement about the sources and sinks that sequester carbon dioxide, which suggests that a carbon market is possible. The largest nonnatural producer of carbon dioxide emissions, fossil fuel consumption, for instance, is well understood (205). And while there is some uncertainty in the calculation of emissions produced through deforestation, this is expected to improve through satellite technology and methodological agreement in monitoring. Carbon dioxide credits for reforestation are also thought to be feasible, although there is potential contestation over land ownership and subsequent land use (207).

This brief account suggests that out of all the greenhouse gas emissions, a market for carbon dioxide emissions permits is feasible because the *agencement* of the emitter can be identified, carbon dioxide emissions permits allocated, and a market framed. As a result, different *agencements* are able to make calculations as to whether they will purchase more permits or credits from *agencements* of emitters or credit producers. By trading carbon credits, they can entangle and disentangle themselves with pollutants and pollutant sinks. But from Victor's perspective, the cost of calculating and governing this market is very high, and thus the benefits of a market approach to carbon dioxide emissions are questionable. Another issue is how market frames are shaped and governed. What accounts for which relationships and concerns are included and excluded in market frames? Should, for instance, national developmental differences between the United States and China be taken into account in setting emissions targets? And how are transactions between enterprises to be governed? How does a firm decide whether to trade permits with a firm that might be considered environmentally destructive? These are questions that remain to be addressed satisfactorily. Thus, although, as Andrew Barry (2002, 270) shows, calculative practices like economics are often able to close off political debate from spheres such as the market, "placing limits on the possibilities for debate and confrontation,"[1] in this case, the developing market for carbon reveals uncertainty and controversy in market boundaries and shows that they are open to negotiation. Thus debate in the identification, calculation, and allocation of carbon credits might actually "heat up" (see Callon 1998b) the environmental arena by producing controversy, which makes economic calculation near impossible. The measurements necessary to operationalize carbon trading, such as quantifying the different forms of pollution each company produces or where they pollute and the types of environments affected, may generate further debate by showing the arbitrary and uncertain nature of allocating carbon credits. In this case, the market is employed as a benign technology but has very real political consequences. Callon (1998b, 260) describes these situations as "hot" because there is no agreement on the boundaries and nature of flows in the market; in other words, the market and its governance are unclear.

The "alternative" markets and their processes of framing and transaction highlighted earlier in this chapter are governed by a range of factors, including ethical decision making and moral governance (Smith 2005; Elyachar 2005). Market transactions and entanglement–disentanglement–entanglement, for example, can be shaped by ethical decision making. This is demonstrated by Smith (2005) in her analysis of the Edinburgh housing market. Smith shows how price and other economic indicators typically associated with market agency are displaced by negative and positive emotional values, such as fear and luck, in situations of speculation. She demonstrates how buyers are entangled with homes through notions of choice and wealth, infused with "an ethic of care" (13). Choice over which home to buy and which neighborhood one might buy into is a "hallmark of owner occupation" and involves the entanglement of buyers and their potential homes in geographies of care that can provide for their material and social needs (13). "Householders may want markets to work differently," Smith writes, "to meet needs as much as respond to ability to pay; to enhance the potential for care among close family and intimate friends" (14). Likewise, though not discussed by Smith in this account, the disentanglement of sellers from homes might involve feelings that their homes can no longer meet their health and care needs or might be associated with changes in identity.

Ethics and social relations also govern performative acts of market framing. Whereas research building on Callon's approach tends to focus on the point of transaction (see, e.g., Slater 2002), accounts of "alternative" markets, such as fair trade, show that market transactions are shaped by much broader and longer-lasting relationships. If trading relationships are not satisfactory, for instance, ATOs might work with producers over time to improve the situation (Bezencon and Blili 2006). Smith's (2005) research also demonstrates that it is necessary to look beyond particular transactions and factors like price to understand the multiple relationships framing markets and shaping market activity, such as speculation bubbles that shape market transactions according to chance and luck (6). She notes, "The Edinburgh stories suggest rather that the meaning of price, the value of property, the exercise of choice and the exchange of all kinds of information and misinformation may be less about the economy of markets, and more about their rich sociality; less about their general principles and more about their multiplicity" (7).

How does this broader market sociality actually govern performative acts of framing and the relationships included within market transactions more generally? Recent research methodologies suggest that market frames themselves might reflect the broader sociality of market *agencements*. John Law's (2004a) reading of the baroque sensibility explains how something seemingly so large—the social—is contained within something that is so small: the framed market transaction. The baroque sensibility is a research methodology that involves looking within phenomena to get a sense of the worlds into which they are folded (see Law 2004a). This entails looking within market frames for the detail, complexity, and wider sociality of market *agencements*. The baroque is an approach akin to the weak theoretical stance discussed in chapter 1 in that it describes "'detail,' rather than . . . 'the broader picture'" for which strong theory strives (19). As such, it embraces heterogeneity and multiplicity over coherence and sameness (19). For example, rather than theorizing market performances as a mechanism of capitalist accumulation (Harvey 2003), a researcher might examine the way in which a variety of moral systems are contained within and come to shape market frames (Elyachar 2005). The baroque corresponds with the perspective of overdetermination mentioned in the introduction to this book as it draws attention to how, in complex and overdetermined contexts, phenomena like the sociality of the market "*manifest* themselves specifically" (Law 2004a, 20). Law's (2004a, 22) work suggests that the researcher can focus attention on one part of the *agencement,* the human actor, for instance, without falling back into divisions between human and nonhuman agency because everything is interconnected and already within that particular part of the *agencement* in view. The sociality embodied by market actors was in fact a chief concern of early political economists, such as Adam Smith, whose work is generally taken as the inspiration for market societies and is more popularly associated with the "market." Can Smith's understanding of the social and moral nature of economic existence provide a way of thinking about how embodied *agencements* govern market transactions?

Ethical Markets

Adam Smith's *The Theory of Moral Sentiments* ([1759] 2002) and *The Wealth of Nations* ([1776–78] 1937) provide much insight into how one might view embodied market sociality or, put in other words, the embodied geography of markets. *The Theory of Moral Sentiments,* published nearly twenty years before *The Wealth of Nations,* is generally placed in the tradition of moral philosophy and takes as its subject the "nature of moral judgement" (Raphael 1985, 29). *The Wealth of Nations,* in contrast, is thought of as focusing on economic growth and the division of labor (Raphael 1985, 29). At the heart of both books, however, and Smith's vision of functioning market societies more generally, is the moral individual. *The Theory of Moral Sentiments* develops a complex psychological understanding of this individual (Raphael 1985). Smith's moral individual involves three different types of being: the actor; the conscience, which refers to a form of society contained within the actor that is used to judge action and is often called the impartial spectator or "man within the breast"; and an idealized image of an agent that freely exercises moral judgment in accordance with the impartial spectator (Watson 2006, 47–48). This understanding of the moral individual and the virtues governing their different parts, such as self-command, prudence, and sympathy (see Brown 1994), is the key to understanding how, for Smith, markets function and are governed.

In *The Wealth of Nations,* Smith develops a theory of economic growth centered on markets and the way that they encourage labor specialization and division, and thereby increase production and trade. Smith's argument is based on the belief that to increase their wealth, individuals specialize their production and thereby create surplus produce to exchange (Raphael 1985). In the process, an increasingly heterogeneous and economically interdependent market is constituted (Raphael 1985). At the heart of the market is the individual drive to further one's own interests and, through conspicuous consumption, to appear wealthy. The combination of conspicuous consumption with the virtue of self-command is thought to increase wealth and drive the accumulation of capital (Smith [1776–78] 1937; see also Fitzgibbons 1995, 145–48). But as Watson's (2006) reading suggests, in *The Theory of Moral Sentiments,* Smith argues that conspicuous wealth and egotism do not result in true happiness. True happiness relates to the third dimension of being and is realized through the attainment of the idealized image of the self as a moral agent. Smith further argues that following one's self-interest does not necessarily ensure an orderly market society, which is thought to require respectful behavior between individuals (Watson 2006). Whereas commercial life is initiated by individuals following their own interests, capitalist growth and orderly markets are produced through restraint. It is by follow-ing one's own conscience that an individual gains self-command, prudence, and the capacity to forgo immediate pleasures to save money (Fitzgibbons 1995; Watson 2006). This is what fuels the wealth of a nation.

Listening to one's conscience in making judgments and calculations involves imagining oneself in another's shoes (Raphael 1985, 30–31). The conscience compels one to make moral judgments and take responsibility for others, which, in turn, "creates a social bond" and operates like a "social-ising agent" (Raphael 1985, 31). To understand how we make judgments of our own actions in relation to others' in a market society, Smith develops the idea of the impartial spectator (Brown 1994, 33). The impartial spectator is seen as society within; it is how we imagine our own actions are seen and judged by others who are as equally informed as we are about our situation (Watson 2006). To correspond with the perceived sentiments of a fully informed society, an individual adjusts her passions, affecting "indulgent humanity," moral action, and self-command (Raphael 1985, 33). The impar-tial spectator is thought to govern individual interests in the marketplace through the virtue of self-command. Self-command refers to the ability to restrain the desire to follow one's own passions, which in commercial society is for highly visible displays of wealth and consumption (Watson 2006, 53). Rather than simply following an aspiration to be like the wealthy in society, individual interests are restrained and shaped by the impartial spectator, leading to the realization that happiness is not to be found in displays of high consumption (Watson 2006, 48).

While the embodied geography of collective action explored through the WSF in chapter 3 extends beyond the human in the sense that it is the hybrid collective made up of human and nonhuman parts that can potentially move bodies and create new possibilities for action, Smith's thinking on the impar-tial spectator and what we would today understand as empathy (putting oneself in another's shoes) centers on human social agents. For the concept of the impartial spectator to be the basis for a market ethics that can take into account the geography of market framing, a different or broader take on empathy is required, one that can include more-than-human others. The idea of putting oneself in another's shoes is also problematic because it assumes one has access to another's state of mind and that there is an objec-tifiable "state" of mind that can be accessed (Slaby 2014). It is in response to this latter problem that Jan Slaby suggests an understanding of empathy based on "mutual interactive engagement and on marked forms of co-presence or 'being-with' one another" (255). This is an approach that is, potentially, much more open to the more-than-human world. The basic idea here is that empathy be centered on an understanding of another's "felt coalescence" that evolves through "joint agency" or "co-engagement" in an activity (255). As Slaby further explains,

> within this shared perspective, experiential responses to intentions, desires, thoughts, feelings and, above [all], actions of the partner are enacted, albeit not in the form of a succession of discrete mental states but in the manner of a seamless relating inextricable from the ongoing unfolding of the joint activity. (255)

Slaby does not have nonhumans in mind here in developing this action-centered account of empathy whereby one comes to be affected by another while at the same time recognizing the other as an animate living and changing subject whose mind cannot be objectified. However, it does not seem like too much of a stretch to include the more-than-human world within the ambit of such an approach to empathy.[2]

With this broader view of empathy in mind, the impartial spectator can be viewed as an embodiment of the sociality of market *agencements* that govern performative acts of market framing. The impartial spectator shapes which relationships are taken into account in market framing and thus whether, for example, market transactions are performed as calculated or self-serving. Fair trade markets are an excellent example of this. Third world producers have experienced devastating effects from international trade, being hit hard by rapidly changing prices, growing competition, and other trade disadvantages (Raynolds and Wilkinson 2007). From the outset, fair trade aimed to connect producers and consumers by reducing supply chains and ensuring that market transactions are guided by the consideration of others in the *agencements,* such as third world farmers and farming ecologies (see Nicholls and Opal 2005). Fair trade thus aimed to do two things: (1) to include a broad range of issues, such as environmental and labor standards, into market frames and (2) to entangle consumers with fair trade products by establishing practices of ethical decision making in the consumption of goods (Bezencon and Blili 2006; Nicholls and Opal 2005). One might expect that the broadening of market frames to include a whole host of issues would greatly slow the speed and rate of market transactions. However, through the FLO, fair trade markets have in fact been able to speed up and expand in scale and quantity (Bezencon and Blili 2006).

To cope with such growth, fair trade supply chains have expanded to include a range of distributors and traders (Bezencon and Blili 2006). As long as they meet the standards of fair trade, FLO has not discriminated between many of the *agencements* included in the fair trade market. For instance, it has not discriminated between traders, such as the NGO Oxfam and the multinational corporation Nestle. And in Switzerland, to provide another example, McDonald's has had a contract to sell fair trade coffee at the same time that it has been embroiled in labor disputes and accused of causing environmental degradation (Bezencon and Blili 2006, 188–89). The fair trade market has also expanded to incorporate producers other than small-scale farmers, including plantation producers, and this can marginalize smaller producers (Renard and Perez-Grovas 2007). Although fair trade initially only included plantation production for goods not produced by small-scale farmers, as supermarket demand and competition against fair trade goods has grown, plantations have been incorporated to provide some of the same products as small-scale farmers, such as bananas (Renard and Perez-Grovas 2007, 150). FLO can thus be seen to have reduced the number and range of issues taken into account in framing fair trade markets and the need for differentiation between the many *agencements* involved. Certification also limits the scope of the impartial spectator as a label takes the place of the consumer's ability to ethically discriminate between different traders, such as Oxfam and Nestle (see Bezencon and Blili 2006). The fair trade label may, indeed, reflect displays of wealth and status (as the products are generally thought to be more expensive and can be associated with a particular identity). Thus, as framed by the FLO, consumers of products might be more able to follow their personal desires for wealth and status rather than being guided by the impartial spectator and a sense of joint participation in markets with distant producers and producing ecologies.

The way that fair trade markets are framed and how consumers are entangled with fair trade goods have been key tensions in the fair trade movement, in particular between FLO and the WFTO (Bezencon and Blili 2006). In contrast to FLO's focus on market expansion via certification, WFTO seeks to develop a strong and lasting connection and awareness between all elements involved in fair trade markets so that, for example, the worst-off producers are taken into account in market activity. It is concerned with educating consumers to discriminate between different actors involved in markets, such as between different traders (Bezencon and Blili 2006). WFTO can be understood as attempting to give rise to an impartial spectator that takes into account a much wider range of relationships in market framing, including developmental and political relationships. Through education, WFTO has also sought to entangle consumers with goods by installing practices of ethical decision making in consumption. In other words, WFTO aims to slow fair trade market activity. It thus enacts what Isabella Stengers (2002) describes as a politics of slowing down. One important way in which politics can be slowed is by extending processes of ethical decision making and participation in political life (Stengers 2002, 251). The WFTO perspective confirms Smith's belief that large and highly specialized (and fast) markets that drive national growth have negative effects on social and moral judgments. Like WFTO, Smith ([1776–78] 1937) believed these matters should be addressed through public education (Raphael 1985, 52).

Adam Smith's impartial spectator gives a sense of the values governing market framing. The ATOs and cooperative producers in WFTO, for example, support and monitor each other and report deviations from fair trade standards to WFTO (see Bezencon and Blili 2006; Renard and Perez-Grovas 2007). Julia Elyachar's (2005) research on traditional market networks between craft producers in Egypt provides another example. She is interested in the different values that shape market life. She is particularly interested in relational value, which she describes as "the positive value attached to the creation, reproduction, and extension of relationships in workshop life" (143). Elyachar employs Smith's impartial spectator to understand the way in which relational value shapes market activity and maintenance. The pursuit of short-term gains or transactions that impact negatively on others in the market *agencement* are, she argues, judged in the eyes of the impartial spectator and single out that individual for bad times. Elyachar uses the notion of the evil eye to describe this relationship:

This conscience embodies the eyes of one's neighbours and community and is part of the formation of the self. He who ignores the internalized eye of the conscience, and pursues short-term individual interest without constraint, invites the attack of another eye, the evil eye. An attack of the evil eye can wipe out all the gains made by a master over a lifetime of work. The confluence of the evil eye and interest makes sense only when we better understand the nature of workshop production. (149)

The evil eye operates by excluding individuals from market frames so that they are no longer taken into account in market activity. The sociality em- bodied in the market actor in the form of the impartial spectator governs this process. Though it plays an important role in governing market perfor- mances, the impartial spectator does not "fix" market frames and the rela- tionships included within them. Rather, performative acts of framing can be responded to by those who are excluded. Elyachar's study shows that ostracized and disgraced craftsmen can respond to their exclusion and chal- lenge the evil eye's sight on them. For instance, one craftsman responded to the evil eye by becoming "publicly religious" (162). This action enabled the craftsman to attain the position of managing "the finances of the main mosque," which, in turn, transformed his business reputation: "this involve- ment with the mosque gave him cover from the evil eye, despite his rapid eco- nomic success" (162). Elyachar documents several other acts in the "medium of the scared" that can be taken in response to the evil eye (163). This indi- cates a broad geography of acts that coalesce around market framing, that is, a broad geography of marking framing. The actions of the disgraced craftsmen can be viewed as periperformative utterances (see my discussion of Sedgwick's periperformative in chapter 2), that is, utterances about, in response to, and surrounding the performative act of the evil eye, that inflect their economic status with religiosity and thereby challenge the impartial spectator's evaluation of them and, with this, the market frame. Moreover, this example suggests that a politics of the market is at work, one that relates to market *agencements* and the actions of that which is gathered around and affected by them. Adam Smith's work read through actor network theories of markets, then, not only offers a view to ethical market action but also, as Elyachar's research suggests, raises questions of market transformation.

Transforming Markets

The concept of overflowing is used by Callon (1998b) to think about what coalesces around performative acts of framing. The idea of overflowing relates directly to market externalities that arise when markets produce unaccounted-for effects, that is, when something moves beyond market frames. These effects are not taken into account in market activity because they create relationships that lie outside the ambit of the impartial spectator. The effects of overflowing are negative when they create social costs (such as contaminated water) or positive when market benefits are socialized (such as through the creation and unintended dissemination of new knowledge). Market overflows whereby entities spill over their framed boundaries produce affected people and things (Callon 1998b). Callon and Rabeharisoa (2008) use the term *affected groups* to describe the collectives of people and things that form in response to market overflows. A second kind of group gathered around market frames that Callon and Rabeharisoa (2003; 2008) identify is an orphan group. Orphan groups are produced through their outright exclusion from market frames. The needs of these orphan groups are not accounted for through existing markets, nor are they considered by the impartial spectator. As discussed in chapter 3, in France, an orphan group of patients with muscular dystrophy and their families joined together in response to the lack of recognition of people with muscular dystrophy in medical markets (Callon and Rabeharisoa 2003). The fact that people with muscular dystrophy were considered to be outside the ambit of modern medicine suggests that they were excluded from the form of sociality and felt presence embodied in the impartial spectator.

It is in ways like this that markets can be seen to give rise to a variety of new social or civil society groups. Like the master craftsmen excluded from markets through the evil eye, these groups can respond to markets that affect or exclude them. In doing so, these groups enact a politics of the market and can be viewed as agents of social transformation. The film *Erin Brockovich* (Soderbergh 2000) nicely illustrates how overflows of contaminated water can have terrible effects on local communities and gestures toward the way affected groups might be mobilized in response (Leet and Houser 2003). Another example of this is social movement groups that have formed in response to fast-food markets. McDonald's, in particular, has been attributed with causing obesity, health problems, and ecological destruction, and there have been a range of attempts to hold the corporation responsible (Klein 2001). The Slow Food movement is one response to fast-food markets that has created an alternative premised on local food and an awareness of food production and that pursues the goal of maintaining biodiversity.[3]

These various concern groups have enacted a politics of the market by forming hybrid collectives. Hybrid collectives identify market affects and exclusions from market frames and develop relationships between those concerned. As discussed in chapter 3, they put the affects of market framing and overflowing into words through processes of dialogue, which might involve testimony to experiences of market affects and witnessing of that testimony. This process of dialogue about experiences of market overflows is an opportunity to create social bonds and connect to other affected people and things. Through this process, concern groups begin to develop a new collective vision of the market in concern and, in Callon's (1998b, 258) words, "self-awareness" of their relationships within this market. The development of such an awareness of the self in relation to others can be understood as a process that calls forth an impartial spectator. This impartial spectator has a view to the concern group's position within the market frame. The film *Erin Brockovich* shows how this process might be played out. The film presents residents of the town of Kinkley affected by contaminated water gathered in meetings with Erin (Julia Roberts) to share their experiences. Through these meetings, in which experiences of market affects are discussed, residents of Kinkley develop an awareness of their common concern and decide to join together in a class action legal battle with the company responsible for the contamination. Later in the film, at a town meeting, some residents who feel that they have been more affected by contamination than others move to pull out of the group and to fight for what they perceive to be a fairer share of the settlement. However, guided by an impartial spectator who has a view of the entire community implicated in the market frame, these residents are aware that their actions would have a negative effect on the legal battle of others, and they decide to remain within the group. The film shows how people and things concerned with markets develop a sense of their interconnectivity and come to embody the broader sociality of the impartial spectator.

While the experience of negative health affects might bring people together in dialogue and put these affects into words, market overflows affecting these groups and the relationship between the overflowing entity and the health of those in concern groups must be identified. Research technologies can play an important role in this process, especially in accounting for overflows (Callon 1998b, 258). In the film *Erin Brockovich,* Erin carries out research on market overflows and affect by collecting water samples and records, documenting testimonies, and so on. Such research can assist in mapping the performative act of market framing and all of the relationships it entails, including those excluded from the frame yet greatly affected by it.

Other technologies are also employed by concern groups in countergovernmentality strategies to reframe markets. Concern groups can take action to transform market performances and the experiences they generate by revealing, documenting, and politicizing overflows and their affects. One example that demonstrates a reframing of fast-food markets is the "McLibel" case, in which the McDonald's Corporation sued environmental activists for publishing and disseminating a pamphlet about the negative effects of its market (Klein 2001). Two activists decided to fight the libel suit in court. The lengthy case that ensued can be viewed as a technology of reframing, giving truth to many of the effects published in the pamphlet, including the exploitation of children and labor, cruelty to animals, and health risks from consuming McDonald's food (Klein 2001, 433). Furthermore, the court case and public discussion surrounding it constituted a political space in which the effects of the McDonald's market were discussed and affected groups, such as children, were identified. There are many more examples of such affected groups and the related technologies of reframing. The film *Supersize Me* (Spurlock 2004) is another account of the effects of the McDonald's market, including, very graphically, the effect of consumption. This film covers a wide range of affected people and things to create a relational and political space through which affected groups can form. Whether as a direct result of these efforts or as a result of a growing health consciousness of which these efforts are a part, McDonald's now promotes healthy food, offering, for example, fruit and salads. This suggests that a reframing, albeit limited, of the McDonald's market has taken place, with the result being the provision of healthier meal options.

Concern groups can also create alternative market frames. For example, the overflows and effects of fast-food markets can be seen to have produced groups that have purposely excluded themselves from these markets and created alternatives. In this case, representations of the negative affects of fast-food markets appear to have operated in a way that disentangles consumers from fast-food products. Originating in Italy, the Slow Food movement is one example of an alternative food market. The Slow Food movement is an international member-supported organization developed to "counteract fast food and fast life, the disappearance of local food traditions and people's dwindling interest in the food they eat, where it comes from, how it tastes and how our food choices affect the rest of the world."[4] Centered on the concept of "ecogastronomy," the Slow Food movement takes into account all of the relationships that are involved in the production of food—"between plate and planet." The Slow Food movement seeks to reframe food markets to include the culture and history connected with food production, biodiversity, animals, and labor. This involves a politics of slowing down, of taking into account a diverse range of relationships in food markets. Research has played an important role in facilitating this framing, particularly research undertaken at the University of Gastronomic Sciences, which was set up in 2004 to create and distribute expert knowledge of all aspects of slow-food markets (Pietrykowski 2004).

The Slow Food movement also seeks to activate "co-producers—an eater who is informed about where and how their food is produced and actively supports local producers, therefore becoming part of the production process."[5] Coproducers embody the impartial spectator of slow-food markets, symbolized by the sensation of taste. As Pietrykowski (2004, 312) notes, taste is connected not only with the palate but also with "habits, norms, rituals, and taboos." Taste can guide how food markets are framed and which relationships associated with food are taken into account in market transactions. The impartial spectator can be seen to govern the slow-food market frames in other ways, too, for instance, producers are committed to local produce and risk a loss of reputation and community if they deviate from using or threaten the production of local foods (316). This movement also seeks to entangle consumers with locally produced food through "the pleasure of the table," a symbol of community and place (314). Like fair trade, slow-food markets seek to entangle consumers with local produce by instilling practices of ethical decision making into food purchases (316).

Viewing markets as performatively constituted by *agencements* gives a sense of a broader geography of markets that includes performative acts of framing that enable market transactions. It also gives a sense of the overflows and exclusions that might lead to a process of reframing. The sociality of the *agencement* embodied in actors, that is, the impartial spectator, governs which relationships are taken into account in acts of framing. One form of contemporary collective action is the politics of the market enacted by concern groups. This is a politics that calls forth an impartial spectator to reframe which relationships are taken into account in market activity. This approach to the politics and ethics of markets provides a strong case for attention to the *geography* of collective action.

Performing a Recycling Market

The creation of alternative markets demonstrates that market framing is a form of collective action that can achieve social justice and dignity. This is exemplified by the performance of recycling markets. Drawing on research that explores the creation of recycling markets in the majority world, in the following case study, I portray the geography of markets as a means of collective action that can potentially transform the lives of trash-pickers. I highlight the way that, in the cities studied, trash-pickers have formed collectives to create and reframe recycling markets to improve their livelihoods and status in society.

Just as I witnessed very different reactions to markets at the 2005 WSF, I also saw several different forms of rubbish collection. Beyond the forum, in the streets of Porto Alegre, I witnessed trash-pickers sorting through rubbish left on the streets, footpaths, and walkways. The forum itself involved a highly developed rubbish collection system that required participants to separate recyclable materials and organic waste. I was told by another participant that rubbish collection at the forum was organized by a cooperative of trash-pickers. Brazil has a number of trash-picker cooperatives linked through the nonprofit association Brazilian Business Commitment for Recycling (CEMPRE).[6] This association aims to raise the profile and awareness of recycling and improve the livelihoods of trash-pickers through the formation of cooperatives. In addition, Porto Alegre's "curbside recycling program" includes trash-pickers (Medina 2000, 61).

In the context of uneven development, urbanization, and housing and land scarcity, trash-picking is common in majority world cities. One estimate in 2000 suggested that scavengers made up 2 percent of the population in the cities of Asia and Latin America (Medina 2000, 52). Seldom has scavenging been treated as a viable economic practice, and there is enormous stigma associated with scavenging (Gonzales 2007; Medina 2000). In large majority world cities, governments struggle to collect discarded waste: "despite spending 30–50% of their operational budgets on waste management, Third World cities collect only between 50 and 80% of the refuse generated" (Medina 2000, 52). Waste is a serious threat to quality of life, and picking through waste poses even more health risks (Appadurai 2002; Medina 2000). Thus it is not at all surprising that the response to trash-picking has so often been negative. Martin Medina's (2000) research in Latin America and Asia, for instance, documents "social cleansing" to remove scavengers from society.

He further highlights the exploitation of scavengers by middlemen, especially in markets where there is only one buyer of recyclable goods; the operation of illegal, "underground" markets through which scavengers are further exploited; the illegalization of scavenging; and authorities turning a blind eye, thus leaving scavenging invisible. These responses suggest that scavenging is often viewed as limited to the individual who is sustained by what the individual collects or who is part of an unseen economy through which scavengers are exploited.

The preceding discussion provides a framework through which to view the potential of waste and scavenging practices to contribute to struggles for social justice and improved livelihoods. Waste can be viewed as a market overflow, as an unaccounted-for entity flowing from market frames onto the streets, into dumps and other sites. Waste has multiple effects beyond market frames; perhaps most obvious are the negative effects on the environment (Gonzales 2007; Medina 2000). Alongside such negative effects, waste can also be viewed as having a positive effect on the economically marginalized in that it provides trash-pickers with material goods that they can easily obtain and entangle with (thus Gonzales 2007 describes waste as an "asset"). Once entangled, trash-pickers transform the value of waste by turning it into a tradable item (Gonzales 2007). They may also add value to waste by sorting and cleaning it (Gonzales 2007). Trash-pickers can then trade waste with dealers. This transaction, the disentanglement of trash-pickers with waste and its entanglement with dealers, might be facilitated by a range of mediators. These mediators include research that identifies and calculates the value of waste and NGOs that link pickers with dealers (Gonzales 2007; Medina 1998). Often, however, the recycling market in these contexts is framed in a way that excludes the needs of trash-pickers, including needs for housing, medical services, welfare, and safety. It also excludes their positive relationship to the environment, industry, and government (Gonzales 2007). In other words, the market is framed in a way that devalues and degrades trash-pickers.

Trash-pickers have attempted to counter this devaluation by forming associations or collectives that create waste as a site of collective action. One type of association is patron–client relationships. Another is cooperatives. Groups gathered around waste involve a whole range of people and things, including trash-pickers, NGOs, animals, means of collecting and distributing waste, tools that add value to waste, and so on. Some of these groups might have a particular self-awareness, an impartial spectator that governs how recycling markets are framed and the way in which trash-pickers and their concerns are included or excluded in this framing. For example, research conducted in Delhi, India, describes the social differentiation of the trash-picking industry and the way in which this shapes recycling markets (Hayami, Dikshit, and Mishra 2006). In Delhi, there are two groups of trash-pickers: "pickers," who sort freely available waste from public sites, and "collectors," who purchase waste from households and other waste producers, such as industry. Both groups are made up of migrants whose ethnic networks shape their entry into different markets and afford different standards of living, especially in relation to housing conditions, income, and working conditions. The framing of collectors—who are mostly from the Uttar Pradesh region—in markets is guided by moral values that take into account collectors' welfare, the transportation of waste, the social mobility of collectors, and various other issues (53). Dealers are compelled by the impartial spectator to take collectors on as apprentices and to provide them with a cart, the initial capital to buy waste, access to emergency assistance, and a guaranteed purchaser of waste, albeit at a low rate. Through savings schemes, capital from social networks, and personal savings, collectors are also able to move up the recycling hierarchy to become buyers themselves (54). In turn, the impartial spectator compels collectors to remain loyal to one dealer. Breaking with the impartial spectator may lead to the exclusion of the collector from the market frame; that is, it may precipitate the end of the collector's relationship with the dealer and all of the benefits that this relationship entails, including the loss of reputation and social ostracism, leading to exclusion from the market more generally (53).

Pickers from the "remote Eastern regions" tend to have little access to collectors' markets and are thus largely restricted to picking waste and selling it to scrap dealers (Hayami, Dikshit, and Mishra 2006, 52). Pickers' markets are framed in a way that limits them to smaller operations, public collection sites, and selling materials to dealers for cash without any of their other needs taken into account. In contrast to collectors, who on average earn more than the minimum wage, pickers face chronic poverty (49). The pickers in Delhi, however, have the potential to respond to the acts of market framing through which they are excluded. By gathering around the market framing, one response by pickers might be to begin a hybrid collective to reframe the market and, possibly, develop a cooperative. And the experience of trash-picking and its affects might be one way in which to develop an alternative vision of market frames.

In Latin America and Asia, trash-pickers have formed cooperatives in response to their common experiences of exploitation, such as by middlemen who restrict which goods can be traded, or the experience of displacement after an open dump is closed (Medina 2000, 60, 62). NGOs have played an important role in the formation of cooperatives, providing financial assistance, linking scavengers to others involved in the market, and providing market information (Gonzales 2007; Hayami et al. 2006; Medina 2000). Cooperatives work to reframe markets to exclude middlemen and include a range of other relationships. Gonzales (2007, 434–35[7]) describes the way in which trash-picker and business associations in the Philippines have changed the way that waste is collected and dumped to include trash-pickers in the collection of waste from its source. Here cooperatives also accumulate, sort, and sell materials directly to industry, avoiding other agents, such as scrap buyers and wholesalers (Medina 2000). Recycling goods enables trash-pickers to increase their income and standard of living in comparison to that of other agencies who gather from dumpsites (Gonzales 2007; Medina 2000). This also has the added benefit of reducing the cost of recycling for local authorities and industry (Gonzales 2007; Medina 2000). Cooperatives have also reframed markets to include social and cultural development, for instance, scholarships are provided for education, and some cooperatives provide insurance (Medina 2000).

Trash-picker collectives might also engage with research on recycling as a means of countergovernmentality. Research has shown that recycling not only adds financial value to waste material but also creates environmental and social value (Gonzales 2007; Hayami et al. 2006; Medina 2000). For instance, Gonzales (2007) discusses the environmental benefits to soil and land as well as the preservation of raw materials. Similarly, Medina (1998, 120) quantifies one component of this value in noting that "recycling aluminium cans uses 95% less energy than producing them from virgin [raw] materials." He also suggests that in reducing the cost of aluminum, "scavengers play an important role in improving the competitiveness of the aluminium industry" (121). Recycling both reduces the negative externalities associated with extracting raw materials and creates positive externalities, such as reduced pollution (Hayami et al. 2006). The social value aggregated by Hayami et al. (2006, 62) includes the income of waste collectors and pickers; a surplus income for waste producers, such as households and industry, that sell their waste to collectors; and savings for governments. The research associated with trash-picker cooperatives offers a new vision of trash-pickers—in Medina's words, giving them "dignity." As Medina (2000, 67) puts it, "scavenger co-operatives can be a means of achieving a better standard of living for its [*sic*] members, dignify their occupations, and strengthen their bargaining power with industry and authorities." Reframing recycling markets has thus established a political space for scavengers to come together, form a common self-awareness, and transform their stigmatized and individualized existence.

Implications for Researchers

This chapter has developed a relational and performative conceptualization of markets. It has drawn attention to the geography of relationships clustered around performative acts of framing that constitute markets. Attention to this geography is important because it relates to the relationships that are taken into account and those that are excluded from market frames and market activity. Whereas the market advanced under neoliberal policies attempts to limit occupation of the market frame to homo economicus, the diverse markets discussed in this chapter make explicit the role of an impartial spectator in the market who takes into account a range of different relationships, such as those with the environment. One way of transforming and creating alternative markets is through a politics of collective action that calls forth common awareness of an impartial spectator who has in its sights a broad range of people and things gathered around market frames. As a geography of the market embodied within actors, the impartial spectator can facilitate market reframing to include multiple factors and relationships that are excluded in neoliberal frames.

Rather than resisting the "market," the project of market transformation calls for intellectual participation that aims to equip those involved in market networks to respond to contemporary social challenges. Research can play an important role in market processes, especially hybrid "research" collectives, by representing overflows, translating market affects into collective discourse, and calculating how overflowing entities can be transformed and traded. Susan Smith (2005), for example, looks beyond the role of economists and neoclassical economic calculation to "lay" actors and their thinking in housing market performances. She develops the concept of a diverse market network shaped by "rich sociality," in which emotions and care influence market transactions. Her research is no less politically engaged than that which examines the ways in which markets are depoliticized and constituted as amoral networks occupied by the rational economic actor. As Smith so eloquently puts it,

> perhaps the politics and ethics of markets can be challenged not by arguing against markets, but by making a bid for them; by embracing a thousand tiny markets whose ethics are not given but made; whose political geography might be different. From this perspective, the diversity of actually existing markets, and the multitude of normative ideas and practices that are, or could be, built into them, is not just a new economic geography, or a social curiosity: it is a far reaching political resource. (17)

This chapter joins the project of conceptualizing these "alternative" markets to contribute to their performation.

If research is viewed as an element in the performance of markets, then researchers might also embody an impartial spectator, an awareness of their relationships with others involved in market performances. The impartial spectator compels researchers to take into consideration all of those involved in market performance and imparts a sense of responsibility for the market *agencements* they study. This chapter suggests that the impartial spectator activates "sensitivity" to one's multiple relationships in action (Lingis 2002, 36). A researcher is responsible not only for the performative effects of that person's research, that is, what the research works to bring into being, but also for the others involved in and enabling that action. Taking a relational approach to performative action is one technique with which to make the relationships in and clustered around markets visible. The performative approach to markets enables an exploration of that which enables and is affected by markets. This is a vital starting point to facilitate a response to contemporary market frames.

5

Dignified Humanity, Dignified World

No one who has passed the last couple of decades with their eyes open can deny that we have been faced with the need to work out in new ways the relationship between what had been familiar as the working class and now its many others—the prisoners, overwhelmingly black, the immigrants, queers, or, for that matter, the gays in the military, our institutional others who are adjuncts, the aged, the sick, the angry janitors, the triumphant UPS part-timers, the migrant cyberworkers who are the high-tech braceros, all our youth who are organizing.

—AMITAVA KUMAR, *Class and Its Others*

In a world where it seems no-one agrees on anything, a world where politics divides, religion divides, and race and even cultural borders seem to divide, dignity is something that everyone can agree on.

—Global Dignity cofounders

Rethinking the Collective Subject of Economic Struggle

As Amitava Kumar (2000) highlights in his foreword to the book *Class and Its Others,* and as I discussed in chapter 2 of this book, the working class can no longer be taken for granted as the privileged collective subject of economic struggle. This was brought home to me at the 2005 World Dignity Forum (WDF), which presented a strong challenge to this positioning. The WDF is a special forum held within the World Social Forum (WSF) for all those concerned about the effects of neoliberalism and who are engaged in contemporary struggles for social justice across many arenas of life. It was established in 2004 to support the Dalits' struggle for dignity in India. In

2005, at the WSF I attended and discussed at length in previous chapters, the WDF assembled an array of diverse groups and provided a platform for testimonies by descendants of slave communities, indigenous peoples, Dalit representatives, and many others. As with the larger WSF, the WDF responds to Kumar's call to rethink the relationship between the working class and other collectives. The WDF seeks to assemble a wide range of cultural groups in economic struggle and experimentation by shifting the motivation for left politics from class opposition to exploitation to a more general concern that economic life be evaluated in terms of human dignity:

> The *right* to work, to a place to live, to sustenance, health and education, affirmative action in the public and private sectors, the *right* to land and to remain on it (the "right to stay"), the defence of the interests of non-organized laborers, agrarian reform and the *right* of peoples to guarantee and protect their environment from attempts to destroy and privatize their natural resources, are central issues for guaranteeing *dignity* and social justice, not only for Dalits and Adivasis, but also for women of African descent, and other minorities and the oppressed and repressed populations of the world. (World Dignity Forum 2005, emphasis added)

This quotation comes from a pamphlet I picked up at the 2005 WDF. It suggests that the WDF has folded an economic politics centered on workers' rights into a broader politics of human rights and the struggle for human dignity. At the 2005 WDF, it seemed to me that "dignity is something that everyone can agree on,"[1] as suggested by the cofounders of Global Dignity, one of the many international organizations focused on dignity. Seeking a more inclusive form of collective, those struggling for human dignity are thus asking us to consider ourselves not as separate political–economic groups but as a single collective—humanity.

Of course, struggles for human dignity extend beyond the WDF and have been part of various forms of collective action for some time. Karl Marx ([1844] 1964), for instance, used the term *dignity* in his *Manuscripts of 1844* to describe the kind of human being that is realized in socially just economies. And today, as the affects of climate change begin to be felt around the world, collective struggles for dignity also extend beyond struggles of the tradition left, their ability to combine concerns about economic injustice with concerns about environmental injustice bringing together a wide range of people across the globe. What is particularly interesting about these contemporary struggles for human dignity is that they must face the proposition that it is the very collective they are struggling to improve the conditions of—humanity—that has caused climate change and now threatens not only human dignity but more fundamentally the existence of our species and that of other beings. In this chapter, I examine this proposition by taking a closer look at humanity or the human species more specifically as a political collective in our era of climate change.

Collective struggles for dignified humanity in our era of climate change coincide with the call from scientists to consider ourselves, not as a number of different groups, but as a single, universal and transhistorical collective, as a species. This call is tied to the announcement of a new geological epoch—the Anthropocene. The Anthropocene presents the human species as a collective geological force, one that is undermining humanity's conditions of existence or "evolution itself" (Davis 2008). As Paul J. Crutzen (2002, 23) describes it, after centuries of "anthropogenic emissions of carbon dioxide, global climate may depart significantly from natural behaviour for many millennia to come." He thus suggests, "It seems appropriate to assign the term 'Anthropocene' to the present, in many ways human-dominated, geological epoch, supplementing the Holocene—the warm period of the past 10–12 millennia" (23) that has been vital to the evolution of the human species. Likewise, social theorists argue that understanding climate change and the challenges it presents to humanity requires that we think in terms of species (Chakrabarty 2008; 2009). Collectives striving for humanity's dignity in the Anthropocene must consider humanity as a species that is not only a political–economic collective but one that has become geological.

In both the announcement of the Anthropocene and for many collectives gathered around concerns about human dignity and economic and environmental injustices, the human species is viewed as *the* dominant force shaping our world. For example, it is up to us humans to come up with a technological or other fix to climate change, and, like the global class struggles, the majority world is pitted against the minority world in a struggle to curb CO_2 emissions.[2] Although curbing emissions is certainly a priority, I am concerned that the understanding of the human species tied to these views fits all too easily with the modernist assumption of human mastery over nature (Plumwood 2002). In her book on Australia's Murray Darling Basin, Jessica Weir (2009, 4) demonstrates the devastating consequences of such thinking, highlighting in particular the impact of Rene Descartes's belief that "science and philosophy would empower men to be the masters and possessors of nature" on water management, resulting in the Murray Darling Basin being treated as if it were a plumbing system. When it comes to climate change more generally, the proposed technofixes are not only proving impossible to agree upon but also risk magnifying the problem (Hobson 2008). Kersty Hobson (2008) highlights, for example, work showing that energy-saving innovation can lead to cheaper appliances, increases in appliance use, and, ultimately, increases in energy consumption. In this chapter, I ask whether there is another way to understand the human species as a political–economic collective, one that gets us away from this sense of human domination of the world that has brought about our environmental crisis. In pursuing this question, and reflecting my overall concerns in this book with the geography of collective action, I am particularly interested in teasing out a relational geography of the species as a political–economic collective.

There are already moves to think about the human species in different ways. Dipesh Chakrabarty (2009, 217) argues, for example, that in the Anthropocene, the history and future of the human species must be understood in terms of "life on this planet, the way different life-forms connect to one another, and the way the mass extinction of one species could spell danger for another." His work suggests that the idea of species does not need to be premised on modernist binaries between human and other forms of life but might be used to think about humanity's interdependence with others. Furthermore, Chakrabarty challenges essentialist understandings of species as a group of organisms with fixed traits (214–15; see also Ereshefsky 2010), highlighting Daniel Lord Smail's work on deep history and neurology, which states, "Natural selection does not homogenize the individuals of a species. . . . Given this state of affairs, the search for a normal . . . nature and body type [of any particular species] is futile." This work suggests that species can be thought of as a transforming and transformative category.

Though the acknowledgment of our species's interdependence with other species is certainly not news to ecologists, what is particularly interesting about Chakrabarty's (2009, 222) work is his call for us to go further, to also consider our species as a political collective:

> Yet climate change poses for us a question of a human collectivity, an us, pointing to a figure of the universal that escapes our capacity to experience the

world. It is more like a universal that arises from a shared sense of catastrophe. It calls for a global approach to politics without the myth of a global identity, for unlike a Hegelian universal, it cannot subsume particularities. We may provisionally call it a "negative universal history."

Chakrabarty's work suggests that we might think of the human species collective as a "negative universal," one that cannot be fully grasped, pinned down, or experienced (222). Species, then, might refer to a kind of political collectivity without essence, a "virtuality" (Dyer-Witheford 2004a, 6).

Although we may not be able to directly experience our existence as a species, several scholars have suggested that we can think about the relationship between our species and the experience of particular modes of living, of which the human might be thought of as one "historical instantiation" (see Dyer-Witheford 2004a, 7). Chakrabarty (2009) notes, for example, that the Anthropocene is not the end of an inevitable path of our species. While he acknowledges the contingent alignments that have brought about the Anthropocene, Chakrabarty writes, "The way to it [the Anthropocene] was no doubt through industrialisation" (217). In doing so, he associates a particular mode of living with the coming of the Anthropocene. In light of this work, it seems that the idea of species can get us thinking about the relationship between our collective existence as a species and various historically and contextually specific modes of living or being human, such as a dignified humanity. In other words, the relational geography of species can be seen to perform particular modes of humanity. Changing our mode of being human is vital to our continued existence as a species: as Val Plumwood (2007, 1) writes, "if our species does not survive the ecological crisis, it will probably be due to our failure . . . to work out new ways to live with the earth, to rework ourselves. . . . We will go on in a *different mode of humanity*, or not at all." In this chapter, I ask whether a dignified humanity offers a new way to live with the earth in the Anthropocene.

Before the nexus between our existence as a species and various modes of living can be explored, including that of human dignity, and most important new modes of humanity experimented with, there is a need to further open up the idea of the species as a political–economic collective. In particular, I am interested in how other species are implicated in the species transformations affecting our humanity. To me, this question seems central to living ethically with others in the Anthropocene. I thus devote the first half of this chapter to further exploration of the concept of species as a political–economic collective and focus in particular on the relational geography of the species collective. To do so, following Chakbrabarty's lead, I turn to Marx's ([1844] 1964) theorization of our species-being, a concept that can be described as the capacity of the human species to transform its conditions of existence and thus humanity itself. As Marx puts it in the *Manuscripts of 1844,* species-being is "life-engendering life" (113). Marx's writing is, however, not surprisingly shaped by modernist binaries that separate and privilege human life from animal life. This is likely to prove problematic for conceptualizing our species interdependence and the possibility of ethical relations between humans and other species. Given this concern, I draw on Bertall Ollman's (1971) elaboration of Marx's theory to read Marx against Marx and unsettle the modernist binaries shaping Marx's writing.

Marx's theory of species-being has provided a starting point to flesh out the relationship between species and the creation of different modes of humanity. I am inspired by contemporary scholars who are using Marx's theory of species-being to understand what is at stake in political activism that is struggling to transform our humanity (especially Dyer-Witheford 2004a; 2004b; Grant 2005), and in the second part of this chapter, I take up the idea of species-being to theorize social movements creating different ways of living with others in the Anthropocene. Although attention has been given to an alienated mode of being human associated with capitalism (Dyer-Witheford 2004a; 2004b; Chakrabarty 2009), I am interested in social movements that are enacting modes of humanity sensitive and responsive to our interdependence with others. Picking up on the more general theme of embodied geographies of performative collective action explored in this book and resonating the embodied processes of learning discussed in chapter 3, I pay particular attention to how our interdependent relationships with human and nonhuman others come to be embodied and shape action. Through the examples discussed, I hope to open up further exploration of the relationship between species-being and dignified modes of humanity that might be able to respond to the environmental crisis.

Rereading Marx's Theory of Species-Being

Marx ([1844] 1964) develops his thinking on species-being in the *Manuscripts of 1844.* The relationship of this "early work" with Marx's later writings has been much debated within Marxism—notably by Althusser (1990), who suggested a break between Marx's early humanist understanding of history and the later Marx's emphasis on structural dynamics as the force of change (Dyer-Witheford 2004a, 4). In this chapter, I take inspiration from and draw directly on the reevaluation of Marx's early work by post-structuralists, who have returned to Marx's early writings to develop an anti-essentialist reading of Marx's humanism that can be applied to contemporary political activism (see especially Dyer-Witheford 2004a; Grant 2005).

Marx's theory of species-being stems from his philosophical engagement with Hegel and other post-Hegelian contemporaries (see Rockmore 2002) and from his political concerns about the estrangement of workers in nineteenth-century capitalist industry. He was interested in how the large-scale mechanized production of commodities, the division of labor, wage work, and the ownership of the means of production by nonworkers in the modern factory were affecting the human condition. Marx formulates his thinking into the now-famous theory of alienation in which he discusses species-being. Marx thus theorizes species-being in light of an alienated mode of humanity tied to the rise of capitalism. In other words, his theory of species-being is historicized through the negative example of alienation under capitalism. In what follows, I discuss alienation briefly; then, with the assistance of Bertall Ollman (1971), Judith Grant (2005), and Kelly Oliver (2009), I move to a more transhistorical exploration of the species-being concept.

There are a number of interrelated dimensions of Marx's ([1844] 1964) theory of alienation, including the alienation of workers from the objects they produce, the alienation of workers from the activity of production, and the alienation of workers from their species-being. Marx suggests that workers are alienated when they are estranged from the objects they produce. He writes that labor gives life to objects and that, as labor is separated from these objects, under capitalist commodity production, part of the workers' lives is estranged from them. In this process, the object gains a life of its own and a kind of "power" over the worker (108). Marx notes that when this happens, the "sensuous external world" or "nature" becomes an "alien" object on which the worker depends for work and a means of subsistence (108–9). One could say that Marx is troubled by alienating work because it separates the worker from nature, which then stands opposed to workers as an alien force. Workers who are alienated from the object produced through their work are also likely to be alienated from the activity of work itself. In this aspect of alienation, work becomes a means to another ends, an activity without spontaneity or creativity that comes to "belong" to someone other than the worker (110–11). Marx describes this as "self-estrangement" (112). Finally, Marx suggests that workers are alienated from their species-being (112). Here Marx distinguishes between estrangement from nature, humans' physical relationship with nature that enables their existence, and estrangement from species "life-activity." He argues that the human species is distinctive when humans are consciously and freely engaged in life-activity. When workers are unable to participate in their species life, "life-activity" or "productive life" becomes a means to "physical existence" (113). Alienation "turns the *life of the species* into a means of individual life" (112). Marx suggests that workers are thus also separated from each other (114).

To show what is happening to humanity under capitalism, and in particular to explain the separation of workers from their species-being, Marx distinguishes between natural-being, or physical existence, and species-being, or life-activity. To do so, he makes a conceptual separation between human life and animal life. Specifically, he employs the figure of the animal to distinguish between activities that are solely "a means to life" and those that are the "species activity" of humans:

> The animal is immediately identical with its life-activity. It does not distinguish itself from it. It is *its life-activity*. Man makes his life-activity itself the object of his will and his consciousness. He has conscious life-activity. It is not a determination with which he directly merges. Conscious life-activity distinguishes man immediately from animal life-activity. It is just because of this that he is a species being. Or rather, it is only because he is a species being that he is a conscious being, i.e., that his own life is an object for him. Only because of that is his activity free activity. Estranged labour reverses this relationship, so that it is just because man is a conscious being that he makes his life-activity, his *essential* being, a mere means to his *existence*. (113)

Marx recognizes that animals and humans share activities, such as procreation (111); however, when these activities are a "sole and ultimate ends," he suggests that "they are animal." Despite his concern about the separation of humans from nature or the object they produce, Marx's discussion of alienation thus assumes a separation between human and other species. This separation does not imply that there is only a difference between the life of human and other species but is historically coded as a ranking—Marx's assertion that species-being is humans' "advantage over animals" gives a sense of human superiority to, and therefore potentially the capacity for mastery over, animals (114). This is likely to prove something of a barrier when the theory of species-being is taken up in an investigation into the modes of humanity that might respond to other species in the Anthropocene.

A closer look at the concepts of natural and species-being outside of the formulation of alienation offers a vision of human connectedness to others and a way to read against the human–animal binary shaping Marx's writing. At least, this is what I would like to suggest here. To do so, in addition to Marx's writing, I draw on Bertell Ollman's (1971) elaboration of the connectedness between humans and other species in natural-being and species-being in his book *Alienation*. Centered on practices that sustain life, Ollman suggests that natural-being involves powers or capacities and needs or desires that are directed toward and realized in the external world:

> Take eating as a natural power, man's impulses which drive him to eat are clear enough: he is hungry. The abilities which enable him to eat include all that he does when eating. The tendencies which direct him toward satisfactory objects are his taste and his general knowledge as to what is edible and what is not. (80; see also 76–79)

Because powers are directed toward and realized through the external world, powers and the external world are fundamentally intertwined. Citing Marx, Ollman continues,

> If man's powers can only manifest themselves in and through objects, he needs these objects to express his powers. Hunger is an example of such a need for objects. Marx says that hunger "needs a nature outside itself, an object outside itself . . . to be stilled. Hunger is an acknowledged need of my body for an object existing outside it indispensable to its integration and the expression of its essential being." (80)

Ollman places corporeal intertwining with the world at the heart of practices that sustain life. The capacity to eat, in this example, rests on the interaction of the body with external elements (81). More generally, the senses come to be known "through what they come into contact with and where they reside. Thus, Marx can say that man 'is established by objects,' and that objects 're-side in the very nature of his being'" (81). What is distinctive about natural-being in Ollman's reading is that there is no unique human; man is "*not yet* a man," he writes, "man is like an animal in being 'identical with his activity'" (82). More recently, Nick Dyer-Witheford (2004b, 476) has described natural-being as an "embodied, ecologically-embedded existence."

If natural-being can be understood as a form of embodied interdependence with others, what about species-being? Marx ([1844] 1964, 88) suggests that species-being is realized through social relationships with others, that is, when others are regarded as social objects and beings. In contrast to a relationship of possession or ownership, fully social relations are "sensuous," affecting and transforming human "subjective capacity." Marx writes,

> Each of his *human* relations to the world—seeing, hearing, smelling, tasting, feeling, thinking, observing, experimenting, wanting, acting, loving—in short, all the organs of his individual being, like those organs which are directly social in their form, are in their *objective* orientation or in their *orientation to the object,* the appropriation of that object. The appropriation of *human* reality, its orientation to the object is the *manifestation of the human reality,* it is human *activity* and human *suffering,* for suffering, humanly considered, is a self-indulgence of man. (138–39)

For Marx, species-being reflects social activities through which humans develop their senses and a sense of self in relation to others. Species-being transforms the possibilities of being/the world. In species activity, human individual and social being come together (140).

Ollman's reading of Marx's early writing elaborates on this interconnected character of species-being. His work helps to draw out the tension in Marx's writing between the human–animal binary and the relational character of species-being. Ollman (85) suggests that species powers extend natural powers and build on the already ecologically embedded character of human life (natural-being). Species powers include all of the senses through which human beings gain an awareness of themselves in relation to others and are affected by this awareness. Our sensuous engagement

> makes us aware of certain aspects of entities that would have remained unknown to us if we had never seen, heard, etc. something in connection with them. They are all "vehicles" carrying a mutual effect between the individual and the object (joined together in an internal relation), altering both to a greater or lesser degree. (89)

Ollman suggests that the extension of species powers through the senses is captured in Marx's understanding of appropriation. As Ollman explains it:

> "Appropriation" means to utilize constructively, to build by incorporating . . . . For Marx, the individual appropriates the nature he perceives and has become orientated to by making it some way a part of himself with whatever effect this has on his senses and future orientation. To "capture" a sunset, it is not necessary to paint, write or sing about it. It becomes ours in the experience of it. The forms and colors we see, the sense of awakening to beauty that we feel and the growth in sensitivity which accompanies such an event are all indications of our new appropriation. To paint the sunset, or to write or sing about it, if joined by genuine emotions, would achieve an even higher degree of appropriation, would make this event more a part of us. (91)

Appropriation here can be read as a process in which bodies interact with and are affected by sensuous engagement with the world. Appropriation affects the experiences humans can have and their stance toward the world. Moreover, appropriation transforms species powers; in the preceding case, it increases one's ability to differentiate color and appreciate a sunset. Ollman's elaboration of appropriation thus shows that species-being can be read as a relational concept (and corresponds to Latour's theory of learning to be affected discussed in chapter 3). This is a different sense of appropriation from appropriation as the objectification of someone or something, such as in taking or reducing another to the self. Instead, as I am reading it, appropriation in species-being refers to the interdependence of the human species with "earth others" (Plumwood 2002) as they become part of, transform (and are transformed by), and thereby constitute humanity.

Judith Grant (2005) offers a similar reading of Marx's species-being concept. Responding to the suggestion that Marx's writing could be taken as "a claim for the domination of nature by man," Grant draws our attention to Marx's writing that suggests nature and the human body are cotransformed through species-being (62). She thus states,

> Sure, self-directing, democratic-communist humans would be free to decide to treat "nature" (trees, animals, etc.) more respectfully than they are treated in capitalist economies. Of course, they might still decide not to. It is likely that they would, I think, since Marx makes the radical claim that *these aspects of*

nature are extensions of the human body. It might follow then that to mistreat nature is to mistreat self. (63, emphasis added)

Grant provides an antiessentialist reading of Marx's writing on the human body and nature, where nature becomes part of the human body through free production and both are "transformed and transforming" through this species-being activity (62, 73). Furthermore, as nature is part of the body (and thus to hurt nature is to hurt oneself), the vulnerability of nature also becomes part of the human body's vulnerability, and nature is, in turn, changed by that humanity. The effects of appropriation, of nature's vulnerability becoming part of humanity's, including whether this facilitates an ethical relationship to nature, must be explored in particular contexts. Under capitalist relationships, for example, the experience of our co-vulnerability with others is disavowed through alienation, limiting the development of ethical relationships with others.

Ollman's and Grant's elaborations of species-being bring out an important tension in Marx's and others' writing on species-being. On one hand, Marx uses animals to hierarchically define and distinguish humans from other species. On the other hand, Marx's concept of appropriation suggests that the human species is fundamentally interdependent with other species in a way that affects our very humanity and self-awareness. Kelly Oliver's (2009) recent book *Animal Lessons* suggests that this can be treated as a productive tension. Oliver criticizes philosophers writing on human life for disavowing their dependence on animals (what she calls "animal pedagogy" [5]) in their thinking about the human or humanity. The problem is that the denial of animal pedagogy "repeats the very power structure of subject and object, of us versus them, of human versus animals" (5). In *Animal Lessons,* Oliver shows how, in key philosophical work from Jean-Jacques Rousseau to Julia Kristeva, animal figures "bite back," betraying the philosopher's attempts to put them in their place in relation to the human by undermining the very conceptualization of humanity each philosopher is trying to make. This action of biting back suggests, I think, that animals cannot simply been seen as inert objects used by humans but have agency, they bite back. Oliver argues that humans are not in fact masters of animals but instead conceptually dependent on them (as well as physical and other forms of dependence). This acknowledgment that our conception of the human relies on animals, who are our teachers rather than our subordinates, places relationships with others at the center of questions concerning human life and directs our attention in particular to the question of "how to share our resources and life together on this collective planet" (22). Starting from relationships shifts debates over our sameness and difference with others to what Oliver calls "sustainable ethics, one based on responsibility to our founding possibility, the earth, animals, and other people, without which we could not live" (48).

Oliver's work helps me to turn the tension in Marx's writing on species-being into a source for creative thinking. She draws our attention to the dependence of Marx's conceptualization of species-being on animals. His thinking on the difference between natural-being and species-being is dependent on what he can say about animal life. In addition, Ollman's elaboration of Marx's writing through the idea of appropriation shows that species-being is realized through, and in fact depends on, human interactions with others, interactions through which both are affected and the potentialities of human experience (and thus modes of being human) transformed. Put simply, it is through our relationships with others that we become human and our humanity is transformed. In the process of appropriation, others become part of humanity and, biting back, their vulnerability becomes inseparable from that of humanity's. The acknowledgment of this interdependence with others unsettles the sense of human superiority and potential mastery over animals conveyed in Marx's early writing and opens up ground for a response. Furthermore, it challenges the distinction between animal and human life as both can be seen as intertwined. This acknowledgment also releases the idea of human freedom found in Marx's early writing from its association with human independence from others. The concept of appropriation implies that human freedom is actually intertwined with others. With this in mind, I now explore whether the idea of species-being might be used to mobilize modes of humanity that are responding to the diverse range of participants in our economies.

Dignified Humanity in the Anthropocene

In this section, I respond to Val Plumwood's (2007, 1) statement that "we will go on in a different mode of humanity, or not at all," by seeking out modes of humanity premised on a shared sense of vulnerability and coexistence or belonging with others. And I return to the theme of dignity to identify and describe these modes of humanity. As I mentioned earlier, Marx used the term *dignity* in his early writings on alienation to characterize the kind of human being that might be realized in just economies. Although collective struggles for dignity might appear to focus on the human, dignity can be understood to reflect both a mode of being human and the dignified world in which this is possible (Malpas and Lickiss 2007, 4). As Jeff Malpas and Norelle Lickiss (2007, 4) explain,

> The sense of human dignity that is at issue here involves, one might say, a feeling of and for the human—although this should not be taken to mean that it is in some way exclusionary of that which is other than the human, that it involves a lack of feeling for, one might put it, the wider world. If the humanities and the arts can be seen to open up a proper sense of dignity through opening up a space for human being in which the human appears as human, then what must also appear there is the world within which such humanity is itself possible. A proper sense of the dignity of the world.

To elaborate this interconnected sense of the dignity of humanity and the world, I return to the social movement activism with which this chapter began, or what Dyer-Witheford (2004a, 11) calls "species-being movements," a term he uses to characterize the antiglobalization struggle, a movement that brings together working-class politics, feminism, environmentalism, and a multiplicity of other movements in the creation of other worlds (see chapter 3). His work suggests that each of these movements might be viewed through the lens of species-being. Here I take a closer look at a few of these movements, starting with one that chiefly concerned Marx.

Marx was keenly interested in bringing into being a dignified mode of humanity. He was particularly interested in the species-being movement of the working class (see also Dyer-Witheford 2004a, 8). As I have already mentioned, Marx was concerned about the dehumanizing nature of work in early industrialization. Take, as an example, the image of a nineteenth-century miner who is dirty, works close to the rock he is chipping at with a pick, and earns very little income. This was, and still is in many places, dangerous and dehumanizing or alienating work. In response to such dehumanizing work of early industrialization, the nineteenth-century British trade union movement initially focused on workers gaining participation in a different kind of appropriation from that which I have used to rethink species-being. Specifically, in addition to struggling for the right to participate in political democracy through voting, this early Marx- and Robert Owen–inspired labor movement aimed to reconfigure surplus production, appropriation, and distribution so that workers, not only owners, had rights to decision making over the surplus produced through their labor (see Gibson-Graham 2003; 2006b). What Marx means by surplus here rests on his distinction between necessary and surplus labor. Necessary labor is "the quantity of labour time necessary to produce the consumables customarily required by the direct producer to keep working" (Resnick and Wolff 1987, 115). Consumables might include food and shelter or, more broadly, leisure time and all else considered a necessity (Gibson-Graham 2006b, 89). Surplus labor is "the *extra* time of labor the direct producer performs beyond the necessary labor" (Resnick and Wolff 1987, 115). In capitalist economies, exploitation occurs when capitalists appropriate surplus labor and compensate direct producers for their necessary labor, which today is generally in the form of a wage (Resnick and Wolff 1987; Amariglio and Madra 2009). Marx used this distinction between necessary and surplus labor in his accounting of the labor that contributes to our economies and also to highlight the exploitative relationships through which surplus labor is extracted (Roelvink and Gibson-Graham 2009, 149). The working-class struggle for workers' participation in decision making concerning surplus is realized today through the cooperative movement. In cooperatives, such as the famous Mondragón Cooperative Corporation, there is typically a structure for workers, who are also owners, to have the final say in matters of surplus. Cooperatives have created a mode of humanity—communism—characterized by dignified worker-owners. With the coming of the Anthropocene, many cooperatives are now experimenting with how they might change this mode of humanity in response to other species (see Gibson-Graham 2010).

However, as the working-class movement has historically developed, again, for example, in the United Kingdom, workers have gained formal or civil political rights but not the right to participate in matters of surplus. Instead, decision making about surplus has been privatized and hidden through the wage system in which the worker is seen to receive "fair" pay for his work. The working-class struggle for dignity shifted from installing communist class relations to focusing more clearly on working conditions, labor laws, pay, and so on. Thus, though undoubtedly improving the conditions for workers in some ways, the working-class movement in some parts of the world has perhaps also helped to instantiate a mode of humanity in which not only is participation in decision making about surplus limited but also, importantly for my project, the appropriation of others in a way that affects species-being is limited. In contrast to the image of a nineteenth-century miner, in Australia today, we typically imagine miners whose work conditions are very comfortable; specifically, we think of workers mining in huge air-conditioned trucks that enable them to gouge out vast amounts of minerals and who receive a high rate of pay. Yet this mode of humanity is precisely what has led us to the Anthropocene. In no way has it contributed to a dignified world or led to a greater sensitivity to the environment. I think the challenge for the working-class movement today is to expand the focus on dignified workers to also consider a dignified world, that is, to consider how we might participate in both senses of appropriation that I have discussed here—appropriation of surplus and of other species through our species-being activity. To explore this further, I now turn to briefly considering two other species-being movements that are creating dignified modes of humanity with others.

Grant's (2005) research suggests that feminism might be viewed as another example of a species-being movement. Specifically, her work suggests that feminism has created a mode of humanity characterized by gender equality. With Marx, Grant argues that gender equality increases the possibilities of species-being or, to use her words, of human creativity and freedom. Thus Marx, Grant notes, suggested gender relations as a marker of the development of the human species (65). Grant is interested in rescuing Marx's early writing for feminism. She argues that, because they have focused on what Marx says about women rather than gender relations, feminists have too easily dismissed his early work. Grant highlights Marx's criticism of "Utopian socialists" and in particular their aim to extend property to all as communal ownership rather than to transcend the property relationship itself (65). She suggests that the value of Marx's writing to thinking about gender relations lies in his criticism of bourgeois and communal marriage. Marx saw bourgeois marriage as a property relation that restricts women's freedom and men's creativity to "physical desires," thus limiting species-being (68). Marx criticized the utopian socialist understanding of communal ownership for maintaining this property relation: "The complaint is that women are treated as property in bourgeois marriage and would also have that status in communal marriage. . . . All are versions of the same animalistic/nonhuman relation" (as quoted in Grant 2005, 66).

Marx's alternative to bourgeois marriage is a marriage relationship in which women are treated as human beings. Grant suggests such a "human marriage" is an "ethical relationship":

> Authentic human marriage should be more like a friendship than a property relation. It ought to be a relation based on freedom rather than necessity. When based on necessity (e.g., lust, procreation, or economic necessity), the relation is not human and takes on the character of an alienated property relation. But when the union is based on ethics, friendship, and choice, it is transformed into an authentic human relationship. (67)

In a marriage based on friendship, men and women relate to and experience each other as social beings, creating a mode of humanity based on gender equality. Importantly, this expands the possibilities of species-being. While Grant does not put it this way, marriage based on friendship might be viewed through the lens of appropriation, that is, as a relationship through which a person is affected by another who transforms the former's orientation to the world. Grant appears to imply just this when she quotes Marx, who writes, "In this relationship is also apparent the extent to which man's need has become human, thus the extent to which *the other human being, as human being has become a need for him,* the extent to which he in his most individual existence is at the same time a social being" (Marx, quoted by Grant 2005, 68, emphasis added). I may be stretching Grant's analysis too far. However, her work clearly suggests that ethical gender relations create a mode of humanity that expands the possibilities for species-being. Grant's extension of Marx's writing to feminism is an important contribution to the theory of species-being because she shows that species-being can be analyzed in terms of intersubjective relations. In other words, Grant's work emphasizes the needs and powers of the subject in question and also, importantly, those of the other in becoming human, in this case, women. I now want to look at an emerging social movement that suggests other species subjects can also shape humanity.

J. K. Gibson-Graham and I have investigated ethical economic relationships between humans and other species through which interdependence is recognized and new modes of humanity are created (see Gibson-Graham and Roelvink 2010; Roelvink and Gibson-Graham 2009). We have explored these relationships in the context of ethical decision making involved in the production, appropriation, and distribution of surplus, paying particular attention to whether this decision making can be expanded to account for the contributions of other species, which often end up as part of an undifferentiated residual surplus (the surplus left over after the costs of production have been met) (Roelvink and Gibson-Graham 2009, 153). In other words, we are interested in modes of surplus extraction that involve ethical relations between humans and between humans and other species, relations through which interdependence and the "commonality of being" are realized (see Gibson-Graham 2006b, 86).

The theory of species-being potentially broadens the concept of appropriation as we, along with others rethinking Marxism, have theorized it. Combining Marx's theory of species-being, and in particular the idea of appropriation as it is elaborated by Ollman, with a Marxian class analysis provides a framework with which to explore both the relationality of economic activity (the ethical negotiation of surplus as well as other coordinates of economic decision making; see Gibson-Graham 2006b) and the relational constitution of modes of humanity in diverse economies. With this expanded view of appropriation, we might investigate the different modes of humanity that are constituted as surplus is negotiated in a variety of different class relations and in diverse sites of the economy, such as in families and enterprises. We could then ask whether we live in ways that respond to our shared vulnerability and interdependence with other species.

In my work on landscape-repairing agriculture, I have begun to explore modes of humanity centered on ethical economic relationships with other species. I am interested in the case of "unconventional farmers," a term I have taken from Lisa M. Hamilton's (2009) book *Deeply Rooted*. Hamilton is concerned about the role of farmers in agriculture amid the widespread dehumanization of agribusiness in the United States. The images that come to mind about agribusiness are similar to those of Australian miners today: working conditions and pay may be good compared to other so-called unskilled sectors, but the connection among workers, the environment, and other species is limited. In addition to these dehumanizing conditions, other troubling consequences of agribusiness are well known and include, for example, chemical-resistant pests and diseases that are crossing species boundaries.

Hamilton (2009, 3) focuses her attention on farmers who have decided to continue farming "as humans":

As they see it, agriculture is not an industry on the periphery of modern civilization. It is a fundamental act that determines whether we as a society will live or die. What binds these people is not a particular farming method, but rather the conviction that *as humans, the contributions they make are essential.* Conventional agriculture doesn't need people for much more than to run the machines and carry the debt, but these people refuse that lifeless role. To the work, they bring their intellects and their consciences, their histories and their concerns for the future. In quiet ways, in quiet places, they have set about correcting the damage that has come from believing agriculture could actually be reduced to numbers alone. The first step: reclaim their place in the center of the equation.

While placing humans at the center of the agricultural equation may set off alarm bells for those who see human-centered life as a key part of the environmental problem (such as some deep ecologists), unconventional farmers are radically different from those celebrating human mastery over nature. From the perspective I am developing in this chapter, unconventional farmers exhibit a mode of humanity constituted through ethical economic interactions with other species. Through their relationship with other species, these farmers appear to be transforming the potentialities of the species-being of humans.

I am particularly interested in the story of one unconventional farmer in Australia, on which I draw here to gesture toward a dignified mode of humanity for the Anthropocene. John Weatherstone (2003) has always been at the cutting edge of farming innovation, working with scientists and other farmers to develop the most efficient and productive agricultural practice. Recalling this period, Weatherstone writes, "At the time we were unaware of the burdens this would place on the land—costs that we would have to pay over the longer term" (4). Indeed, the effects of these practices combined with years of drought on the landscape and other species have led to the recent period of farmers being provided with government assistance to "leave land with dignity" (ABC News Online 2005). Weatherstone, however, has not left the land. Instead, he is leading the way in the creation of a dignified mode of farming in the Anthropocene. He pinpoints one moment in particular that led to this shift in practice. In the context of this chapter, I would like to interpret Weatherstone's story through the lens of appropriation and species-being transformation.

Weatherstone recalls the "day from hell" as the moment he decided to change his agricultural practices (5). At this time, the drought was so bad that he was faced with the prospect of having to kill all the newborn lambs as there was nothing to feed them. He describes this prospect as "horrible," a "gruesome task" (5). As the topsoil blew away across his farm after years of drought, Weatherstone went out to survey his land:

> On the afternoon on that bleak day I took my camera and went out to take some pictures. . . . Little did I anticipate the impact that taking those few photos was to have on my life and the future of Lyndfield Park.
>
> While photographing I climbed over the boundary fence along the highway to get a better angle from which to take a photo. On the highway side of the fence the grass had not been grazed. This remaining grass, along with the netting on the boundary fence, had caught soil and organic matter, including cover burr, which had been blown from our paddocks by the drought winds. It was like a huge organic sponge. In some places it was almost knee deep!
>
> . . . This was the moment I made a solemn commitment that if we survived that drought I would do everything in my power to ensure that Lyndfield Park would never look like that again. (5–6)

Like Ollman's description of appropriating a sunset, Weatherstone's story can be read as the appropriation of his farm in drought. As he surveyed his property, he was devastated by seeing that all his well-managed, cutting-edge farming practice had produced a dustbowl, while neglected areas, such as the roadside, were able to retain soil coverage and in fact capture the top soil blowing off his property. Like Ollman's discussion of the appropriation of a sunset, Weatherstone was deeply affected by viewing the farm in this light, so affected that he could no longer see the farm in terms of the "prevailing philosophy at the time . . . 'If you farmers are going to make money, you need to produce more food and fibre; you need to make your land work harder'" (6). This experience transformed his relationship to the landscape and other species.

Weatherstone has gone on to transform his farming practices by, for example, reducing livestock and chemical use, ensuring there is surplus grass for the soil, and planting a diverse range of trees for seed production. Rather than choosing trees on the sole basis of efficiency and profitability, he has planted trees that attract birds, provide shade and fodder for cows, and provide for his own need for seeds to generate an income. Likewise, Weatherstone ensures that the soil has the organic matter it needs to flourish through "the creation of smaller paddocks and the use of perennial pastures, rotational grazing, reducing cropping, and no stubble burning" (8). Weatherstone might be seen to be taking other species into account in his economic decision making, initially deciding to reduce his cash income and work in a way that also meets the needs of the landscape and other species and enables them to replenish after agricultural production. Although further empirical and theoretical work needs to be done here on how exactly earth others are included in the appropriation of surplus (such as how this transforms individual appropriation), in this example, it is clear that the contributions of the environment are taken into account on Weatherstone's farm rather than simply ending up in the residual that, in practice, we often identify as surplus (see Roelvink and Gibson-Graham 2009). I also want to suggest Weatherstone's story as an example of a moment in which he recognized that the needs of the landscape and other species are also his own needs, that is, a moment in which he recognized and then responded to coexistence. Perhaps one could even say that the capacities and limits of the landscape and other species became part of Weatherstone's own capacities and limits. This in turn led to new possibilities for agriculture.

The cases of unconventional farmers and feminism demonstrate, I hope, dignified modes of humanity centered on ethical relationships with others and a politics of dignity focused on coexistence. This is, however, a contested political terrain, one that is also occupied by a narrow human-centric understanding of dignity expressed, perhaps, in the labor movement, especially when jobs are pitted against environmental concerns. The task of research might thus be to help understand which modes of humanity recognize and respond to the world that makes them possible and to thereby magnify their presence. I pick up on this research challenge in the concluding chapter.

Focusing on Humanity in the Anthropocene

In this chapter, I have begun to think about our species as a political–economic collective in the Anthropocene. With the help of Bertall Ollman, Judith Grant, and Kelly Oliver, I have found in Marx's writing a theory of species that, despite the modernist binaries shaping his thinking, appreciates the role of others in the constitution of humanity. Importantly, this theory provides insight into the relational geography shaping our existence as a species collective. My overall aim in this chapter is to see if Marx's theory of species-being can help us to think about the relationship between our existence as a species and the performance of different modes of humanity in the Anthropocene, especially those characterized by a dignified human *and* a dignified world. In the second half of this chapter, I investigated species-being movements that are transforming our mode of humanity. In this contested terrain, which I have characterized as a politics of dignity, the cases of feminism and unconventional farmers are distinctive because they show how other subjects, women and other species, are affecting species-being and creating new dignified modes of humanity in which coexistence and interdependence are recognized and responded to.

Like all concepts, Marx's idea of species-being has a checkered history. It has been dismissed by many and has been read in a number of different ways. Typically known as Marx's humanism, the theory of species-being has been criticized by some scholars as an "essentialist concept of human nature" and dismissed as anthropocentrism (see Dyer-Witheford 2004a, 4). Thus the species-being concept may seem unsuitable to investigating dignified modes of humanity centered on our interdependence with others. In contrast to humanist interpretations of Marx's early writings, in this chapter, I hope to have shown the value of a "posthumanist" approach to the species-being concept. As Cary Wolfe (2009, xv) describes it, "posthumanism . . . isn't posthuman at all—in the sense of being 'after' our embodiment has been transcended—but is only posthuman*ist,* in the sense that it opposes the fantasies of disembodiment and autonomy, inherited from humanism itself." I hope to have shown that modes of humanity for the Anthropocene deeply embody and, in doing so, are shaped by a geography of interdependence with human and nonhuman others. Marx's writing on species-being, then, provides a rich resource for posthumanist thinking, which, as Wolfe (xv–xii) argues, demands attention both to our coevolution with earth others and the radical challenges to our mode of humanity at this historical moment.

Conclusion
Doing Research Together

Researching Contemporary Social Movements

In the late 1990s, a number of different activists gathered around growing political economic concern. They included "unions, debt campaigners, peace activists, economists and landless farmers" who were all concerned about the destruction caused by neoliberal reform and desired alternative ways to organize economic life (Kingsnorth 2003, 210). In 2001, this gathering, timed to coincide with the World Economic Forum and located in Porto Alegre, Brazil, was called the World Social Forum (WSF). In 2005, I arrived in Porto Alegre in search of alternatives to neoliberalism, a political economic rationality that I had studied for several years. What I found in Porto Alegre was overwhelming: the 2005 WSF brought together innumerable people, things, and concerns representing diverse experiments in living from around the globe. While trying to absorb and process as much of the WSF as I could, I came to realize that the strong thinking tools I had used to understand social change were of little use for appreciating what these diverse collectives were doing. My ability to look for patterns, align different entities into a single vision, and expose an underlying historically driven system was not what I needed and, as I came to discover, was something of a hindrance to the social activists gathered at the WSF. While de-legitimating and fueling resistance to neoliberalism, techniques of thinking that expose neoliberalism as part of the system of capitalism and align a range of diverse entities under its umbrella create a representation of neoliberalism that renders the diverse heterogeneous alternatives actually under way as futile, easily ignored, destroyed, or co-opted into the capitalist political economy. In this book, I have argued that other techniques of thinking about political economy that are oriented toward the unknown, the diverse, and the contingent are better able to assist social movement struggles because they represent neoliberalism as fragile, ineffective, and open to change.

The 2005 WSF highlighted another limitation of my thinking. Unlike others who were "documenting" the forum, such as journalists, I registered as a participant. However, as a researcher, I struggled to understand the nature of my participation and found myself slipping into the observational, note-taking methods employed by some researchers in the field site. As a result, I found it difficult to participate in the discussions, and I felt isolated from the broader experiment that is the WSF. I further found that my isolation was not minimized by seeking out other academics. I think that this "participation challenge" reflected my inability at the time to see my research and myself as a researcher as having an active role in the collective experiments gathered at the WSF and thus in the creation of new economies. These challenges to thinking about the productive force of collective experimentation and the role research plays in shaping our world prompted several of the themes explored in this book.

Around the time I attended the WSF, I read J. K. Gibson-Graham's book manuscript that came to be called *A Postcapitalist Politics.* Her first book, *The End of Capitalism (As We Knew It),* challenged the discursive hegemony of the capitalist economy. In the years following its 1996 publication, Gibson-Graham embarked on a project to create space for, and bring into being, other economies. Performativity is central to this project. The theory of performativity radically departs from the view that social life is the outcome of an unfolding structural logic and suggests instead that social life is constituted through discourse that is interwoven with bodies and practices. It also suggests that social transformation occurs through the slippage and difference that result from repeated performances. Gibson-Graham's work on performing the economy has been a central starting point for my thinking about how collective experiments can change the world. *A Postcapitalist Politics,* and more so Gibson-Graham's (2008) later work, also suggests ways that research might directly participate in and contribute to the performance of alternative economies. Gibson-Graham's work offers thinking techniques and intellectual stances with which to make visible and viable that which is marginalized by dominant discourse and critical practices of inquiry.

Equipped with this knowledge, I have been able to see how my research participates in collective action. Yet more than this, with this understanding of research as an active participant in social struggle has come a sense of responsibly to the myriad others involved in research. I have had to reflect, for example, on what my work on neoliberalism was doing in terms of the possibilities for action it opens up for those struggling against neoliberal reform, and I have had to consider the effects of another story of the "market" on trash-pickers forming markets to improve their livelihoods. And while I had already begun to consider the more-than-human world in my research, with the coming of the Anthropocene, I have been compelled to go beyond simply considering the role of the more than human in economic action (although this is not a simple task) to also exploring how we might become sensitive to the capacities and needs of earth others and how collective action effects this. In my thinking about collective action for farmers' dignity, for instance, I have had to consider all the nonhuman participants in farming (soil, plants, cattle, and others) and their capacities for resilience as well as the dignity of the world more generally (see also Roelvink and Gibson-Graham 2009; Roelvink 2015). Such an exploration of geographies of collective action facilitates the practice of "relational ethics," that is, ethical consideration of the hybrid others with which one is corporeally connected (Whatmore 2002). In what follows, I look back at these others involved in research and consider how researchers can practice relational ethics in hybrid collectives.

In doing so, in this conclusion, I recall and extend several of the overlapping themes and concerns that have prompted this book. I start by discussing the politics and geography of performativity as a way to appreciate how collective experimentation can change the world and create alternative economies. I then offer some thoughts on the role of research in collective experimentation and the challenges of doing research together in the Anthropocene. This brings me to consider the responsibility researchers have to those within the networks in which their research participates. I argue that awareness of the intertwining of research and collective struggle is vital to ethical performances of new economies.

Expanding the Politics of the Performative

This book employs the lens of the performative to understand the ways in which the diverse collectives that characterize contemporary political struggle are creating new economies. A performative view of politics has been advanced by the extension of linguistic understandings of the performative to thinking about the constitution of social life. Described as a "politics of language" (Gibson-Graham 2006b, xxxiv), this politics aims at "dislocating" representations of the "economy" to make way for the inclusion of other objects, concerns, and groups in economic representation, thus remaking economy. However, discursive politics has been critiqued for its neglect of the geographical, material, and interrelational nature of the social world and for the way it is practiced. For instance, Nigel Thrift and John-David Dewsbury (2000, 414) suggest that Butler's influential work provides little insight into how others can respond to performative acts and thus little insight into the interrelational character of performative action. In addition, discursive forms of politics are often based on the problematic assumption of a division between the material body and conscious thought, an assumption that limits politics to cognitive thought and linguistic expression (Connolly 2002). Early understandings of performative politics have led critics to ask questions about other registers of social construction, including those that are embodied, and how collectives might use these forces to change the world.

In response to such criticism, a politics of the performative has been taken in many different directions. Scholars and activists have turned their attention to the relationship between the material and the discursive, in particular to ideas about embodiment and affect. Gibson-Graham (2006b), for instance, shows how affect—captured in feelings and emotions—can be employed to both resist and bring into being new economic subjectivities. Categorized by Thrift and Dewsbury (2000; see also Thrift 2008) as nonrepresentational theory, such work focuses on the material processes and practices that take place before representation. The challenge of how we might think about the constitutive role of practice has also been taken up in governmentality studies. Research on the constitution of economy, for instance, has shown that governmental rationalities and technologies shape material realities, such as economic relations, which then appear to be nondiscursive preexisting entities (Mitchell 1998, 91). For Timothy Mitchell (2007), the power of economics lies precisely in its ability to produce material effects; the economy is created through "sociotechnical arrangements" that shape the world in ways that have enabled economics to flourish. Aware of the ways in which governmental power operates, marginalized collectives can use technologies, such as census data collection, to create the conditions in which they become visible to government and can access citizenship entitlements, such as food rations (see Appadurai 2002).

Theorists of contemporary forms of capitalism share governmentality scholars' concerns with the practice of power. They argue that consumption has shifted toward purchases that enable one to carry out certain practices and have particular experiences, such as purchasing entry to theme parks or buying software packages (Massumi 2002a; Thrift and Dewsbury 2000, 423). Alongside this growing intellectual attention to experience, leftist political activists have taken up the idea of performance as a way to create alterative realities, thus taking the politics of the performative in another direction. Theatrical performance has been employed to make visible the experiences of silenced or marginalized subjects and to reveal the social construction of their subordination (Carlson 1996). Criticism suggesting that a politics of exposure reinforces the powers it seeks to dismantle has led to a rethinking of the representational nature of performance. This rethinking has focused on the ways in which dominant discourse can be subverted to alternative agendas through mime, play, and a reformatting of the relationship between the subject–object, performer–audience (Carlson 1996). Marvin Carlson highlights Thi Minh-Ha Trinh's (1991) work as an example, drawing attention to her use of dialogue to include the audience in the creation of the performance. As a result, "performance is no longer created by someone for someone, but is the expression of a plurivocal world of communicating bodies, where difference is 'conceived of not as a divisive element, but as a source of interactions; objects and subject are neither in opposition nor merged with each other'" (182).

Performances centered on communicating bodies confirm that, on its own, linguistic representation is often limiting, using only existing and recognizable expressions to create common understandings and thus presenting a challenge to the creation of the new (Massumi 2002a). Brian Massumi argues that linguistic systems can never fully capture experience; experiences are always more than the words that describe them and, despite common linguistic meaning, are always different for different people. He suggests that some forms of expression, however, come close to revealing this excess of meaning from which the new emerges. One form of expression utilized in political performance is humor (Hynes et al. 2007). Maria Hynes, Scott Sharpe, and Bob Fagan (2007) have shown, for example, the political power of theatrical performance through an examination of the Yesmen's performance of the dissolution of the World Trade Organization (WTO). Hynes and colleagues argue that this hoax bypassed many of the "representational structures" that constitute the politics of globalization and instead acted through the realm of affect—shaming the WTO when it attempted to shut down the hoax. Going beyond the disabling affect of shame, they suggest that, unbounded from empirical reality and the "facts" of the world, the humorous and surprising nature of the performance that dissolved the WTO gave viewers a sense of possibility.

One of the early insights of feminist political performance was the way in which theatrical performance, unlike other art forms, such as painting, gains its force through emotions rather than particular, refined skills (Carlson 1996, 148). Massumi (2002a) highlights how particular forms of expression, such as humor, poetry, or anger, mediate between multiple and heterogeneous nondiscursive experiences and that which is represented through discourse to generate something new. Likewise, Thrift and Dewsbury (2000) argue that the constitutive force of theatrical performances is centered on practices, processes, and experiences that cannot be articulated in discourse yet create knowledge, visions, and imaginations forming the world. The expression and communication of the emotions and feelings generated through these experiences is one way in which new visions are thought to arise (Anderson 2006, 749).

In this growing field of research on performativity and social struggle, the geographical nature of collective action has received much less explicit attention than other dimensions that constitute the world. Yet, in the context of concern about climate change and viruses that ignore species and geographical boundaries, we are becoming increasingly aware that action exceeds the ambit of the individual human to encompass a broad geography of people and things. This book suggests that the geography of collective association should also been seen as a significant political strategy to bring about change. I have drawn on Sedgwick's (2003) discussion of the geography of performative utterances and actor network theories of action to theorize the relational geography of collective action. Just as the force of the performative utterance is constituted by a range of people clustered around it, in chapter 2, I showed that economic performances rely on an arrangement of human and nonhuman witnesses and call for their response. Not only this, but Sedgwick suggests that the spatial relationship between performative utterances and other utterances is also open to examination, particularly the periperformative utterance that responds to and makes a statement about the performative. Applied to the economy and the possibilities of collective action, the geography of the performative broadens the view of what is involved in economic performances to include a whole range of humans, things, and concerns. And the periperformative utterance offers a way for social movements to contest and respond to economic discourse. Reassembling the relationships on which the performative relies is thus key to opening up new economic possibilities. This geography of the performative is not merely a one-dimensional landscape that surrounds the performer. Drawing on nonrepresentational theory and classical political economic thought, I have shown that the geography of the performative is embodied and in this way also shapes action. Embodied forces of affect and emotions play a central role in generating new possibilities for economic experimentation, and ethical economic action can be guided through an embodied awareness of others either directly involved in or implicated by that action.

A geography of the performative and performance offers more than another dimension with which to perform new worlds. It also provides a view to this vast landscape of different representational and nonrepresentational forces that interact to shape the world. Collective action cannot be characterized by *either* nonrepresentational forces like affect *or* representational forces like discourse. Our world is shaped in a much more complex fashion (Latour 2004b). Affect, for instance, involves what the body does and can potentially experience, the new relationships prompted through that experience, and dialogue that produces new discourse. It thus operates through the body, through arrangements of people and things, and through language. In chapter 3, I argued that social movement collectives employ affect to translate their experiments in living into a shared discourse that in turn shapes economic relationships and identities. This is collective action at work. The collective under discussion in this chapter refers to a hybrid collective, a heterogeneous asssemblage of human and nonhuman actants. And action here is the process that brings the hybrid collective into being; it gathers social movements, translates their diverse experiences into a shared discourse, and creates an arrangement through which further action is shaped. As a whole, this book traces some of the many different forces that are employed in contemporary collective action. Bruno Latour (2004b) argues that, in the context of collectives that are made up of multiple actants that operate on the world in different ways, social scientists need to take a closer look at how these collectives are assembled, the different forces mobilized, and the multiple trajectories of action. In this book, I have shown how opening up the geography of performative collective action might facilitate such a project.

Moreover, this book begins to develop a posthumanist view of collective action. This is not to suggest that collective action comes after the human; rather, my aim has been to offer an embodied view of the human in relation to others that enable collective life. In doing so, I extended from a relational and geographical view of collective performativity developed in chapters 2 and 3 to explore in chapter 4 markets as framed relationships between humans and the many others that enable market action. Economic action is constituted by a hybrid of interacting actants. The human, I argue, may be identified as an ethical economic actor, engaged, for example, in dignifying economic life, but the possibilities of being human lie in hybrid collectives. The Marxian concept of species extended in chapter 5 helps us to think further about the kind of collective that provides the conditions for dignified human being. I have only just begun to think about how to represent nonhuman elements in the production of alternative futures. To extend Gibson-Graham's work on the inclusion of diverse others in economic ethics in this way means taking a step back from Jean-Luc Nancy's (1991) idea of "being in common" that underpins the community as a praxis of ethical coexistence. It means considering the hybridity of being itself and the way particular subjects are figured through hybrid collective action. It further means opening the "being" in the idea of "being in common" to more-than-human possibilities.

Researching in Hybrid Collectives

It is generally accepted that research, and thinking more generally, plays an important role in the way we live our lives. To recognize the importance of research is, of course, nothing new—we need only think of the celebration of Newton's discovery of gravity or of breakthroughs in medical science. Today, however, in some circles at least, attention has shifted from seeing research primarily as a means of discovery that unveils truths that have always been present to exploring the performativity of research and the role that research has in bringing its subjects into being. This perspective abandons understandings of research as an objective and apolitical reflection of an external reality and instead embraces an ethics and politics of research. Before turning to the question of ethics, in this section, I discuss the performativity of research with reference to the hybrid collective and the research undertaken in this book.

A performative understanding of research as an active force that shapes life encourages researchers to utilize the discursive and affective registers of the performative to bring about change. For instance, Gibson-Graham's participatory action research uses a politics of language combined with the production of experiences that generate positive affect to prompt new subject positions that facilitate ethical community development (Gibson-Graham 2006b). More broadly, with Gibson-Graham, researchers have worked to resignify the economy to make present the multiple and diverse economic institutions and practices that are available to support life (Gibson-Graham 2006a; 2006b; Leyshon, Lee, and Williams 2003). In light of these and many other developments, research has come to be seen as a tool for bringing about social, economic, cultural, and environmental justice and as a way for activist academics to equip social movements with the tools to better take up their struggle for alternatives (Callon and Caliksan 2005; Gibson-Graham 2006b). With my interest in the performative, in this book, I have focused on the constitutive force of research in and of itself rather than the impact of research on the field site. However, both areas must be taken into consideration to judge the success of the performation of research, that is, the ongoing success of research in shaping the reality it describes (Callon and Caliskan 2005, 28). But this kind of judgment has not been my aim. Rather, inspired by the growing body of work on the performativity of knowledge, I have set out to offer some research and thinking techniques that might aid collective struggle for change. I began with struggle against neoliberalism. Much is known about neoliberalism, and whatever one's political intentions, Julia Elyachar's (2005) book *Markets of Dispossession* is a good example of a tendency in research to foreground neoliberalism when it might instead contribute to the alternatives it backgrounds (see also Roelvink 2007). To enable a different role for research in social movement struggles, in writing this book, I set out to develop thinking and research techniques oriented toward the creation of new economies. I have offered two techniques of thinking and research in particular, the periperformative and dialogue, that are currently utilized in research found beyond the traditional confines of the academy, that is, in documentary films and in research conducted by social movement groups. These techniques of research operate through a range of different forces. In addition to the discursive, these performative forces or registers include relational and embodied geographies.

I have placed these research techniques within a broader mode of politics: a politics of collective action. A politics of collective action gathers diverse concerns, peoples, and things around performative utterances such as TINA ("there is no alternative") and "the capitalist economy efficiently provides for all." In doing so, a politics of collective action establishes a space to gather diverse experiences and knowledge. It also provides a space for others coalescing around performative utterances to respond to, and thereby reconfigure, the relationships constituting economic action. I am interested in a politics of collective action performed by hybrid collectives. As I see it, the hybrid collective generates new discursive visions from the diverse economic experiences of social movements and offers an infrastructure for these visions to be enacted in everyday life.

I am especially interested in the role that research can play in a politics of collective action. In chapter 4, I analyze the diverse groups gathered around markets and, in doing so, develop a relational understanding of collective action that is open to a range of interventions, including intervention by research. Market sociality embodied through the impartial spectator governs which relationships are taken into account in market transactions. I demonstrate that research participates in collective action by reformulating these relationships. In other words, research offers a technique for the realignment of the relationships framing markets. It can do so in several ways: as part of the networks we call markets, research can play a role in the formation of concern groups; it can also identify market overflows that can be utilized by concern groups, as demonstrated by the case of trash-pickers; and finally, research that maps performative economic acts can cultivate an awareness of the hybrid collective in the production, appropriation, and distribution of surplus and can prompt an ethical orientation to economic relationships. Research can thus facilitate the economic experimentation of hybrid collectives in different ways. I have offered just a few possibilities (for other possibilities, see Law 2004a; 2004b; Mol 1999). Yet whether the political economic realignments that are potentially initiated by these techniques will succeed remains to be seen. To explore the impact of these techniques and the economic experimentation they help to initiate requires continued engagement. Performativity does not operate simply by socially constructing a world that is then fixed in place. Research that seeks to operate performatively is also open to things not turning out according to plan (such as projects failing to achieve a particular goal or creating an effect quite different from the one expected); after all, many other actants and actions are already in play. As Butler (2010, 152) notes, "performative processes" involve the "reiteration of a set of social relations," which means performative actions are necessarily open to change.

How, then, might we support the performance and reiteration of the research techniques offered in this book and the economic experimentation in which they participate? One place to look might be the academy itself, and in particular movements directed at making "other academies" to support the enactment of alternative economies (Gibson-Graham 2008, 629; see also Appadurai 2000). The Community Economies Collective (CEC) is one example of a hybrid collective including academic and community researchers in Australia, North America, Europe, and Southeast Asia, organized to support and proliferate collective economic experimentation.[1] It demonstrates perhaps how an "other academy" might operate. The collective gathers people interested in supporting ethical economic practices and institutions through research. It does so in part by generating, sharing, and spreading research techniques designed to perform economic diversity and, in particular, ethical forms of economic life and by participating in the creation and maintenance of hybrid collectives able to performatively reiterate these processes. Ann Hill's (2014) doctoral research is an excellent example. Hill, a member of the CEC, sees the CEC as a hybrid collective of people, things (a website and e-mail list), and the ghost of the late Julie Graham, to name just a few of the human and nonhuman actants assembled and committed to researching together. In addition to developing a posthumanist theory of the CEC, Hill's research employs collective research practices, such as the "cross-appropriation" of ideas from different fields (agroecology and social enterprise development) in practical workshops and online dialogue to build hybrid collectives cultivating ethical food economies in the Philippines (on cross-appropriation, see Spinosa, Flores, and Dreyfus 1997; Gibson-Graham 2006b). With these and other techniques Hill aims to support and privilege collective subject formation over that of the individual in food economies so that communities can respond together to freak weather events and food insecurity, concerns becoming all too common in our era of climate change. The CEC and Hill's theorization of it show how other academies can operate as hybrid collectives and take advantage of their hybridity in the creation, cultivation, and circulation of research practices. Furthermore, through processes of collective knowledge production, Hill's research in particular aims to create opportunities for ethical encounters (particularly through affective experience) between humans and between the human and the more-than-human world. This opens up the question of how researchers are to be included in relational ethics.

Including Researchers in Relational Ethics

This book theorizes the performative force of hybrid collectives. From the performative utterance, to affect modulation, to market transactions, to struggles for human dignity, I argue that we can no longer think of economic action as a product of human beings or any other singularity. This opens up the constitution of social life to participation by a whole range of actants, including that which we call research. My argument that research should not be seen as separate from its field of inquiry and my suggestion of a number of research techniques with which hybrid collectives can create new economies have ethical implications for researchers. First, the performative approach places ethics at the forefront of research; that is, in contrast to a model of research that assumes one must first have the results of the project before considering possible interventions, when taking a performative perspective, from the very outset of the project, researchers see their work as an intervention with possible effects (Cameron, Manhood, and Pomfrett 2011). Second, to consider the ethics of research, the researcher must look to a wide range of possible participants in the research. In this section, I flesh out this idea by applying Sarah Whatmore's (2002) conceptualization of "relational ethics" to the project undertaken in this book (see also Routledge 2003). Relational ethics concerns our ethical connection to others in hybrid assemblages and the collectives discussed throughout this book. These connections are formed in everyday embodied life. Moreover, they enable existence and shape the possibilities of our, always collective, action. I am particularly interested in teasing out the role of research in ethical collective action directed at the big challenges that face us today, especially climate change. In what follows, I argue that sensitivity and responsibility are central to ethical collective action.

As Jane Bennett (2010, 37) describes in her account of confederate agency, a collective understanding of action "broadens the places to look for sources" of the effects of action. From this perspective, it seems futile to point a finger at a single location of responsibility or blame, whether a corporation or an individual. Rather, Bennett argues that we need to look at "strings of events" when considering the ethics of action (37). In the case of farming, for exam-ple, one would need to consider how action affects the capacities of all those involved—not just the farmer's income and the farm's profitability, as is often the case, but also the impact of farming on bird life, soil sustainability, insect life, and so on. Research has an important role to play in identifying the participants and the effects of action and can in fact be viewed as a part of the experiments in living in which the "presence" of co-constituting others comes to be "felt" (Whatmore 2002, 161). Moreover, research can help to give presence to, or at least provide space for, co-constituting others. In doing so, it might increase "our possibilities for interaction with and perception of the world" (Plumwood 2002, 175). Throughout this book, I have explored a num-ber of different techniques with which to cultivate sensitivity and awareness of all that which co-constitutes economic action. For instance, mapping eco-nomic performances reveals a variety of human and nonhuman entities that need to be taken into account in a relational ethics. Mapping economic per-formances contributes to understanding the co-constituting roles of humans and nonhumans in collective action and offers techniques through which the nonhuman might come to assert a stronger presence in our collective responses to contemporary and future challenges.

Although I have explored a number of techniques for change, researchers can go further in using these techniques as research *methods* to understand and respond to contemporary challenges, most notably climate change. For instance, in chapter 3, I developed Bruno Latour's idea of learning to be affected as a way to increase our ability to differentiate co-constituting others, thereby transforming our worlds and the possibilities for action within them. Picking up on this and other work, Jenny Cameron, Craig Manhood, and Jamie Pomfrett (2011) have used the idea of learning to be affected as a per-formative and collective method in their research on community gardens. Noting that gardeners already learn to be affected by the more-than-human world, registering and responding to differences in plant and insect life as seasons change, Cameron and colleagues set out to create opportunities for community gardeners to learn to be affected by each other and a range of different community gardens. In doing so, they have helped to broaden and strengthen each community garden collective. Although there are many ways to respond to climate change, learning to be affected is significant here because it increases our sensitivity to the world and, through this increased sensitivity, diversifies the collectives of which we are part. A gardener aware of a great number of actants shaping the garden can also see a wider range of possibilities for action and is therefore likely to be more resilient to climatic changes. Cameron and colleagues' research demonstrates that learning to be affected can be used as a method in research aiming to participate in the performance of new worlds. As governments call for citizens to become backyard scientists and document the effects of climate change (Cubby 2010), learning to be affected offers a way to think about how we might develop responses to climate change through the very process of documentation rather than after it.

Cameron et al.'s (2011) work provides an excellent demonstration of how research can shape collective life. The idea of relational ethics also has important implications for the *kinds* of collectives researchers cultivate to face major challenges. With Bennett (2010, 37–38), we can question our participation in the various collectives that we research by asking, "Do I attempt to extricate myself from assemblages whose trajectory is likely to do harm? Do I enter into the proximity of assemblages whose conglomerate effectively tends toward the enactment of nobler ends?" Rather than being detached from the process of research, the researcher becomes much more like an activist and spokesperson who takes an active role in the assemblages through which presence of the more than human is felt (Latour 2004c). We cannot know for sure which assemblages will be harmful or contribute to nobler ends, but by developing sensitivity to how collectives are framed, how strong those frames are, and others that enable action outside these frames, we can begin to get a better idea. For example, a carbon market has emerged in parts of the world in which the emitter is identified, carbon dioxide emission permits are allocated, and a market is framed. In the process, however, other greenhouse gas emissions (such as nitrous oxide, methane, and tropospheric ozone) are excluded, and the focus on carbon marginalizes other factors that might also contribute to climate change, such as the impact of reduced cloud coverage and increased solar radiation caused by changes to the hydrological cycle due to deforestation (a theory developed by the Sustainability Science Team of the Nature and Society Forum led by Walter Jehne and discussed by Mathews 2011). In such a contested context, the researcher as spokesperson can take the role of questioning and opening up how concerns about the cause and response to climate change have become "fact" through *agencements* like that of carbon trading. In the process, the researcher can examine how statements are performed through particular *agencements* and how the more-than-human world might assert its presence and capacity to thrive through other kinds of *agencements* (see Mathews 2011 for an excellent example of the latter).

Freya Mathews (2011) picks up on Jehne's research on the impact of changes to the hydrological cycle on the planet to suggest that, in responding to climate change, we need to make space for capacities of natural systems, such as the reforestation of the planet. We might see climate change research, then, as enabling human beings to develop a greater awareness of the earth's capacities to respond to climate change and as an investigation of the ways in which we can participate in (rather than dictate) this response (Mathews 2011). This is a radically different approach to research than the one that exposes and predicts and thereby seeks to shock people into taking action against an apocalypse brought about by climate change. Instead, it suggests that we need to look beyond the human in developing a collective response to climate change and environmental degradation. As Magdalena Zolkos and I have found in our research on the experience of environmental degradation, our affective connections with the more-than-human world can transform thinking and generate new possibilities for progressive action (see Roelvink and Zolkos 2011). For example, John Weatherstone, whose story is discussed in chapter 5, came to see his farm in a new way following the experience of its devastation and a moment of deeply felt connectively with the land (see also Roelvink and Zolkos 2011). Following this experience, he could no longer farm with only profit and efficiency in mind but came to see that the resilience of the soil and of other species was central to the farm and must be taken into account in economic planning and decision making. Although humans are not in control of other species or the planet, we can, as the preceding example suggests, work toward collective responses to mitigate the worst effects of climate change.

Sensitivity is a term that has come up several times in this discussion, particularly when it comes to taking an ethical position in relation to the more-than-human world. I have suggested that research has an important role to play in the cultivation of a sensitivity that is so vital to a relational ethics. This sensitivity shapes one's relationship with and responses to co-constituting others. One might also think about the response of researchers in hybrid collectives as a form of responsibility. Alphonso Lingis (2002, 35) describes the relationship between sensitivity and responsibility in his conversation with Mary Zournazi:

> To be sensitive to the other person is to be responsive. Responsibility is connected with the notion of answering to the other, responding to the other's moves and to the other's sensibility. It's too weak to say that the other person is not responsive to my feelings. It is much more than that. It is more to do with a kind of sensibility—the way I perceive things, the way I make sense of the whole environment about me.

One's ability to be sensitive to and respond to others involves perception and the ability to feel, sense, and perceive the relations one has with others. In hybrid collectives, the researcher is thus responsible not only for the performative effects of the research, that is, what the research works to bring into being, but *also* to the others involved in and enabling that action. A first step for a researcher in taking up responsibility is for the researcher to become sensitive to the broader relationships of which the research is a part. In undertaking the research that has gone into this book, I have taken this first step. By providing some techniques with which to perceive the relational and embodied geography of collective action, I have sought to contribute to such sensitivity.

Acknowledgments

Building Dignified Worlds argues that research is a collective endeavor. Although I acknowledge here only a few of the relationships that have shaped this book, I hope the work conveys to readers its broader relational geography, which includes, for instance, those gathered at the 2005 World Social Forum, a vast range of scholars and scholarship, and much more.

Building Dignified Worlds is inspired by and a direct engagement with J. K. Gibson-Graham's research. It takes off from the ground experimentally explored by Gibson-Graham and the growing community economies research collective and networks. Gibson-Graham is the persona of Katherine Gibson and Julie Graham, who have collectively and individually guided me through the early stages of this project. I am deeply grateful to Katherine, my primary mentor, for her encouragement in experimenting with my most exciting and difficult ideas, while also pushing me to develop these ideas to the highest standards of scholarship. Her strength and passion for research were of great inspiration throughout my doctoral candidature. Katherine's and Julie's generous spirits and stances toward research have had a profound impact on me and are something I will always treasure.

As part of my mentorship by Katherine and Julie, I was very fortunate to have been introduced to and later become a member of the Community Economies Collective. The collective has provided me with much inspiration and intellectual support for my research endeavors and has led to many exciting collaborations. Though the members of the collective are too numerous to mention individually, a few stand out for their intellectual engagement with my research, including Jenny Cameron, Stephen Healy, Ann Hill, Kelly Dombroski, Ethan Miller, and Kevin St. Martin.

I would particularly like to say a special thank-you to my dear friend and colleague Magdalena Zolkos. Working with Magdalena has extended, and continues to extend, my thinking in unimaginable ways, and I have never before worked with such a humble and caring colleague.

I would also like to thank several scholars at the Australian National University and the University of Western Sydney who, over the past few years, have engaged with my ideas and prompted my exploration into new areas. In particular, I benefited from Barry Hindess's doctoral supervision, and my work is much stronger as a result of his comments and advice. I am also grateful to Kersty Hobson, Scott Sharpe, Maria Hynes, Larry Saha, Tim Rowse, Katharine Rankin, Joe Painter, David Craig, Wendy Larner, Dipesh Chakrabarty, David Ruccio, Michel Callon, George DeMartino, Jacqui Poltera, Allison Weir, Anna Hutchens, Amanda Cahill, Michelle Carnegie, and Tina Jaskolski for their willingness to listen to or read my work and for their encouragement to pursue my ideas further.

Thank you to Jason Weidemann from the University of Minnesota Press for his continued interest in this project and helpful feedback along the way. I would also like to thank the three reviewers of my manuscript for the University of Minnesota Press, whose constructive criticism has strengthened *Building Dignified Worlds*.

Thank you to my family, Jenny, Harry, and Jochem Roelvink, for their ongoing support while I have followed my dreams in distant countries. My regular chats over the phone and Skype video calls to Jenny and Harry have been invaluable in connecting me with my home and family and have provided me with the love and care required for combining family and work lives. Finally, a special thank-you to my partner, Brett Bowden, to our daughter, Elke Bowden-Roelvink, and to our son, Lucien Bowden-Roelvink, for their love and encouragement. As an academic, Brett has played a range of supportive roles during my research career and has often been placed in the difficult position of giving me intellectual criticism hard to hear from a partner. Like Brett, Elke and Lucien have become some of my most important teachers, particularly when it comes to knowing when to slow down and be mindful of the wonders of life around me. Thank you to Lucien, Elke, Brett, and everyone who has supported me in the research that is *Building Dignified Worlds*.

Notes

Introduction

1. The Community Economies Collective is a good example of one such community; see http://www.communityeconomies.org/Home.

1. The Discontents of Knowing Neoliberalism

1. See http://www.forumsocialmundial.org.br/main.php?id_menu=4&cd_language=2.

2. Spatializing Economic Concerns

1. See http://www.thecorporation.com/.
2. See http://www.thetake.org/.

3. Affective Collective Action

1. http://www.forumsocialmundial.org.br/main.php?id_menu=19&cd_language=2.

2. The last meeting in one location before the forum took a polycentric form.

3. This is not to simply dismiss violent protest outright and thereby move toward the assertion of a single strategy for social transformation. As Isabelle Stengers notes, "the matter is not to demand a unifying principle which would be stronger than divergence, but to learn how to work together not in spite of but through the divergence" (Stengers 2002, 255).

4. Kathleen Stewart's (2007, 4) work is instructive on other creative ways of evoking the force of affect or, as she describes it, "to find something to say about ordinary affects by performing some of the intensity and texture that makes them habitable and animate."

5. Connolly, too, notes that the play of affect is also expressed through "the timbre of our voices, the calmness or intensity of our gestures, our facial expressions, the

flush of our faces, the rate of our heartbeats, the receptivity, tightness, or sweatiness of our skin, and the relaxation or turmoil in our guts" (76).

6. See http://www.nu.ac.za/ccs/.

7. Transcript from the 2005 WSF session "Change the World without Taking Power," http://www.all4all.org/2007/06/3160.shtml.

8. Ibid.

9. Ibid.

4. Transforming Markets

1. Callon (1998b, 261) describes these situations in which calculation determines the transaction as "cold." In cold situations, agreement has been reached on the boundaries of the market and, in particular, on those issues that are included or excluded from its frame.

2. As recently advanced by Owain Jones at the Workshop on Environmental Post-humanities, UMEA University, Sweden, October 15–16, 2014.

3. See http://www.slowfood.com/.

4. http://www.slowfood.com/international/1/about-us.

5. http://www.slowfood.com/international/2/our-philosophy.

6. See http://www.cempre.org.br/.

7. Page numbers refer to a prepublished version of the chapter.

5. Dignified Humanity, Dignified World

1. http://www.globaldignity.org/view/about.

2. See, e.g., the website of the humanitarian organisation CARE, which has the motto, "Defending Dignity. Fighting Poverty." CARE seeks to draw attention to the "human face of climate change" by calling on U.S. president Obama to tackle climate change, stating, "Effectively addressing climate change requires a global response based on a shared sense of community. It also requires leadership to make and implement difficult decisions. The United States is the critical actor that can help forge and implement an international plan by the power of its example" (see https://my.care.org/site/Advocacy?cmd=display&page=UserAction&id=344).

Conclusion

1. See http://www.communityeconomies.org/Home.

Bibliography

ABC News Online. 2005. "Leave Land with Dignity, Farmers Urged." http://www .abc.net.au/news/newsitems/200505/s1375510.htm.

Achbar, Mark, Jennifer Abbott, and Joel Bakan, dirs. 2003. *The Corporation.* DVD. Canada: Big Picture Media Corporation, Madman Cinema.

Althusser, Louis. 1990. *For Marx.* Translated by B. Brewster. London: Verso.

Amariglio, Jack L., and Yahya M. Madra. 2009. "Karl Marx and Ethics." In *Handbook on Economics and Ethics,* edited by Irene Van Staveren and Jan Peil, 325–32. Cheltenham, U.K.: Edward Elgar Press.

Amin, Ash. 1994. "Post-Fordism: Models, Fantasies, and Phantoms of Transition." In *Post-Fordism: A Reader,* 1–39. London: Blackwell.

Anderson, Ben. 2006. "Becoming and Being Hopeful: Towards a Theory of Affect." *Environment and Planning D: Society and Space* 24, no. 5: 733–52.

Andreotti, Vanessa, and Emma Dowling. 2004. "WSF, Ethics, and Pedagogy." *International Social Science Journal* 56, no. 182: 605–13.

Appadurai, Arjun, ed. 1986. *The Social Life of Things: Commodities in Cultural Perspective.* Cambridge: Cambridge University Press.

———. 2000. "Grassroots Globalization and the Research Imagination." *Public Culture* 12, no. 1: 1–19.

———. 2002. "Deep Democracy: Urban Governmentality and the Horizon of Politics." *Public Culture* 14, no. 1: 21–47.

Austin, John Langshaw. (1955) 1962. *How to Do Things with Words: The William James Lectures Delivered at Harvard University in 1955.* Oxford: Clarendon Press.

Bakan, Joel. 2004. *The Corporation: The Pathological Pursuit of Profit and Power.* New York: Free Press.

Barnett, Clive. 2005. "The Consolations of 'Neoliberalism.'" *Geoforum* 36, no. 1: 7–12.

Barry, Andrew. 2002. "The Anti-political Economy." *Economy and Society* 31, no. 2: 268–84.

Bennett, Jane. 2010. *Vibrant Matter: A Political Ecology of Things.* Durham, N.C.: Duke University Press.

Berlant, Lauren. 2007. "Politics and the Political in a Post-liberal Age." Paper presented in the Friday Forum series, the Research School of Humanities, Australian National University, July 27.

Bezencon, Valery, and Sam Blili. 2006. "Fair Trade Channels: Are We Killing the Romantics?" *International Journal of Environmental, Cultural, Economic, and Social Sustainability* 2: 187–96.

Brenner, Neil, Jamie Peck, and Nik Theodore. 2010. "Variegated Neoliberalization: Geographies, Modalities, Pathways." *Global Networks* 10, no. 2: 182–222.

Brown, Vivienne. 1994. *Adam Smith's Discourse: Canonicity, Commerce, and Conscience.* New York: Routledge.

Butler, Judith. 1988. "Performative Acts and Gender Constitution: An Essay in Phenomenology and Feminist Theory." *Theatre Journal* 40, no. 4: 519–31.

———. 1990. *Gender Trouble: Feminism and the Subversion of Identity.* New York: Routledge.

———. 1997. *The Psychic Life of Power: Theories in Subjection.* Stanford, Calif.: Stanford University Press.

———. 2010. "Performative Agency." *Journal of Cultural Economy* 3, no. 2: 147–61.

Callenbach, Ernest. 2002–3. "The Gleaners and I (Les Gleaners et la Glaneuse)." *Film Quarterly* 56, no. 2: 46–49.

Callon, Michel. 1998a. "Introduction: The Embeddedness of Economic Markets in Economics." In Callon, *Laws of the Markets*, 1–57.

———. 1998b. "An Essay on Framing and Overflowing: Economic Externalities Revisited by Sociology." In Callon, *Laws of the Markets*, 244–69.

———. ed. 1998c. *The Laws of the Markets.* Oxford: Blackwell.

———. 2005. "Why Virtualism Paves the Way to Political Impotence: Callon Replies to Miller." *Economic Sociology: European Electronic Newsletter* 6, no. 2: 3–20.

———. 2007. "What Does It Mean to Say Economics Is Performative?" In MacKenzie et al., *Do Economists Make Markets? On the Performativity of Economics,* 311–57.

———. 2015. "How to Design Alternative Markets: The Case of Genetically Modified/Non-Genetically Modified Coexistence." In Roelvink et al., *Making Other Worlds Possible: Performing Diverse Economies.*

Callon, Michel, and Koray Caliskan. 2005. "New and Old Directions in the Anthropology of Markets." Paper presented at the Wenner-Gren Foundation for Anthropological Research: An International Panel, Wenner-Gren Foundation, New York, April 9.

Callon, Michel, and John Law. 1995. "Agency and the Hybrid Collectif." *The South Atlantic Quarterly* 94, no. 2: 481–507.

Callon, Michel, and Vololona Rabeharisoa. 2003. "Research 'in the Wild' and the Shaping of New Social Identities." *Technology in Society* 25, no. 2: 193–204.

———. 2008. "The Growing Engagement of Emergent Concerned Groups in Political and Economic Life." *Science, Technology, and Human Values* 33, no. 2: 230–61.

Cameron, Jenny, and Katherine Gibson. 2005. "Participatory Action Research in a Poststructural Vein." *Geoforum* 36, no. 3: 315–31.

Cameron, Jenny, Craig Manhood, and Jamie Pomfrett. 2011. "Bodily Learning for a Climate (Changing) World: Registering Difference through Performative and Collective Research." *Local Environment* 16, no. 6: 116–29.

Carlson, Marvin. 1996. *Performance: A Critical Introduction.* London: Routledge.

Carrier, James G. 1998. Introduction to *Virtualism: A New Political Economy,* edited by James G. Carrier and Daniel Miller. Oxfrod: Berg.

———. ed. 1997. *Meanings of the Market: The Free Market in Western Culture.* Oxford: Berg.

Carter, Helen. 2002. "Agnes Varda." *Senses of Cinema,* September. http://sensesofcin ema.com/2002/great-directors/varda/.

Carter, Ian. 2001. *Railways and Culture in Britain: The Epitome of Modernity.* Manchester, U.K.: Manchester University Press.

Castree, Noel. 2006. "Commentary: From Neoliberalism to Neoliberalisation— Consolations, Confusions, and Necessary Illusions." *Environment and Planning A* 38, no. 1: 1–6.

Chakrabarty, Dipesh. 2008. "The Public Life of History: An Argument Out of India." *Public Culture* 20, no. 1: 143–68.

———. 2009. "The Climate of History: Four Theses." *Critical Inquiry* 35: 197–222.

Chandhoke, Neera. 2002. "The Limits of Global Civil Society." In *Global Civil Society,* edited by London School of Economics and Political Science, Centre for the Study of Global Governance and Centre for Civil Society, 35–53. Oxford: Oxford University Press.

Coldcut. 1997. "Every Home a Prison" (musical performance). On *Let Us Play!* Ninja Tune IFPI L135, 2 compact discs.

Collier, Stephen J. 2012. "Neoliberalism as Big Leviathan, or . . . ? A Response to Wacquant and Hilgers." *Social Anthropology* 20, no. 2: 186–95.

Connolly, William E. 2002. *Neuropolitics: Thinking, Culture, Speed.* Minneapolis: University of Minnesota Press.

Craig, David, and Douglas Porter. 2006. *Development beyond Neoliberalism? Governance, Poverty Reduction, and Political Economy.* London: Routledge.

Crutzen, P. J. 2002. "Geology of Mankind—the Anthropocene." *Nature* 415, no. 6867: 23.

Cubby, Ben. 2010. "Green Groups Call for Backyard Scientists." *Sydney Morning Herald,* September 4. http://www.smh.com.au/environment/conservation/green -groups-call-for-backyard-scientists-20100903-14ufg.html.

Davis, Mike. 2008. "Living on the Ice Shelf: Humanity's Meltdown." *Tomdispatch* 26. http://www.tomdispatch.com/post/174949.

de Sousa Santos, Boaventura. 2004. "The World Social Forum: Toward a Counterhegemonic Globalisation (Part I)." In Sen et al., *World Social Forum: Challenging Empires,* 235–45.

Dewsbury, John David, Paul Harrison, Mitch Rose, and John Wylie. 2002. "Enacting Geographies." *Geoforum* 33, no. 4: 437–40.

Dyer-Witheford, Nick. 2004a. "1844/2004/2044: The Return of Species-Being." *Historical Materialism* 12, no. 4: 3–25.

——. 2004b. "Species-Being Resurgent." *Constellations* 11, no. 4: 4776–91.

Edwards, L. 2007. Paper presented at Event 271: Money, Money, Money, Sydney Writers Festival, Sydney, N.S.W., June.

Elyachar, Julia. 2005. *Markets of Dispossession: NGOs, Economic Development, and the State in Cairo.* Durham, N.C.: Duke University Press.

——. 2011. "The Political Economy of Movement and Gesture in Cairo." *Journal of the Royal Anthropological Institute* 17: 82–99.

Ereshefsky, Marc. 2010. "Species." In *The Stanford Encyclopaedia of Philosophy.* http://plato.stanford.edu/entries/species/.

Findlay, Peter. 1994. "Conscientization and Social Movements in Canada: The Relevance of Paulo Freire's Ideas in Contemporary Politics." In McLaren and Lankshear, *Politics of Liberation: Paths from Freire,* 108–22.

Fitzgibbons, Athol. 1995. *Adam Smith's System of Liberty, Wealth, and Virtue: The Moral and Political Foundations of the Wealth of Nations.* Oxford: Clarendon Press.

Forum Social Mundial. 2005. "Programacao 2005." http://www.forumsocialmundial.org.br/dinamic.php?pagina=programa_fsm2005_ing.

Freire, Paulo. 1996. *Pedagogy of the Oppressed.* London: Penguin Books.

Gaudiano, Edgar Gonzalez, and Alicia de Alba. 1994. "Freire—Present and Future Possibilities." In McLaren and Lankshear, *Politics of Liberation: Paths from Freire,* 123–42.

Gibson, Katherine. 2001. "Regional Subjection and Becoming." *Environment and Planning D: Society and Space* 19, no. 6: 639–67.

Gibson-Graham, J. K. 2003. "Enabling Ethical Economies: Cooperativism and Class." *Critical Sociology* 29, no. 2: 123–61.

——. 2006a. *The End of Capitalism (As We Knew It): A Feminist Critique of Political Economy with a New Introduction.* Minneapolis: University of Minnesota Press.

——. 2006b. *A Postcapitalist Politics.* Minneapolis: University of Minnesota Press.

——. 2008. "Diverse Economies: Performative Practices for 'Other Worlds.'" *Progress in Human Geography* (OnlineFirst). doi:10.1177/0309132508090821.

——. 2010. "A Feminist Project of Belonging for the Anthropocene." Paper presented in the Centre for Citizenship and Public Policy Seminar Series, Centre for Citizenship and Public Policy, University of Western Sydney, March 26.

Gibson-Graham, J. K., Jenny Cameron, and Stephen Healy. 2013. *Take Back the Economy: An Ethical Guide for Transforming Our Communities.* Minneapolis: University of Minnesota Press.

Gibson-Graham, J. K., and Gerda Roelvink. 2009. "Social Innovation for Community Economies." In *Social Innovation and Territorial Development,* edited by D. MacCallum, F. Moulaert, J. Hillier, and S. Vicari Haddock, 25–38. Aldershot, U.K.: Ashgate.

———. 2010. "An Economic Ethics for the Anthropocene." *Antipode* 41, no. 1: 320–46.

Gonzales, Eugene. 2007. "Wastes as Assets: Limits and Potentials." In *Reclaiming Nature: Environmental Justice and Ecological Restoration,* edited by J. Boyce, S. Narain, and E. Stanton, 416–47. London: Anthem Press.

Grant, Judith. 2005. "Gender and Marx's Radical Humanism in the Economic and Philosophic Manuscripts of 1844." *Rethinking Marxism* 17, no. 1: 59–77.

Gregson, Nicky, and Gillian Rose. 2000. "Taking Butler Elsewhere: Performativities, Spatialities, and Subjectivities." *Environment and Planning D: Society and Space* 18, no. 4: 433–52.

Gudeman, Steve. 2001. *The Anthropology of Economy: Commodity, Market, and Culture.* Oxford: Blackwell.

Hamilton, Lisa M. 2009. *Deeply Rooted: Unconventional Farmers in the Age of Agribusiness.* Berkeley, Calif.: Counterpoint.

Hardt, Michael, and Antonio Negri. 2000. *Empire.* Cambridge, Mass.: Harvard University Press.

Harvey, David. 2003. *The New Imperialism.* Oxford: Oxford University Press.

———. 2012. *Rebel Cities: From the Right to the City to the Urban Revolution.* London: Verso.

Hayami, Yujiro, A. K. Dikshit, and S. N. Mishra. 2006. "Waste Pickers and Collectors in Delhi: Poverty and Environment in an Urban Informal Sector." *Journal of Development Studies* 42, no. 1: 41–69.

Higgins, Vaughan. 2014. "Australia's Development Trajectory: Neoliberal or Not?" *Dialogues in Human Geography* 4, no. 2: 161–64.

Hill, Ann. 2014. "Growing Community Food Economies in the Philippines." PhD diss., Australian National University.

Hinchliffe, Steve. 2003. "'Inhabiting'—Landscapes and Natures." In *Handbook of Cultural Geography,* edited by K. Anderson, M. Domosh, S. Pile, and N. Thrift, 207–25. London: Sage.

Hindess, Barry. 1996. *Discourses of Power: From Hobbs to Foucault.* Oxford: Blackwell.

Hobson, Kersty. 2008. "Values, Behaviour, and the Hope of 'Creative Maladjustment' in the Anthropocene." Paper presented in the Fenner School Seminar Series, Fenner School of Environment and Society, Australian National University, Canberra, December 4.

Holloway, John. 2002. *Change the World without Taking Power.* London: Pluto Press.

Hynes, Maria, and Scott Sharpe. 2009. "Affected with Joy: Evaluating the Mass Actions of the Anti-globalisation Movement." *Borderlands* 8, no. 3: 1–21.

———. 2015. "Affect: An Unworkable Concept." *Angelaki* 20, no. 3: 115–29.

Hynes, Maria, Scott Sharpe, and Fagan, Bob. 2007. "Laughing with the Yes Men: The Politics of Affirmation." *Continuum: Journal of Media and Cultural Studies* 21, no. 1: 107–21.

Jessop, Bob. 1995. "The Regulation Approach, Governance, and Post-Fordism: Alternative Perspectives on Economic and Political Change?" *Economy and Society* 24, no. 3: 307–33.

Johnston, Jose E., and James Goodman. 2006. "Hope and Activism in the Ivory Tower: Freirean Lessons for Critical Globalization Research." *Globalizations* 3, no. 1: 9–30.

Johnston, Ron, Derek Gregory, Geraldine Pratt, and Michael Watts. 2000. *The Dictionary of Human Geography.* 4th ed. Oxford: Blackwell.

Jones, O. 2014. "Life Is in the Transaction." Paper presented at the workshop Environmental Posthumanities, Department of Historical and Religious Studies, UMEA University, Sweden, October.

Keraghel, Chloe, and Jai Sen. 2004. "Explorations in Open Space: The World Social Forum and Cultures of Politics." *International Social Science Journal* 56, no. 182: 483–93.

Kingsnorth, Paul. 2003. *One No, Many Yeses.* London: Free Press.

Kitchin, R. M., and P. J. Hubbard. 1999. "Research, Action, and 'Critical' Geographies." *Area* 31, no. 3: 195–98.

Klein, Naomi. 2001. *No Logo.* London: Flamingo.

Kumar, Amitava. 2000. Foreword to *Class and Its Others,* edited by J. K. Gibson-Graham, Stephen A. Resnick, and Richard D. Wolff. Minneapolis: University of Minnesota Press.

Larner, Wendy. 2000. "Post-welfare State Governance: Towards a Code of Social and Family Responsibility." *Social Politics* 7, no. 2: 244–65.

———. 2003. "Neoliberalism?" *Environment and Planning D: Society and Space* 21, no. 5: 509–12.

———. 2014. "Coexist as Post-politics? Rethinking Radical Social Enterprise." In *Spectres of the Political: The Post-political and Its Discontents,* edited by J. Wilson and E. Swyngedouw, 189–207. Edinburgh: Edinburgh University Press.

Larner, Wendy, and Maria Butler. 2005. "Governmentalities of Local Partnerships: The Rise of a 'Partnering State' in New Zealand." *Studies in Political Economy* 75, Spring: 79–102.

Larner, Wendy, and William Walters. 2002. "Globalization as Governmentality." Paper presented at the ISA Panel RC18: "Governing Society Today," International Studies Association Congress, Brisbane, Australia, July 7–13.

———. 2004. "Globalization as Governmentality." *Alternatives* 29, no. 5: 495–514.

Latour, Bruno. 2004a. "Why Has Critique Run Out of Steam? From Matters of Fact to Matters of Concern." *Critical Inquiry* 30, no. 2: 225–48.

———. 2004b. "Nonhumans." In *Patterned Ground: Entanglements of Nature and Culture,* edited by S. Harrison, S. Pile, and N. Thrift, 224–27. London: Reaktion Books.

———. 2004c. *Politics of Nature: How to Bring the Sciences into Democracy.* Cambridge, Mass.: Harvard University Press.

———. 2005a. "From Realpolitik to Dingpolitik: or How to Make Things Public." In Latour and Weibel, *Making Things Public: Atmospheres of Democracy,* 14–41.

———. 2005b. *Reassembling the Social: An Introduction to Actor-Network-Theory.* Oxford: Oxford University Press.

Latour, Bruno, and Peter Weibel, eds. 2005. *Making Things Public: Atmospheres of Democracy.* Cambridge, Mass.: MIT Press.

Laub, Dori. 1992. "Bearing Witness, or the Vicissitudes of Listening." In *Testimony: Crises of Witnessing in Literature, Psychoanalysis, and History,* edited by Shoshana Felman and Dori Laub, 57–74. New York: Routledge.

Law, John. 2004a. "And If the Global Were Small and Noncoherent? Method, Complexity, and the Baroque." *Environment and Planning D: Society and Space* 22, no. 1: 13–26.

———. 2004b. *After Method: Mess in Social Science Research.* New York: Routledge.

Lee, Roger. 2006. "The Ordinary Economy: Tangled Up in Values and Geography." *Transactions of the Institute of British Geographers* 31, no. 4: 413–32.

Leet, Don, and Scott Houser. 2003. "Economics Goes to Hollywood: Using Classic Films and Documentaries to Create an Undergraduate Economics Course." *Journal of Economic Education* 34, no. 4: 326–32.

Lemke, Thomas. 2002. "Foucault, Governmentality, and Critique." *Rethinking Marxism* 14, no. 3: 49–64.

Lewis, A., dir. 2002. *Gustavo Benedetto: Presente!* DVD. Canada: Canadian Broadcasting Corporation.

Lewis, Avi, and Naomi Klein. 2004. *The Take.* DVD. Canada: National Film Board of Canada and Barma-Alper Productions, Madman Cinema.

Leyshon, Andrew. 2010. "Review: *The End of Capitalism (As We Knew It): A Feminist Critique of Political Economy.*" *Progress in Human Geography* 34: 117–27.

Leyshon, Andrew, Roger Lee, and Colin C. Williams, eds. 2003. *Alternative Economic Spaces.* London: Sage.

Lingis, Alphonso. 2002. "Murmurs of Life—with Alphonso Lingis." In Zournazi, *Hope: New Philosophies for Change,* 22–41.

Longhurst, Robyn. 1995. "Viewpoint: The Body and Geography." *Gender, Place, and Culture: A Journal of Feminist Geography* 2, no. 1: 97–106.

———. 1997. "(Dis)embodied Geographies." *Progress in Human Geography* 21, no. 4: 486–501.

MacKenzie, Donald, Fabian Muniesa, and Lucia Siu, eds. 2007. *Do Economists Make Markets? On the Performativity of Economics.* Princeton, N.J.: Princeton University Press.

Malpas, Jeff, and Norelle Lickiss. 2007. "Introduction to a Conversation." In *Perspectives on Human Dignity: A Conversation,* edited by J. Malpas and N. Lickiss, 1–8. Dordrecht, Netherlands: Springer.

Marx, Karl. (1844) 1964. *Economic and Philosophic Manuscripts of 1844.* Edited by D. Struik. Translated by M. Milligan. New York: International.

Massey, Doreen. 2005. *For Space.* London: Sage.

Massumi, Brian. 2002a. "Navigating Movements—with Brian Massumi." In Zournazi, *Hope: New Philosophies for Change,* 210–43.

———. 2002b. *Parables for the Virtual: Movement, Affect, Sensation.* Durham, N.C.: Duke University Press.

Mathews, Freya. 2011. "Moral Ambiguities in the Politics of Climate Change." In *Climate Change and Environmental Ethics,* edited by Ved P. Nanda, 43–64. Livingston, N.J.: Transaction.

McLaren, Peter, and Colin Lankshear, eds. 1994. *Politics of Liberation: Paths from Freire.* London: Routledge.

Medina, Martin. 1998. "Border Scavenging: A Case Study of Aluminium Recycling in Laredo, TX and Nuevo Laredo, Mexico." *Resources, Conservation, and Recycling* 23: 107–26.

———. 2000. "Scavenger Cooperatives in Asia and Latin America." *Resources, Conservation, and Recycling* 31, no. 1: 51–69.

Meyer, Andrea. 2001. "Interview: 'Gleaning' the Passion of Agnes Varda: Agnes Varda." http://www.indiewire.com/article/interview_gleaning_the_passion_of_agnes_varda_agnes_varda.

Miller, Daniel. 2005. "Reply to Michel Callon—Daniel Miller." *Economic Society: European Electronic Newsletter* 6, no. 3: 3–13.

Mitchell, Timothy. 1998. "Fixing the Economy." *Cultural Studies* 12, no. 1: 82–101.

———. 2007. "Rethinking Economy." *Geoforum* 39, no. 3: 1116–21.

———. 2008. "Culture and Economy." In *The Sage Handbook of Cultural Analysis,* edited by T. Bennett and J. Frow, 447–66. Thousand Oaks, Calif.: Sage.

Mol, Annemarie. 1999. "Ontological Politics: A Word and Some Questions." In *Actor Network Theory and After,* edited by J. Law and J. Hassard, 74–89. Oxford: Blackwell/Sociological Review.

Moulaert, Frank, Flavia Martinelli, Erik Swyngedouw, and Sara Gonzalez. 2005. "Towards Alternative Model(s) of Local Innovation." *Urban Studies* 42, no. 11: 1969–90.

Naidoo, Prishani. 2005a. "The Struggle for Water, the Struggle for Life: The Installation of Prepaid Water Meters in Phiri Soweto." *Centre for Civil Society RASSP* 1, no. 9: 155–77.

———. 2005b. "Production: Thoughts on the World Social Forum 2005." http://www.europe-solidaire.org/spip.php?page=article_impr&id_article=1813.

Naidu, Suresh. 2012. "Introduction: Economics and Occupy Wall Street." *The Economists' Voice* 9, no. 3. http://degruyter.com/view/j/ev.

Nancy, Jean-Luc. 1991. *The Inoperative Community.* Minneapolis: University of Minnesota Press.

Nicholls, Alex, and Charlotte Opal. 2005. *Fair Trade: Market-Driven Ethical Consumption.* London: Sage.

Oliver, Kelly. 2004. "Witnessing and Testimony." *Parallax* 10, no. 1: 78–87.

———. 2009. *Animal Lessons: How They Teach US to Be Human.* New York: Columbia University Press.

Ollman, Bertell. 1971. *Alienation: Marx's Conceptualisation of Man in Capitalist Society.* London: Cambridge University Press.

O'Malley, Pat. 1998. "Indigenous Governance." In *Governing Australia: Studies in Contemporary Rationalities of Government,* edited by M. Dean and B. Hindess, 156–72. Cambridge: Cambridge University Press.

Osterweil, Michal. 2005. "Place-Based Globalism: Theorizing the Global Justice Movement." *Development* 48, no. 2: 23–28.

Pain, Rachel, and Peter Francis. 2003. "Reflections on Participatory Research." *Area* 35, no. 1: 46–54.

Peck, Jamie. 2004. "Geography and Public Policy: Constructions of Neoliberalism." *Progress in Human Geography* 28, no. 3: 392–405.

Peck, Jamie, and Adam Tickell. 2002. "Neoliberalizing Space." *Antipode* 34, no. 3: 380–404.

Pietrykowski, Bruce. 2004. "You Are What You Eat: The Social Economy of the Slow Food Movement." *Review of Social Economy* 62, no. 3: 307–21.

Piore, Michael, and Charles Sabel. 1984. *The Second Industrial Divide.* New York: Basic Books.

Plant, Sadie. 1998. *Zeros + Ones: Digital Women + the New Technoculture.* London: Fourth Estate.

Plumwood, Val. 2002. *Environmental Culture: The Ecological Crisis of Reason.* London: Routledge.

———. 2007. "A Review of Deborah Bird Rose's Reports from a Wild Country: Ethics of Decolonisation." *Australian Humanities Review* 42, August: 1–4.

Ramsey, Joseph G. 2005. "Left Docudrama 2004." *Socialism and Democracy* 19, no. 1: 169–80.

Raphael, D. D. 1985. *Adam Smith.* Oxford: Oxford University Press.

Raynolds, Laura T., and John Wilkinson. 2007. "Fair Trade in the Agriculture and Food Sector." In *Fair Trade: The Challenges of Transforming Globalization,* edited by Laura T. Raynolds, Douglas Murray, and John Wilkinson, 33–47. London: Routledge.

Renard, Marie Cristine, and Victor Perez-Grovas. 2007. "Fair Trade Coffee in Mexico: At the Centre of the Debates." In *Fair Trade: The Challenges of Transforming Globalization,* edited by Laura T. Raynolds, Douglas Murray, and John Wilkinson, 138–56. London: Routledge.

Resnick, Stephen A., and Richard D. Wolff. 1987. *Knowledge and Class: A Marxian Critique of Political Economy.* Chicago: University of Chicago Press.

Rockmore, Tom. 2002. *Marx after Marxism: The Philosophy of Karl Marx.* Oxford: Blackwell.

Roelvink, Gerda. 2007. "Review Article: Performing the Market." *Social Identities: Journal for the Study of Race, Nation, and Culture* 13, no. 1: 125–33.

———. 2015. "Performing Posthuman Economies in the Anthropocene." In Roelvink et al., *Making Other Worlds Possible: Performing Diverse Economies,* 225–44.

Roelvink, Gerda, and David Craig. 2005. "The Man in the Partnering State: Regendering the Social through Partnership." *Studies in Political Economy* 75, Spring: 103–26.

Roelvink, Gerda, and J. K Gibson-Graham. 2009. "A Postcapitalist Politics of Dwelling." *Australian Humanities Review* 46: 145–58.

Roelvink, Gerda, Kevin St. Martin, and J. K. Gibson-Graham. 2015. *Making Other Worlds Possible: Performing Diverse Economies.* Minneapolis: University of Minnesota Press.

Roelvink, Gerda, and Magdalena Zolkos. 2011. "Climate Change as Experience of Affect." *Angelaki* 16, no. 4: 43–58.

Rose, Mitch. 2002. "The Seductions of Resistance: Power, Politics, and a Performative Style of Systems." *Environment and Planning D: Society and Space* 20, no. 4: 383–400.

Rose, Nikolas. 1999. *Powers of Freedom: Reframing Political Thought.* Cambridge: Cambridge University Press.

Routledge, Paul. 2003. "Voices of the Dammed: Discursive Resistance amidst Erasure in the Narmada Valley, India." *Political Geography* 22, no. 3: 243–70.

Safri, Malia. 2012. "The Economics of Occupation." *The Economist's Voice* 9, no. 3. http://degruyter.com/view/j/ev.

Sedgwick, Eve Kosofsky. 1993. *Tendencies.* Durham, N.C.: Duke University Press.

———. 2003. *Touching Feeling: Affect, Pedagogy, Performativity.* Durham, N.C.: Duke University Press.

Sen, Jai. 2004. "A Tale of Two Charters." In Sen et al., *World Social Forum: Challenging Empires,* 72–75.

Sen, Jai, Anita Anand, Arturo Escobar, and Peter Waterman, eds. 2004. *World Social Forum: Challenging Empires.* New Delhi: Viveka Foundation.

Sharpe, Scott. 1999. "Bodily Speaking: Spaces and Experiences of Childbirth." In *Embodied Geographies: Spaces, Bodies, and Rites of Passage,* edited by Elizabeth Kenworthy Teather, 91–104. London: Routledge.

———. 2002. "A Geography of the Fold." PhD diss., Department of Human Geography, Macquarie University.

Slaby, Jan. 2014. "Empathy's Blind Spot." *Medical Health Care and Philosophy* 17: 249–58.

Slater, Don. 2002. "From Calculation to Alienation: Disentangling Economic Abstractions." *Economy and Society* 31, no. 2: 234–49.

Smith, Adam. (1776–78) 1937. *An Inquiry into the Nature and Causes of the Wealth of Nations.* Edited by E. Rhys. New York: J. M. Dent.

———. (1759) 2002. *The Theory of Moral Sentiments.* Edited by K. Haakonssen. Cambridge: Cambridge University Press.

Smith, Susan J. 2005. "States, Markets, and an Ethic of Care." *Political Geography* 24, no. 1: 1–20.

Soderbergh, Steven, dir. 2000. *Erin Brockovich.* DVD. United States: Jersey Films.

Sparke, Matthew. 2006. "Political Geography: Political Geographies of Globalization (2)—Governance." *Progress in Human Geography* 30, no. 2: 1–16.

Spinosa, Charles, Fernando Flores, and Hubert L. Dreyfus. 1997. *Disclosing New Worlds: Entrepreneurship, Democratic Action, and the Cultivation of Solidarity.* Cambridge, Mass.: MIT Press.

Spurlock, Morgan, dir. 2004. *Super Size Me.* DVD. United States: Kathbur Pictures.

Stengers, Isabelle. 2000. *The Invention of Modern Science.* Translated by D. Smith. Minneapolis: University of Minnesota Press.

———. 2002. "A 'Cosmo-Politics'—Risk, Hope, Change—with Isabelle Stengers." In Zournazi, *Hope: New Philosophies for Change*, 244–73.

Stewart, Kathleen. 2007. *Ordinary Affects*. Durham, N.C.: Duke University Press.

St. Martin, Kevin, Gerda Roelvink, and J. K. Gibson-Graham. 2015. "Introduction: An Economic Politics for Our Time." In Roelvink et al., *Making Other Worlds Possible: Performing Diverse Economies*, 1–25.

Tallontire, Anne. 2006. "The Development of Alternative and Fair Trade: Moving into the Mainstream." In *Ethical Sourcing in the Global Food System: Challenges and Opportunities to Fair Trade and the Environment,* edited by Stephanie Barrientos and Catherine Dolan, 35–48. London: Earthscan.

Thrift, Nigel. 2008. *Non-representational Theory: Space, Politics, and Affect*. London: Routledge.

Thrift, Nigel, and John-David Dewsbury. 2000. "Dead Geographies—and How to Make Them Live." *Environment and Planning D: Society and Space* 18, no. 4: 411–32.

Thrinh, Minh-ha T. 1991. *When the Moon Waxes Red: Representation, Gender, and Cultural Politics*. London: Routledge.

Torres, Carlos Alberto, and Paulo Freire. 2004. "Twenty Years after Pedagogy of the Oppressed: Paulo Freire in Conversation with Carlos Alberto Torres." In McLaren and Lankshear, *Politics of Liberation: Paths from Freire*, 100–7.

Varda, Agnes, dir. 2000. *Les Glaneurs et la Glaneuse*. DVD. France: Ciné Tamaris, Madman Cinema and Potential Films.

Victor, David G. 1991. "Limits of Market-Based Strategies for Slowing Global Warming: The Case of Tradeable Permits." *Policy Sciences* 24, no. 2: 199–222.

Watson, Matthew. 2006. "Civilizing Market Standards and the Moral Self." In *Global Standards of Market Civilization,* edited by Brett Bowden and Leonard Seabrooke, 45–59. London: Routledge.

Weatherstone, John. 2003. *Lyndfield Park: Looking Back, Moving Forward*. Braddon, A.C.T.: Booklet produced by Greening Australia and Land and Water Australia.

Weiler, Kathleen. 1994. "Freire and a Feminist Pedagogy of Difference." In *Politics of Liberation: Paths from Freire,* edited by P. McLaren and C. Lankshear, 12–40. London: Routledge.

Weiner, Annette B. 1992. *Inalienable Possessions: The Paradox of Keeping-While-Giving*. Berkeley: University of California Press.

Weir, Jessica K. 2009. *Murray River Country: An Ecological Dialogue with Traditional Owners*. Canberra, A.C.T.: Aboriginal Studies Press.

Weller, Sally, and Phillip O'Neill. 2014. "An Argument with Neoliberalism: Australia's Place in a Global Imaginary." *Dialogues in Human Geography* 4, no. 2: 105–30.

Westley, Frances, Brenda Zimmerman, and Michael Patton. 2006. *Getting to Maybe: How the World Is Changed*. Toronto, Canada: Random House.

Whatmore, Sarah. 2002. *Hybrid Geographies: Natures, Cultures, and Spaces*. London: Sage.

Wilson, Jake. 2002. "Trash and Treasure: *The Gleaners and I.*" *Senses of Cinema* 23, November. http://sensesofcinema.com/2002/feature-articles/gleaners/.

Wolfe, Cary. 2009. *What Is Posthumanism?* Minneapolis: University of Minnesota Press.

Wolfwood, Theresa. 2004. "Another World Is Possible: Globalization by the People." In Sen et al., *The World Social Forum: Challenging Empires,* 81–86.

World Dignity Forum. 2005. *World Dignity Forum: Dignity Everywhere.* Pamphlet. World Social Forum, Porto Alegre, Brazil, January 29.

Zournazi, Mary, ed. 2002. *Hope: New Philosophies for Change.* Annandale, N.S.W.: Pluto Press.

Index

GERDA ROELVINK is a senior lecturer in the School of Social Sciences and Psychology at the University of Western Sydney. She is coeditor of special issues on posthumanism and affect for *Angelaki* and *Emotion, Space, and Society* and of the edited collection *Making Other Worlds Possible: Performing Diverse Economies* (Minnesota, 2015). She has published research in *Antipode, Journal of Cultural Economy,* and *Rethinking Marxism.*